Segmentation and Lifetime Value Models
Using SAS®

Edward C. Malthouse

support.sas.com/bookstore

The correct bibliographic citation for this manual is as follows: Malthouse, Edward C. 2013. *Segmentation and Lifetime Value Models Using SAS®*. Cary, NC: SAS Institute Inc.

Segmentation and Lifetime Value Models Using SAS®

Copyright © 2013, SAS Institute Inc., Cary, NC, USA

ISBN 978-1-61290-706-2 (electronic book)
ISBN 978-1-61290-696-6

All rights reserved. Produced in the United States of America.

In Memory of Ted Spiegel

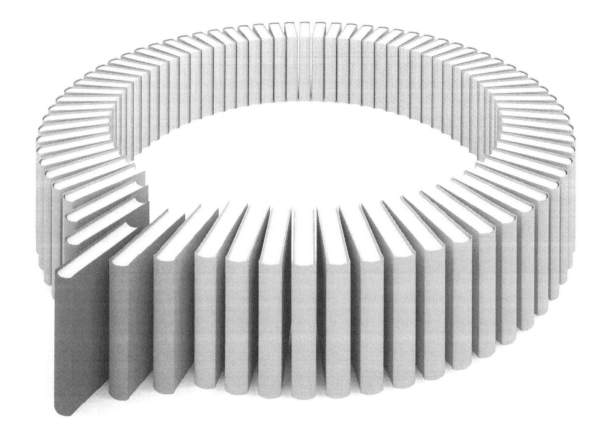

Gain Greater Insight into Your SAS® Software with SAS Books.

Discover all that you need on your journey to knowledge and empowerment.

support.sas.com/bookstore
for additional books and resources.

THE POWER TO KNOW.

Contents

About This Book

Purpose

This book addresses the problem of allocating marketing resources to, and estimating the financial value of different customer groups. For example, how much money can be spent to acquire a customer? What is the financial value of a database of customers (for the purpose of acquiring a firm or valuing the intangible assets of a firm)? How much money can be invested in individual customers? These questions are central to customer relationship management (CRM). This book introduces the reader to segmentation models for identifying groups of customers and different lifetime value models for estimating the future value of the segments. The reader will be exposed to a range of models and understand their strengths and weaknesses. Readers will also learn how to prepare a data set and estimate different models using Base SAS®, SAS/STAT®, SAS/IML® and the SQL procedure.

Is this book for you?

This book applies to any industry that maintains databases of customer information and can target marketing "investments" at individual customers, for example, travel, financial services, insurance, media, cable, telecommunications, retail, healthcare, e-commerce, non-for-profits, and so on. Readers who work in the areas of marketing analytics, customer relationship management, or direct, database or interactive marketing would find this book useful. This book is also of interest to financial analysts. While the book attempts to derive all models from basic probability theory, much of the content can be understood with nothing more than a basic understanding of undergraduate-level probability and statistics.

Prerequisites

This book assumes that readers have had at least two college-level courses in probability and statistics, including introductions to probability theory, multiple linear regression, logistic regression and two-way ANOVA models (interactions). It also assumes that readers already have experience with SAS DATA step programming and the PROCs in SAS/Base and SAS/STAT. Readers should have programming knowledge at the level of the SAS Base Certified Base Programmer. Many of the programs use the SQL procedure and SAS macros, which are covered in the Advanced certification exam (SAS Institute, 2011). Delwiche and Slaughter (2008) is another good reference covering the prerequisite SAS skills. Some sections use matrix arithmetic, and there is an appendix reviewing the necessary results. Readers should also be familiar with the SGPLOT procedure.

Software used to develop the book's content

Most of the examples have been developed using SAS 9.3 running on a Linux X64 platform. A few examples were developed using spreadsheet software.

Scope of this book

This book has three intersecting goals: introduce CLV models, discuss their applications and show how to prepare the data and estimate the models in SAS. This is only an introduction and is not intended to be a comprehensive survey of and not all models. Many models have been omitted, although references are provided. We attempt to develop the models in a rigorous way, assuming an undergraduate level of probability and statistics knowledge (as a point of reference, see (DeGroot, 1975)). Each model's assumptions are clearly identified and discussed, so that the reader will know when a model is appropriate. Analysts should understand more than the models, and the book attempts to give the reader a clear sense of how and when the models are applied. The third goal is computational. We hope that the examples will show the reader how to interact with large databases to prepare the data sets and then how to use SAS to estimate the models. All parts of the book are intended to achieve the three goals of understanding the statistical models, business context, and computational details.

How to use this book

Reading a technical book is not a passive activity and readers must engage with the material by working through the examples and additional problems, and applying the techniques to their own work. It is only through these activities that readers will fully understand and remember the material. The first step in learning should be to replicate the examples and experiment with variations of them. The reader will find suggestions in the text of tasks that will advance understanding. The next step should be to work on additional problems or apply the methods to their own work. A separate file that contains dozens of exercises and worked solutions is available from the author's page at http://support.sas.com/malthouse.

Typographical conventions used in this book

Italic font is used to define new terms and add emphasis. It also used for side headings.

`Courier` font is used for all SAS programming commands and output, and filenames. Words reserved in the SAS language are typeset in all caps and user-selected variable and data set names are set in lower case, for example, `DATA rollup` or `logx = LOG(x)`.

Mathematical content follows these conventions:

- All functions and scalar variables are set in italic, for example, $y = f(x)$, $E(aX) = aE(X)$. Exceptions include multi-letter scalar quantities and functions, for example, MSE, CLV, $\exp(\beta)$ and $\log(x)$.

- Random variables are upper case and realizations of a random variable are lower case, for example, $P(T = t)$.

- Vectors are typeset in lower-case bold and matrices in upper-case bold, for example, $\mathbf{y} = \mathbf{X}\beta + \mathbf{e}$ and $\mathbf{b} = (\mathbf{X'X})^{-1}\mathbf{X'y}$.

- The $\log(\cdot)$ function assumes natural logarithms (base of e).

Data and programs used in this book

All data sets and programs used in this book can be downloaded from the author's page at http://support.sas.com/malthouse.

Output and graphics used in this book

All output was generated using SAS. Unless otherwise noted, graphics were produced using the SGPLOT procedure or the LaTeX picture environment.

Additional resources

Comments or Questions? If you have comments or questions about this book, you may contact the author through SAS as follows. E-mail: saspress@sas.com Fax: (919) 677-4444

Please include the title of the book in your correspondence. For a complete list of books available through SAS Press, visit support.sas.com. SAS Book Report: Receive up-to-date information about all new SAS publications via e-mail by subscribing to bookstore the SAS Book Report monthly eNewsletter. Visit support.sas.com/sbr.

About The Author

 Edward C. Malthouse is the Theodore R. and Annie Laurie Sills Professor of Integrated Marketing Communications and Industrial Engineering at Northwestern University and the Director of Research for the Spiegel Initiative on Database and Digital Marketing. He was the co-editor of the *Journal of Interactive Marketing* from 2005–2011. He obtained his PhD in 1995 in computational statistics from Northwestern University and completed his postdoctoral fellowship at the Kellogg School of Management at Northwestern.

Malthouse's research interests center on media marketing, database marketing, advertising, new media, and integrated marketing communications. He is the co-editor of *Medill on Media Engagement*, and he has published articles in numerous journals, including the *Journal of Consumer Psychology, Journal of Interactive Marketing, Data Mining and Knowledge Discovery, Journal of Broadcasting and Electronic Media, International Journal of Market Research,* and *Journal of Media Business Studies*. He teaches undergraduates, graduates, and executives, and he has been a visiting professor at universities in Japan, China, and Europe.

Learn more about this author by visiting his author page at support.sas.com/malthouse. There you can download free chapters, access example code and data, read the latest reviews, get updates, and more.

x

Acknowledgments

I would sincerely like to thank Ted Spiegel, Bob Kestnbaum and Tom Collinger for introducing me to many of the concepts covered in this book and making sure my teaching of these topics is grounded in the practice of database marketing. The Direct Marketing Educational Foundation (now called the Marketing EDGE), Ralf Elsner, and Bobby Calder provided some of the data sets used in this book for examples. Bobby has also had a strong influence on my thinking about segmentation and subsegmentation. Bob Blattberg originally suggested this project and has been an excellent collaborator on several lifetime value research projects. The IMC process shown in Figure 1.1 and the material covered in Chapter 1 was influenced by discussions with Don Schultz, Frank Mulhern, and Bobby Calder. Scott Neslin and Ben Sylvan provided early feedback on Chapters 3 and 4. Countless students have challenged my thinking and helped shape my presentation of these concepts. Many students found typos and mistakes in the manuscript, including Yan Da, William Chiu and Adrianna Jelesnianska. Bari Lawhorn, Rob Agnelli and Marcia Surratt from SAS technical support answered many questions about the SGPLOT and FMM procedures. George McDaniel, Julie Platt, and Brad Kellam have been great editors, and several anonymous reviewers gave feedback that improved the book substantially. Finally, I would like to thank my family—Elisabeth, Thomas, Niklas, and Ellen—for their support during this project.

Strategic Foundations for Segmentation and Lifetime Value Models

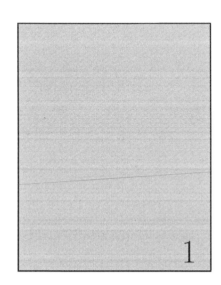

Contents

1.1   Introduction

Customer lifetime value (CLV) is the discounted sum of *future* cash flows attributed to the relationship with a customer (Pfeifer et al., 2005). In simple terms, CLV estimates the "profit" that an organization will derive from a customer in the future. It is an important concept because one of the main goals of for-profit organizations is to maximize CLV. Most models calculate an expected CLV given by:

$$\text{CLV} = \sum_{t=1}^{\infty} \frac{E(V_t)}{(1+d)^{t-1}}, \tag{1.1}$$

where V_t is the customer's net contribution in period t and d is the discount rate (Blattberg et al., 2009).

One of the first applications of CLV was in deciding how much an organization could spend to acquire a customer. A classic example is the Columbia Record Club (Wunderman, 1996), where prospective customers would pay one cent for, say, six records, or later CDs. The cent did not come close to covering the costs of goods sold, shipping, and advertising—Columbia Records was acquiring the customer at a loss. Such a loss could be justified, however, by considering that Columbia Records was also gaining a relationship with a customer and that it could market to this customer in the future. The acquisition costs could be justified if they were less than the customer's CLV. The secret of the business was to identify prospective customers with high CLV, and avoid acquiring those with low CLV. This book shows you how to estimate the future value of a customer.

Record clubs now sound anachronistic, but the business model of acquiring high-CLV customers at a loss is pervasive today across may different industries. Media providers, telecommunications and cable companies, nonprofits, online retailers, and firms in many other industries do exactly this.

This basic logic has been extended to other marketing expenditures, and is changing the way that people think about marketing. Columbia Records was spending marketing resources to acquire a customer, who would generate some expected financial return for the organization. An important shift is that such marketing expenditures should not be viewed as *expenses*, but rather as *investments*. The firm is investing in customers, in the same way, and following the same process, as other investments it makes. Marketing activities should not be thought of as expenses, but as investments in customers having a quantifiable financial return.

For example, the logic can be applied to making decisions about retaining existing customers. If a firm invests resources in retaining customers longer, the *incremental* future profits of the customers should exceed the costs of the retention efforts.

We argue that CLV provides the best rationale for allocating marketing resources: organizations should invest marketing resources only in activities that increase CLV so that it is more than their costs. While this may seem obvious, organizations often do not follow this prescription, relying instead on simple heuristics such as allocating some percentage of sales or what was allocated in the previous year after an adjustment.

CLV is closely related to other concepts and metrics, and we now distinguish it from these other measures of loyalty and profitability. "*Customer profitability* is the difference between the revenues earned from and the costs associated with the customer relationship during a specified period," according to Pfeifer et al. (2005, p. 14). Other measures used in database marketing include *frequency*, the number of previous purchases, and *monetary value*, the sum of revenues earned from a customer during a period in the past. Customer profitability, frequency, and monetary value can be computed by counting or summing variables in a customer database. CLV, in contrast, cannot be directly observed because it occurs in the future, and therefore must be estimated by a statistical model. Many CLV models have been proposed, and the purpose of this book is to introduce some of them and their applications.

Another related term is *long-term value*. The sum in equation 1.1 goes to infinity, indicating that CLV includes the remainder of the customer's life. It is difficult to forecast cash flows far into the future with any reliability. We use the term CLV to refer to lifetime value (letting $t \to \infty$), and *long-term value* to indicate cash flows into a relatively long but finite future window (for example, when three years are being considered). An alternative to truncating the future window is to increase the discount rate, under the rationale that cash flows that are less certain should be discounted more than those with less "risk." We will also see in the next section that CLV can be estimated more reliably at the segment level than at the individual level. It may be optimal to allocate resources based on the expected cash flows over an entire lifetime, but a practical constraint is that managers and firms must demonstrate to their superiors and investors a more rapid return for their actions (Blattberg et al., 2009, Issue 14).

In dealing with uncertainty of future cash flows, one should not lose track of the big ideas. First, the firm should consider cash flows beyond those from the next sale because it can be profitable to acquire a customer at a loss as long as there is a high chance of positive future cash flows. Second, the effect that some marketing action has on CLV provides an upper bound for how much can be spent on the action.

Another related concept is *customer equity* (CE), which is the sum of CLV values over individuals within some group of customers (Blattberg et al., 2001; Blattberg and Deighton, 1996). The group often consists of all customers in a database, but could also refer to segments of customers. CE forecasts the financial value of a customer database, which is an intangible asset of many organizations. The CLV models developed here can be used to quantify the value of a customer database. Such calculations can be useful in assessing whether the stock price of a company is under- or over-valuing the company.

Figure 1.1 The integrated marketing process for increasing CLV

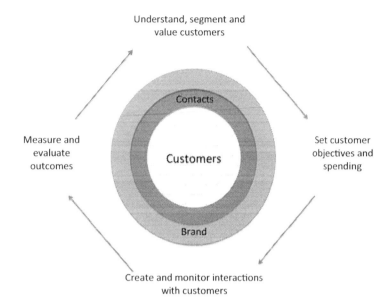

1.2   A process for increasing CLV

If a primary goal is for an organization to increase CLV, then the next question is how? Many processes and approaches have been proposed for managing customer relationships. We use the process in Figure 1.1 for organizing this book. The outer circle involves four broad steps and is consistent with other customer relationship management (CRM) processes. Each subsection below discusses one of the four steps. We first discuss the inner circles and their relationship to the outer CRM process.

The purpose of the process is to manage interactions between an organization and its customers. These interactions will be called *contact points*, or sometimes just *contacts*. Contact points include all customer encounters with a brand. Many contact points are initiated by the organization, such as advertising or direct marketing, but some are not, such as when customers call tech support or use the product. Other customers and non-customers also create contact points, such as when a consumer creates a video and posts it to YouTube or writes a product review on Amazon.

A difficult problem is maintaining the consistency of all the various contact points. A solution to this problem is to have a *brand concept*. By a brand, we mean the idea that the organization wants consumers to have of it. The brand idea explains why a product or service is of value to its consumers, and organizations should usually remind consumers of this value in its contact points. Conflicting contact points that do not support the brand may confuse consumers and be counter-productive.

The outer process in Figure 1.1 consists of CRM activities done by the organization. Customers experience contact points, which are aligned by the brand. The focus of this book is not on creating the brand, but it is important to recognize that the brand plays a critical role in CRM by providing the idea that should be communicated in contact points. Sometimes organizations give a marketing department responsibility for the brand, but other contacts are managed by other departments that do not coordinate their activities with marketing or other departments.

1.2.1   Understand, segment and value customers

An organization's customers will have different wants, needs, preferences, and behaviors. For example, some airline customers fly often while others do not. Some supermarket customers buy organics while others prefer conventional foods. Because of this heterogeneity, a firm should not offer the same contact points with all customers. Offering the marketing contact point of coupons for organic vegetables to a customer who buys only traditional food would not be relevant to the customer and would likely be ineffective, wasting marketing resources. Those flying 100,000 miles a year have different needs than those who fly once every other year, and all contact points—from e-mails and direct mails to security checkpoints—should be tailored to meet the needs of different customers and be justified financially. The ways to increase CLV vary across customers.

An approach to dealing with this heterogeneity is to segment customers into smaller group having similar behaviors, needs, and preferences, which is the first step in the process. Chapter 2 discusses customer segmentation strategies and clustering methods. This first step also involves understanding the motivations and needs of different segments, as well as estimating their value with the CLV models discussed in this book. The honeycomb pattern in the center of the diagram represent different segments of customers.

1.2.2   Strategies for increasing CLV

The second step is to set customer objectives and spending levels. CLV is especially useful in this step. After identifying subsegments of customers, the next step in the process of managing relationships is to specify objectives for each customer segment, which informs the creation of contact points in the next step. *The objectives should generally be to increase, or at least maintain, CLV.* We first consider existing customers, and later discuss acquiring new ones and reactivating lapsed ones.

There are three main ways to increase the CLV of existing customers:

1. Retain them longer.
2. Increase customers' revenues.
3. Decrease the costs of serving them, marketing to them, or both.

Different objectives will be applicable for different customer segments. In many businesses the most effective way to increase CLV is to increase the retention rate. We show in Chapter 3 how small increases in the "period" (for example, monthly) retention rate can have a profound impact on CLV. For example, consider a mobile phone provider who acquires customers and receives monthly payments from customers until they cancel. We will show that increasing the monthly retention rate from 94% to 97.5% will double CLV. Increasing it further to 99.25% doubles it again! Thus, focusing on retaining existing customers longer can be a rewarding strategy. If the objective is to increase retention rates, then the firm will try to understand what leads customers to churn and develop contact points to avoid it. Of course, the cost of such contact points should not exceed their incremental effect on CLV.

The second way of increasing CLV for existing customers is to *increase their revenues*, which is usually done by focusing on one of four approaches. The first is to increase the organization's *share of wallet* by getting customers to purchase more with the focal firm instead of a competitor. Suppose, for example, that a customer of an airline is spending about $5000 per year on airline tickets, but is splitting the purchases equally across two carriers. One carrier can increase this customer's CLV by shifting share. Airline loyalty programs offer strong incentives for travelers to concentrate their purchases with one carrier with "points pressure." Fliers want to reach the next tier of the program so that they will receive special perks such as priority boarding and shorter security queues. A customer who splits her miles with the two carriers might not fly enough to receive perks from either airline, but if she consolidates her flights with one airline, she will clear the "bar." Mutual funds charge lower loads for customers who have invested more than some amount, for example, a 5% rate for those who invest less than $100,000 and a 4% rate for those above $100,000. This is another contact point used to achieve the objective of increasing share of wallet.

A similar strategy is to *cross-sell* other products or services. A cell phone provider may acquire a customer with a basic plan having a small number of minutes and no additional services such as text messaging or Internet data. The provider might attempt to cross-sell additional services, which would increase monthly revenues and CLV. Likewise, an online retailer such as Amazon might attempt to cross-sell a book buyer other products in categories such as music, toys or electronic devices.

Revenues and CLV can also be increased by getting customers to *buy higher-margin products*. This is often called *up-selling*. For example, if we can assume that margins are constant across products then a wine store that can up-sell a customer from a $10 bottle of wine to a $15 bottle will increase revenues. In many categories margins are smaller for the cheapest products than for the intermediate and high-end versions, making the incentive for a firm to up-sell even stronger.

The fourth approach to increasing revenues is to get customers to *buy more often*. For example, if a computer company can get its loyal customers to buy a new laptop every two years rather than every three years, CLV will increase. The same is true for many other electronic devices and durables such as automobiles.

The point is that the way to increase CLV may vary over customers. Therefore, the firm should begin by segmenting customers as shown in Figure 1.1. For some customers, the most effective way to increase CLV will be to up-sell them. For other customers it might be to cross-sell them or increase their share of wallet. Different customers demand different strategies, which imply different contact points.

Organizations can also increase CLV by *making customers less costly to serve*. A famous example from the United States is bank teller fees. Banks realized that they had a substantial segment of customers who were not very profitable because they would visit the bank often and make small withdrawals or deposits with tellers. Tellers are expensive because banks must pay for their salaries and benefits, and because they must maintain branch locations. It would be more cost effective to have customers in this subsegment using ATMs. Many banks announced that they would charge low-profit customers—not all customers—a service fee for visiting the teller, which would increase their CLV by making them less costly to serve. In a similar vein, airlines and hotels commonly charge customers a fee to book a reservation over the phone, but do not charge a service fee for using their web site. The fee is a contact point designed to increase CLV by reducing the cost of serving the customer.

An example of reducing the cost of serving the customer is when the Netflix movie service announced a lower subscription price for people who will only download movies and not use their mail service. Part of the reason is that it is expensive to "pick, pack, and ship" a DVD to a customer, as well as pay for the return shipping, return the DVD to inventory, and account for lost or damaged DVDs. Netflix does not realize any of these marginal service costs when a customer streams a movie over the Internet. Another way to reduce the costs of serving a customer is to get customers to consolidate orders. For example, a grocery delivery service incurs a substantial cost to deliver an order. Customers who place larger, less-frequent orders are therefore more profitable than customers who order the same items in small, frequent orders.

Finally, organizations can increase CLV by *reducing marketing costs*. A common way of achieving this goal is to provide incentives for customer to sign up for longer contracts. For example, magazines and other media organizations will try to sell a two-year subscription instead of a one-year subscription because they will not have to spend marketing resources to keep the subscription until the end of the second year. Likewise mobile phone providers want to sell initial contracts that include substantial penalties for canceling within the first two years or so. Having customers commit to longer contracts should also lower the discount rate because positive future cash flows are more certain. A smaller discount rate also increases CLV in (1.1).

Existing customers can also create value to an organization through *referrals and word of mouth*. Cell phone providers routinely offer family plans as a way of generating referrals. Similarly, product reviews written by customers can influence others. Referrals and reviews are both examples of *customer engagement value* (Kumar et al., 2010).

Our discussion has focused on existing customers, but the same logic of setting objectives to increase CLV also applies to prospective and former customers. The obvious objective for a prospective customer is to get the customer to buy for the first time, but this goal is often too ambitious to achieve in a single step, and organizations might have greater success by breaking it up into smaller sub-goals. For example, perhaps the first step in getting a customer to purchase is to obtain the customer's permission to be marketed to. This would trigger a series of contacts designed to educate the prospect about the organization's product and its value to the consumer. The next step could be to get the prospect to visit the web site for a virtual product experience. There could be additional subgoals before trying to close the initial sale. Each of these subgoals corresponds to a subsegment, and prospective customers migrate between subsegments over time as the sub-goals are achieved.

A similar process applies to lapsed customers. The organization must understand why the customer stopped purchasing before it can develop relevant contact points to bring the customer back. A firm could use marketing research to develop a segmentation of lapsed customers based on the reason why the customer has discontinued the service. In the case of contractual services, this could lead to asking a question during the exit interview that classifies the canceling customer into the subsegment, which would then determine which marketing contacts, if any, the customer will receive in the future.

Another component of this second step is setting spending levels. *The incremental change in CLV informs how much money can be spent on a tactic.* A marketing contact point that costs $20 to increase a customer's CLV by $10 is not a good contact point. A contact costing $20 that increases CLV by $100 is a good one.

Many writers on this subject simplistically advocate "investing more resources in your best customers." This bromide suggests that customer investments should be based on the absolute value of a customer rather than the potential change in CLV due to an intervention. Under this strategy, a firm should invest a $20 contact in a high-value customer with a CLV of $1000 before investing the $20 contact in a customer with CLV = $100, but what if the $20 contact doubles the CLV of the low-value customer while having no effect on the high-value customer? Of course, if not giving the $20 contact to the high-CLV customer causes the customer to defect, changing CLV to 0, then the difference (increment) in CLV is great and the high-CLV customer should get the contact. *Incremental CLV should determine spending levels, not absolute levels of CLV.*

1.2.3   Creating and monitoring contact points

The third step of the integrated marketing process for increasing CLV Figure 1.1 is to create and manage *contact points* with customers.

Contact points include those initiated by the organization such as traditional advertising, sales promotion, and direct marketing, plus responses to consumer-initiated contacts from web sites and interactive media along with participation in consumer-to-consumer and third-party dialogues. In addition, these interactions also include points of contact that are not traditionally found under the "marketing function," such as customer service, technical support, retail distribution, web sites, and the like.

We will not discuss the creation of such contact points in this book. There are many other books (for example, Rossiter and Percy, 1997 or Stone and Jacobs, 2001) that discuss the creation of advertising and direct marketing messages, web site design, call-center management, and so on.

The key point is that the amount of money that can be spent on such tactics is informed by the change that they will have on a customer's CLV. These decisions should *not* be made based on what was spent last year, some percentage of sales, or any related heuristic.

1.2.4   Measuring outcomes

The fourth step is to measure what happens as a consequence of the contact points. This is essential for at least two reasons. First, the organization must know whether a contact point is achieving its objectives so that it can discontinue using ineffective ones. For example, if customers acquired from banner ads displayed on a particular web site turn out to have CLV that is less than the acquisition cost, then the company should stop displaying banner ads on that site.

Measuring the effectiveness of a contact point usually requires some sort of experimental design (for example, a randomly selected set of customers from the segment receive the contact while others do not, making up the control group). See the discussion of *causal designs* in marketing research books or experimental design books for further discussion.

Second, knowing what happened will determine what contacts the firm will make with a customer next. For example, suppose that the objective of a contact was to up-sell a customer to a premium product line. If the marketing contact point is successful and the customer is now buying the premium line, then the next round of contacts should be designed to further increase the customer's CLV. Perhaps the next objective should be to increase share of wallet by cross-selling another category. Or perhaps it should be to get the customer to increase purchase frequency. The process is iterative and customers will migrate between segments over time. Chapter 5 will discuss Markov chains for modeling such transitions between "states" (segments).

In summary, the organization should begin by identifying different segments of customers. Next it should decide on strategies for *increasing* the CLV of customers in each segment and then create contact points. The last step is to measure the outcomes from the contact points to determine whether the contacts work and whether the customer has migrated to a different segment.

We close this section with a caution about CLV. The overarching goal for an organization is to increase CLV. The firm should measure CLV and its components such as retention rates and spending levels as a way gauging its progress toward this goal. But CLV is only half of the story. High values of CLV result from providing value to customers. CLV measures value to the organization, but there should be a parallel set of metrics measuring whether the organization is successfully creating value for its customers.

1.3   A taxonomy of CLV models

The focus of this book is on modeling CLV, but the issues involved in doing so depend on the nature of the business. One helpful way of classifying organizations is according to whether there is a *contractual relationship*, where there is an observable end to the relationship. For example, many services know when a relationship has ended: cell phone customers exit their contract and stop paying their bill; cable TV and Internet service providers observe when customers cancel the service; media content subscriptions end when customers cancel their subscription or fail to renew it; health-club membership expire at a certain time. These are sometimes called *gone-for-good* models, because the models assume customers who cancel the service will not return. The models in Chapters 3 and 4 address this situation. The most important issue in these situations is retaining customers over time, and survival analysis models will be used to study the time until a customer cancels.

The other main class of CLV models is called "always a share." These models do not assume that customer inactivity implies the customer will never return. For example, a customer who does not fly this month might fly again next month. A retail customer who does not buy this month might come back next month. A donor who does not donate this month to some nonprofit might donate again next month. A different class of models will be used for such situations and they are covered in chapters 5 and 6.

Segmentation Models

2

Contents

Segmentation is one of the central concepts in marketing because in almost all situations customers have different wants, needs, preferences, and so on. Marketers call this *heterogeneity*. Whenever such heterogeneity exists, organizations that recognize and accommodate differences can achieve an advantage over competitors in a category. Conversely, organizations that do not accommodate differences across customers and offer only one version of their marketing mix create opportunities for competitors. If customers are heterogeneous then it follows that not all needs will be met with only one offering, and the needs of some customers will not be satisfied as well as they could be. A competitor can offer a better-targeted product and attract such customers.

One approach for addressing heterogeneity is segmentation. Customers with similar wants and needs are grouped into segments so that an organization can better meet the different needs. This chapter discusses models for identifying segments. Before we begin this discussion, it is useful to distinguish between the marketing problems that the models address. A clear understanding of applications can inform many model-building decisions. The focus of the chapter is on the models rather than the marketing strategy, but analysts will have to make many subjective decisions and the more they understand about applications, the more effective they will be. There are two main applications:

1. *Market segmentation* is covered in every marketing management book (for example, see Kotler and Keller, 2012). An entire market is first *segmented* into homogeneous groups. The organization usually *targets* one market segment and develops a product or service and brand for this segment. For example, automotive companies segment the market for cars and develop products or brands for different segments. There is a segment of families, and companies will produce, for example, minivans for this segment. There is also a segment of people seeking more luxury, and there are many cars targeted at this market segment.

2. *Customization and personalization to subsegments.* Within a market segment there will still be heterogeneity. Customization is when a firm allows its customers to configure the marketing mix to meet these heterogeneous needs more closely. It is important to note that, with customization, it is the customers who configure to mix, not the company. The company enables the customization by offering up a menu of options, and the customer decides. For example, consider the Dell web site. Dell recognizes that customers have different needs depending on whom they are buying for: "home," "small and medium businesses," "public sector," or "large enterprise." The Dell landing page asks visitors to select one. Automobile companies allow consumers to configure aspects of a car. Cell phone customers can configure their plans. Note that the company does not target a single subsegment as it did with market segmentation. All subsegments are customers in the targeted market segment, and the organization must determine how to market to each. For further discussion, see Malthouse (2003a), Malthouse and Calder (2005), Calder and Malthouse (2004), and Malthouse and Elsner (2006) for discussion of the strategic issues.

2.1 Introduction to segmentation models

We have a random sample of n people and assume that each person belongs to exactly one of K *unobserved* groups, which will be labeled $1, 2, \ldots, K$. The value K is fixed before estimating any of the models discussed here. By unobserved we mean that we do not know from which group a person comes—the identifying label has not been observed. It will be the job of our model to find these groups and estimate how likely it is that each person comes from each group. Groups will also be called *clusters, types, segments* or *subsegments*. Let $g_i \in \{1, \ldots, K\}$ be the true group membership of person $i = 1, \ldots, n$. The variable g is sometimes called a *latent variable* because it is not directly observed.

Instead of observing group membership, we have measured p variables that indicate group membership. Let x_{ij} be the observed value of variable j on person i. These variables are sometimes called *manifest* or *observed variables* because they are thought to be manifestations of the unobserved latent variable g. We use the notation $\mathbf{x}_i = (x_{i1}, \ldots, x_{ip})$ to indicate the row vector of observed variables for person i.

We now illustrate these terms and motivate the cluster analysis model with two examples that will be used throughout this chapter.

Table 2.1 Crosstab of the time spent reading a newspaper during a week (octile number) and the number of sections read

Time	Number of Sections								Total
	0	1	2	3	4	5	6	7	
0	370	0	0	0	0	0	0	0	370
1	9	127	119	55	34	55	34	21	454
2	3	72	94	68	48	74	48	29	436
3	1	43	107	48	40	63	52	38	392
4	0	21	58	39	32	47	30	25	252
5	0	15	40	23	25	51	38	32	224
6	0	21	67	54	39	90	59	71	401
7	0	15	47	31	51	103	67	96	410
Total	383	314	532	318	269	483	328	312	2,939

EXAMPLE 2.1: Newspaper readership
Table 2.1 gives a crosstab from a random sample $n = 2,939$ Chicago residents of the time spent with a newspaper during a week and the number of sections "read or looked into." In

this example, there are $p = 2$ manifest variables, time spent (x_{i1}) and sections read (x_{i2}). Are there types of newspaper readers? See Malthouse and Calder (2002) for an expanded version of this segmentation.

Solution   With only one or two manifest variables, as we have here, we do not really need cluster analysis or any other segmentation model to identify segments. We can simply inspect frequency distributions, histograms, crosstabs and other descriptive statistics to identify natural groups. When there are more than two manifest variables, such visual methods are less possible. We first read the data into SAS with the following program:

Program 2.1 Read newspaper data

```
DATA np;
   INPUT time sections count @@;
DATALINES;
0 0 370    1 0 9     1 1 127    1 2 119   1 3 55    1 4 34    1 5 55    1 6 34    1 7 21
2 0 3      2 1 72    2 2 94     2 3 68     2 4 48    2 5 74    2 6 48    2 7 29    3 0 1
3 1 43     3 2 107   3 3 48     3 4 40     3 5 63    3 6 52    3 7 38    4 1 21    4 2 58
4 3 39     4 4 32    4 5 47     4 6 30     4 7 25    5 1 15    5 2 40    5 3 23    5 4 25
5 5 51     5 6 38    5 7 32     6 1 21     6 2 67    6 3 54    6 4 39    6 5 90    6 6 59
6 7 71     7 1 15    7 2 47     7 3 31     7 4 51    7 5 103   7 6 67    7 7 96
RUN;
```

Figure 2.1 Contour plot of the newspaper data, where contours numbers show the square root of the counts. The BMW specifies the *bandwidth multiplier*, which controls the amount of smoothing.

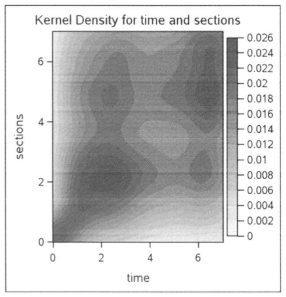

```
DATA rootnp;
   SET np;
   rootcount = SQRT(count);
RUN;

ODS GRAPHICS ON;
PROC KDE DATA=rootnp;
   BIVAR time sections /
     PLOTS=CONTOUR BWM=0.8;
   FREQ rootcount;
RUN;
ODS GRAPHICS OFF;
```

Figure 2.1 uses `PROC KDE` to create a kernel density plot of the crosstab. A kernel density plot is like a two-dimensional histogram, showing the joint distribution of `time` and `sections` by representing areas with higher probabilities with darker shades of red and areas with lower probabilities in blue. The `ODS GRAPHICS ON` statement invokes graphics in the output delivery system. Those using SAS 9.3 or later in the Microsoft Windows environment do not need to include this command, because ODS is invoked automatically.

An inspection of the crosstab and plot shows a very large group of 370 *nonreaders* who spend no time with a newspaper and read no sections. This appears as a dark red peak in the lower left corner of the kernel density plot. The contours are close together showing a steep ascent. It would seem reasonable to have one type of reader to be these nonreaders.

There are also large numbers of people who read very little of the newspaper, with small values of time and sections. There is a peak on the kernel density plot around time = 2 and sections = 2. This type of reader could be called a *light reader*, because those in this group spend little time with the paper and only read a small number of sections.

There is also a peak of *heavy readers* in the upper right corner of people who spend a large amount of time with the newspaper and read most sections. There is another peak in the upper left corner consisting of people who read many sections but do not spend a lot of time with the paper. This group could be called *skimmers*, because they probably skim the many sections they read in the small amount of time they claim to spend with the newspaper.

There is a fifth peak in the lower left corner consisting of people who spend a substantial amount of time with the newspaper, but who only read a narrow set of sections. We call these *selective* readers.

Some alternative ways of visualizing the data are as follows. Figure 2.2 uses `PROC SGPLOT` to make a jittered scatter plot. Jittering adds a small amount of uniform random noise to the values with the `RANUNI` function. Without the jittering we would see one point for each combination of time and sections. Again, darker shades indicate larger counts.

Figure 2.2 Jittered scatter plot of the counts from newspaper data

```
DATA npjitter;
  SET np;
  DO i = 1 TO count;
    Jtime = time + RANUNI(1234)/2-1;
    Jsections = sections + RANUNI(1234)/2-1;
    OUTPUT;
  END;
  LABEL Jtime = "Jittered Time"
    Jsections = "Jittered Sections";
  KEEP Jtime Jsections;
RUN;


PROC SGPLOT DATA=npjitter;
  SCATTER X=Jtime Y=Jsections /
  MARKERATTRS=graphdata2(symbol=circlefilled)
    TRANSPARENCY=.9;
RUN;
```

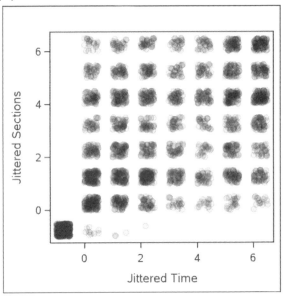

Another way of visualizing the joint distribution is with a *bubble plot*, as shown in Figure 2.3. The bubble plot encodes the number of cases (joint probabilities) using the areas of the plotted circles. The `DATALABEL` option causes the `SGPLOT` procedure to show counts on the top right of each circle.

EXAMPLE 2.2:   Theater attitudes

Five theaters that stage non-musical plays in Chicago joined forces to develop a marketing plan. The group of theaters is called North Shore Live. In addition to the segment of current theater attendees, the group wants to attract people who do not currently attend theater productions. In developing a marketing plan, the group conducted a marketing research study in which they recruited a random sample of approximately 3,000 adults living in the Chicago area to complete a survey. Data for this example are in `theater.csv`.

Figure 2.3 Bubble plot of the newspaper data, where the area of the circles indicate the counts

```
PROC SGPLOT DATA=np;
  BUBBLE X=time Y=sections SIZE=count
    / DATALABEL=count;
RUN;
```

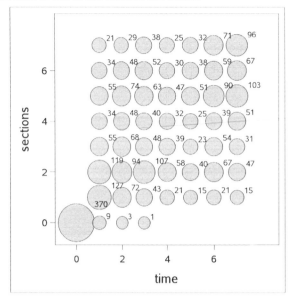

The survey asked respondents 14 questions measuring their attitudes and beliefs about theater using semantic differential scales. For example, respondents were asked to rate the experience of attending live theater using a seven-point scale where 1 equaled "not fun" and 7 equaled "fun." Exploratory factor analysis suggested that 10 questions loaded on a single factor, and that the remaining four questions did not load on this factor nor form another one. We therefore have dimensions:

1. `attitude`: The 10 questions averaged to form this variable are 1 = not fun and 7 = fun, 1 = not exciting and 7 = exciting, 1 = boring and 7 = stimulating, 1 = bad and 7 = good, 1 = uncomfortable and 7 = comfortable, 1 = cannot appreciate and 7 = can appreciate, 1 = irritating and 7 = relaxing, 1 = disliked and 7 = liked, and 1 = not educational and 7 = educational.

2. `planning`, 1 equals "spur of the moment" and 7 equals "requires planning."

3. `parents`, 1 equals "my parents disliked" and 7 equals "my parents liked plays."

4. `goodval`, 1 equals "too expensive" and 7 equals "good value for the money."

5. `getto`, 1 equals "hard to get to" and 7 equals "easy to get to."

We would like to find different types of people with respect to their attitudes toward theater. There are $n = 2,747$ respondents and $p = 5$ manifest variables in this example, `attitude`, `planning`, `parents`, `goodval` and `getto`. With five manifest variables we will be unable to use simple visual methods for identifying clusters and will have to rely on segmentation models.

Segmentation models will be used to answer the following questions:

1. How many segments are there? In practice the analyst will have to decide how many segments are appropriate.

2. For a specified number of segments K and set of manifest variables, what are natural groups? For example, a good segmentation method will use information about the manifest newspaper readership variables, time spent and sections read, to find the five

types of readers discussed above (nonreaders, light readers, heavy readers, skimmers and selective readers). As we saw from the discussion of Figure 2.2, a quantitative way of describing, for example, light readers is that that they have a mean time of about 3 and a mean number of sections of about 2. These means will be called *class-conditional means*, because they are conditional on group membership $E(\mathbf{X}|g)$.

3. How large is each segment? For example, there were 370 nonreaders out of a total of 2,939 respondents, suggesting that about 12.6% of the population is a complete nonreader. The relative sizes of the segments will be given by the *prior distribution*, $P(G = g)$, where G is a random variable indicating the group membership of a randomly selected person from the population.

4. To which segment does each respondent belong, considering the information we have on the person? Segmentations will ultimately be used to develop marketing actions and often personalized marketing contact points. If we want to target a personalized contact at an individual, we will need to know from which segment the person comes. Even if we will not be targeting personalized offers, we will need to know segment memberships to do further profiling. The *posterior distribution*, $P(G = g|\mathbf{x})$, will help us answer this question.

This chapter discusses two models for answering these questions. The first is K-means clustering and the second is the finite mixture model. We will see that it is possible to think of K-means as a special case of the more general finite mixture model. Advantages of the K-means model include that it is comparatively simple to estimate and nearly universally available in commercial statistical software. While not all data sets come from the model assumed by K-means, we can often transform the data before estimation so that it will give a useful solution.

2.2 K-means clustering

2.2.1   The K-means model

The K-means method was originally proposed as a heuristic algorithm for finding clusters (MacQueen, 1967) rather than as a formal statistical model. Since then others (Hastie et al., 2001, §14.3.7 or Venables and Ripley, 1999, p. 340) have noted that the K-means algorithm is estimating the parameters from a specific statistical model that is related to the one-way MANOVA model. We start with the model, and then state the algorithm.

As noted earlier x_{ij} is the observed value of variable j for respondent i, who is assumed to be from unobserved group $g_i \in \{1, 2, \ldots, K\}$. Suppose that the true mean of all members of cluster k on variable j is μ_{jk}. The K-means model hypothesizes that

$$x_{ij} = \mu_{jg_i} + e_{ij}, \tag{2.1}$$

where e_{ij} is an error term with mean $E(e_{ij}) = 0$ and variance σ^2, which is common across all variables and clusters. It is also common to assume that the errors have normal distributions.

This model, with a common error variance, implies that the distribution of points from some cluster is round or spherical. See the section 2.4.1 for further discussion. It also implies that all of the clusters have the same shape and dispersion. When the manifest variables do not fall into *round* clumps of equal size, the K-means model can have problems. For example, the clumps have elliptical shapes instead of round ones. The finite mixture model allows for other shapes and varying sizes. Alternatively, transforming the data before estimating the K-means model may also help to make the clusters more spherical (but transformations will not address the equal-size issue).

EXAMPLE 2.3:   Bivariate Gaussian mixture

We now illustrate this model with a mathematical example. Following the notation from above, generate 100 normal observations from each of $K = 2$ clusters where $\boldsymbol{\mu}_1 = (0, 0)'$, $\boldsymbol{\mu}_2 = (3, 0)'$, and the common variance is $\sigma^2 = 1$. Each mode is a *bivariate normal distribution*, which will be discussed further in section 2.4.1. Plot the true clusters.

Solution   See Figure 2.4 to generate and plot the data. There are two clusters, the blue circles ($\circ$) and red plus signs ($+$). Each cluster has a round shape.

Figure 2.4 Bivariate Gaussian mixture

```
TITLE "Ideal situation for k-means";
DATA clus;
  DO i=1 TO 100;
    x1 = RANNOR(123);
    y1 = RANNOR(123);
    truth=1;
    OUTPUT;
    x1 = RANNOR(123)+3;
    y1 = RANNOR(123);
    truth=2;
    OUTPUT;
  END;
  LABEL x1 = "x (inches)"
    y1 = "y (inches)";
RUN;
PROC SGPLOT DATA=clus;
  SCATTER X=x1 y=y1 / GROUP=truth;
RUN;
```

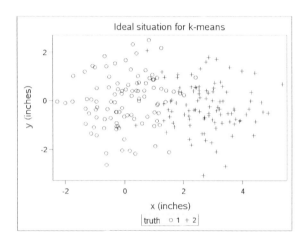

As mentioned in the introduction to this section, this model is related to the one-way MANOVA model. The difference is that the group memberships g_i are unobserved. With MANOVA the analyst knows to which group an observation belongs. For example, some observations were in a control group, some received treatment A, and others received treatment B. With cluster analysis the analyst does not observe cluster membership g_i.

K-means generally works best with numerical variables. If one wishes to include categorical variables the finite mixture models discussed in section 2.4 accommodate categorical variables in a natural way (see, in particular, latent class models in section 2.4.2). Alternatively, there are two other approaches for incorporating categorical variables in a K-mean analysis. The first is to partition—without a model—the observations on important categorical variables and then apply K-mean to each partition. For example, a demographic segmentation system might initially partition households into married couples, single males and single females. One could then apply K-means clustering within each of the marital-status-gender groups, clustering on numerical variables such as age, income, and so on. The second approach is to create dummy variables and apply the variable weighting methods discussed on page 32.

2.2.2   The K-means algorithm

To use K-means effectively it is important to know something about the algorithm that estimates the parameters, which will help you understand the options and output in the FASTCLUS procedure in SAS. The K-means algorithm is as follows:

1. *Initialize.* Select an initial set of *cluster centers*, or *seeds* $\hat{\mu}_{jk}^{0}$, where $k = 1, \ldots, K$ and the superscript 0 indicates the iteration number. Initialize iteration counter $h = 1$. SAS selects a random set of observations to be used as seeds or the user can specify a data set containing seeds with the `SEEDS=` option.

2. *Assign clusters.* Assign observation i to the cluster whose mean is closest. The Euclidean distance[1] between point $\mathbf{x}_i$ and cluster center $\hat{\boldsymbol{\mu}}_k^{h-1}$ is given by

$$d_{ik}^{h} = \sqrt{\sum_{j=1}^{p} \left(x_{ij} - \hat{\mu}_{jk}^{h-1}\right)^2}. \tag{2.2}$$

Observation i is assigned the cluster that is closest, that is,

$$g_i^h = \operatorname{argmin}_k d_{ik}^h$$

The argmin_k indicates that g_i^h equals the value k giving the smallest value of d_{ik}^h.

3. *Compute cluster means.* With cluster assignments fixed, compute *cluster means*, which are reported in `PROC FASTCLUS` output and saved to a data set using the `MEANS=` option. Some authors call them *cluster centroids* or *centers*.

$$\hat{\mu}_{jk}^h = \operatorname{average}\{x_{ij} : g_i^h = k\}.$$

In other words, the new estimate of cluster mean k is the simple average of all observations assigned to it ($g_i^h = k$).

4. *Compute SSE.* This is called the *sum of squared errors* or total *within-cluster variation*.

$$\text{SSE} = \sum_{i=1}^{n} \sum_{j=1}^{p} \left(x_{ij} - \hat{\mu}_{jg_i^h}^h\right)^2 = \sum_{i=1}^{n} d_{ig_i^h}^2. \tag{2.3}$$

The errors are really distances between each observation and its closest center.[2]

5. *Loop.* Let $h \leftarrow h + 1$ and return to step 2 until the *convergence criterion* is satisfied or the *maximum iterations* is exceeded. In the `FASTCLUS` procedure use the `MAXITER` option to specify the maximum number of iterations and the `CONVERGE` option to specify the convergence criterion. The convergence criterion is usually that the change in SSE be small (or, according to Hastie, Tibshirani and Friedman 2001, p. 462, assignments do not change).

This algorithm attempts to minimize SSE, which is a combinatorial optimization problem and is computationally very difficult. In particular, this algorithm is not guaranteed to converge to the optimal solution, and different starting seeds might produce different solutions. Because of these problems, analysts might want to estimate the K-means solution multiple times with different starting seeds and select the solution with the smallest value of SSE. See Example 2.6 below.

2.2.3 K-means examples

This section shows how to use the `FASTCLUS` procedure and interpret its output.

EXAMPLE 2.4:   Bivariate Gaussian mixture (continued)

Continuing Example 2.3, estimate the two-cluster solution using K-means and plot the estimated clusters.

Figure 2.5 Bivariate Gaussian mixture

```
TITLE "K-means solution";
PROC FASTCLUS DATA=clus MAXC=2 OUT=clusout;
  VAR x1 y1;
RUN;
DATA anno;
  SET clusout(WHERE=(truth NE cluster));
  RETAIN function "oval" height width 3
    x1space y1space "datavalue";
RUN;
PROC SGPLOT DATA=clusout SGANNO=anno;
  SCATTER X=x1 y=y1 / GROUP=cluster;
  LINEPARM x=1.456 Y=-0.111 slope=12.08;
  YAXIS MIN=-3 MAX=3;
RUN;
```

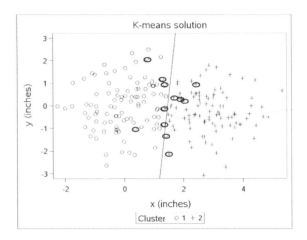

Solution The program next to Figure 2.5 estimates the solution. MAXC= specifies the number of clusters and OUT= saves the cluster assignments in the clusout data set. The scatter plot shows the *estimated*, rather than true, clusters.

   The points are divided by a line: all points to the left of the line are classified as blue circles and all point to the right are classified as red plus signs. The reason that the boundary is a line is that K-means assigns points to the closest center. The line is set of points that are equal distance from the estimated cluster centers.[3] The circled observations are misclassified.

Table 2.2 Cluster means and standard deviations for bivariate Gaussian example

Cluster Means		
Cluster	x1	y1
1	0.030879543	0.007211593
2	2.881756761	-0.228853971

Cluster Standard Deviations		
Cluster	x1	y1
1	0.878636684	1.067440664
2	0.859297893	0.919903954

   The cluster means and standard deviations from the output are provided in Table 2.2. The cluster 1 means $(0.0309, 0.0072)'$ estimate the true value $(0,0)'$ and $(2.88, -0.229)'$ estimates $(3,0)'$. The cluster standard deviations are all around the true value $\sigma = 1$.

EXAMPLE 2.5:   Newspaper readership continued

Find the five-cluster solution for the newspaper data using PROC FASTCLUS. The number of people in the sample with each unique combination of time and section values is given by the count variable.

Solution The program below shows how to estimate the solution. The MAXC=5 argument specifies the number of clusters and CONVERGE=0 indicates that iterations should continue until there is no change in the objective function value. All of the variables that are to be used in defining the clusters should be specified in the VAR statement. Because the count variable indicates the number of responses for each time-sections combination, we use a FREQ statement; it is more common to have one row for each respondent, and then the FREQ statement is not necessary. The DRIFT option requests a slightly different optimization algorithm that sometimes improves the solution.

Program 2.2 Find K-means solution to newspaper problem

```
PROC FASTCLUS DATA=np MAXC=5 CONVERGE=0 DRIFT;
  VAR time sections;
  FREQ count;
RUN;
```

There are several sections in the output. The second column in the output below gives a frequency distribution for the clusters, which we will denote by n_k. For example, $n_1 = 628$ people are assigned to cluster 1. The third column gives estimates of the within-cluster standard deviation, which indicates how heterogeneous the segment is. If $\hat{\mu}_{jk}$ is the final cluster mean of variable j in cluster k, then the RMS Std Deviation for cluster k is

$$\sqrt{\frac{1}{p(n_k - 1)} \sum_{g_i = k} \sum_{j=1}^{p} (x_{ij} - \hat{\mu}_{jk})^2}$$

Cluster 1 has the smallest value, which indicates that it is the most homogeneous. Cluster 5 has the largest. The value 0.6619 is the typical distance (or deviation) from the center of observations in cluster 1.

Cluster Summary					
Cluster	Frequency	RMS Std Deviation	Maximum Distance from Seed to Observation	Nearest Cluster	Distance Between Cluster Centroids
1	628	0.6619	1.6876	2	2.6935
2	606	0.8278	2.2340	1	2.6935
3	428	0.8855	1.9979	4	3.2584
4	607	0.8084	1.6397	3	3.2584
5	670	1.0265	2.2511	2	3.2371

The section of the output below gives measures of the total variation. (Total STD is the typical distance from a single grand mean.) Let $\hat{\mu}_{j\cdot}$ be the overall mean of variable j. Then the Total STD of variable j is its sample standard deviation, which tells us the typical deviation from grand mean $\hat{\mu}_{j\cdot}$.

$$\sqrt{\frac{1}{(n - 1)} \sum_{i=1}^{n} (x_{ij} - \hat{\mu}_{j\cdot})^2}$$

The Within STD for variable j indicates the typical distance an observation is from its respective cluster mean.

$$\sqrt{\frac{1}{(n - K)} \sum_{i=1}^{n} (x_{ij} - \hat{\mu}_{jg_i})^2}$$

It computes R^2 values, indicating the fraction of variation explained by the clusters. For example, $88.0895\% \approx 1 - (0.81831/2.36950)^2$ of the variation in `time` is explained by having five means rather than one grand mean. The Within STD of the OVER-ALL variable equals RMSE and is an indication of the overall fit of the model.

Statistics for Variables				
Variable	Total STD	Within STD	R-Square	RSQ/(1-RSQ)
time	2.36950	0.81831	0.880895	7.395956
sections	2.25379	0.88257	0.846862	5.530065
OVER-ALL	2.31237	0.85105	0.864730	6.392614

The output below gives the final cluster means $(E(\mathbf{X}|g))$, which we earlier denoted by $\hat{\mu}_{jk}$. For example, cluster 1 has a mean of (.42, .58). Referring back to Figure 2.2, cluster 1 corresponds to the nonreaders in the lower left corner. Cluster 2 has a mean of (2.6, 2.1) and matches the light reader segment. Cluster 3, with a mean of (6.1, 2.7), comprises the selective readers in the lower right corner of Figure 2.2. Cluster 4 corresponds to the heavy readers in the upper right corner. Cluster 5 corresponds to the skimmers in the upper left corner. Thus, it appears that K-means has recovered the groups that the plots revealed. As we indicated earlier, with only two manifest variables we could possibly use such plots to identify clusters instead of K-means, but in higher dimensions we will need some clustering model.

Cluster Means		
Cluster	time	sections
1	0.415605096	0.581210191
2	2.627062706	2.118811881
3	6.095794393	2.670560748
4	6.238879736	5.925864909
5	2.473134328	5.352238806

The last part of the output gives the within-cluster (sample) standard deviations for each of the clustered variables. As we saw in the RMS Std Deviation column of the output above, cluster 1 is the most homogeneous and cluster 5 is the most heterogeneous. While the RMS Std Deviation gives an overall typical deviation from the cluster center that is averaged over the dimensions, the cluster standard deviations below break out the typical deviations by manifest variable. For example, the overall RMS Std Deviation for cluster 3 was 0.8855, but the standard deviations below tell us that there is more variation in sections (0.999) than time (0.754). Likewise, there is more variation in the time dimension for cluster 2 than in the sections dimension.

Cluster Standard Deviations		
Cluster	time	sections
1	0.502826255	0.789543183
2	0.897854349	0.751247496
3	0.754490740	0.999471834
4	0.762532733	0.851773457
5	1.039587432	1.013268949

EXAMPLE 2.6: Newspaper example with different seeds

Earlier we suggested that K-means is sensitive to starting values. Estimate the five-cluster solution to the newspaper example with 100 different random seeds.

Solution   The program below accomplishes the task. It consists of macro `multseed`, which is passed the number of starting seeds. We use PROC SURVEYSELECT to select a simple random sample of size N=5 from the original data. The output data set from PROC SURVEYSELECT containing the starting seeds is passed to the SEEDS= option of PROC FASTCLUS.

Program 2.3 The `multseed` macro for finding multiple cluster solutions with different starting seeds

```
%MACRO multseed(n);                              /* stack answers in single data set ans */
%DO i = 1 %TO &n;                                  DATA ans;
  PROC SURVEYSELECT DATA=np OUT=seeds N=5            SET out
    SEED=&i NOPRINT;                                   %IF &i>1 %THEN %DO;
  RUN;                                                    ans
  PROC FASTCLUS DATA=np MAXC=5 CONVERGE=0              %END;
      DRIFT SEEDS=seeds OUTSTAT=out LEAST=2          ;
      NOPRINT MEAN=meanout;                          KEEP seed over_all;
    VAR time sections;                             RUN;
    FREQ count;                                  %END;
  RUN;                                           %MEND;
  DATA out;
    SET out(WHERE=(_TYPE_="WITHIN_STD"));        %multseed(100);
    /* assign seed number to RMSE value */       PROC UNIVARIATE DATA=ans PLOT;
    seed = &i;                                      VAR OVER_ALL;
  RUN;                                              ID seed;
                                                 RUN;
```

Figure 2.6 Histogram of the RMSE values from 100 different K-means solutions using different random seeds

```
TITLE "Distribution of RMSE";
PROC SGPLOT DATA=ans;
  HISTOGRAM over_all /
    SCALE=count
    BINWIDTH=.01;
  XAXIS DISPLAY=(NOLABEL);
RUN;
```

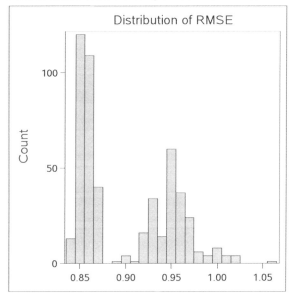

As we noted earlier the algorithm is not guaranteed to converge to the optimal solution. Figure 2.6 gives a histogram of the RMSE values across the 100 starting seeds. Recall that RMSE describes the typical distance of an observation to its closest center and is a measure of the overall fit of the model. The variation across starting values is substantial. The best solution has RMSE = 0.8429, yet some solutions have RMSE = 1.015. Figure 2.7 shows all of the estimated means from different seeds. There is substantial variation in the estimated cluster centers.

We note from the Extreme Observations section of the PROC UNIVARIATE output that there are multiple seeds that produce the best solution, including 31, 60, 93, 99, and 94. The ID statement requests that PROC UNIVARIATE label the extreme values by the seed variable. Program 2.4 estimates the best solution out of these 100 seeds.

Figure 2.7 Estimated cluster centers of 100 different K-means solutions using different random seeds

```
PROC SGPLOT DATA=ans;
  SCATTER x=time y=sections;
RUN;
```

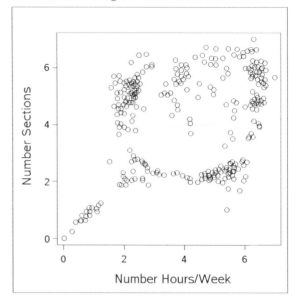

Program 2.4 Best solution to newspaper example (out of 100 seeds)

```
TITLE "Best solution";
PROC SURVEYSELECT DATA=np OUT=seeds N=5 SEED=31;
RUN;
PROC FASTCLUS DATA=np MAXC=5 CONVERGE=0 DRIFT SEEDS=seeds
  OUTSTAT=out LEAST=2 MEAN=meanout OUT=asgn;
  VAR time sections;
  FREQ count;
RUN;
```

The solution is summarized in Table 2.3, which has the minimum information about the cluster solution that one would want to present. The `MEAN=` and `OUT=` options save the cluster means and assignments to data sets and Figure 2.8 plots these means as stars, along with a scatter plot of unique time-section combinations plotted as numbers indicating the cluster to which each point is assigned. Each point is assigned to the cluster mean that is closest to it, and the boundaries are indicated by lines on the plot.

Table 2.3 K-means solution to the newspaper data

Number	Cluster				
	1	2	3	4	5
Name	Nonreader	Light	Skimmer	Heavy	Selective
Cases (n)	509	725	670	607	428
Percentage	17%	25%	23%	21%	15%
time	0.28	2.36	2.47	6.24	6.10
sections	0.25	2.10	5.35	5.93	2.67
Color	Blue	Red	Green	Brown	Purple

The first row of Table 2.3 gives the number of observations assigned to each cluster. A total of 509 observations from the entire data set of 2,939 were assigned to cluster 1, which comprises 17% of the data. Cluster 2 is the largest with $725/2,939 \approx 25\%$ of the cases.

Figure 2.8 Plot showing the best means and cluster assignments for the newspaper example

```
DATA clusout;
  SET clusout meanout(KEEP=time sections);
  LENGTH clus $6.;
  IF cluster=. THEN clus = "Center";
  ELSE clus=PUT(cluster, $1.);
  LABEL clus = "Cluster";
RUN;

DATA myanno;
  DRAWSPACE='datavalue'; FUNCTION='line';
  X1=-.1; Y1=3.5; X2=4.5; Y2=3.5; OUTPUT;
  X1=4.5; Y1=4.5; X2=7.1; Y2=4.5; OUTPUT;
RUN;
PROC SGPLOT DATA=clusout SGANNO=myanno;
  SCATTER X=time Y=sections / GROUP=clus;
  REFLINE 4.5 / AXIS=x;
  LINEPARM X=2.5 Y=0 SLOPE=-1;
RUN;
```

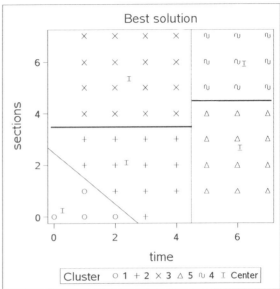

The next two rows give the estimated cluster means, which are plotted as stars on Figure 2.8. All observed combinations of time and sections are also plotted on the scatter plot as colored symbols representing the assigned cluster. Starting in the lower left corner the points are shown as blue circles and are nonreaders. The plot shows that the nonreader label is somewhat misleading because some of the people assigned to the cluster read occasionally, but their readership is very light. The star plotted at (0.28, 0.25) is the cluster center for this group and is the average, weighted by the respondent counts, of all the observations assigned to this cluster: $\{(0,0),(1,0),(2,0),(1,1)\}$. These assignments and the distances between the points and the respective centers are in the `asgn` data set. The lines partition the domain into the clusters and can be thought of as cluster boundaries.

We usually want to generate multiple cluster solutions and visualize them. For example, we may want to compare the five- and six-cluster solutions so that we can decide which is more actionable. Graphs can often help us understand a complex data set more quickly than numerical summaries such as means and standard deviations. A good way to visualize a cluster solution is with a *multi-panel display* using PROC SGPANEL. Each cluster is plotted in what Tufte (2001) calls a *small multiple*, or panel. Information about each variable is shown in the panel. The highest level of summarization would be to show only the cluster mean, but one could instead give box plots showing within cluster dispersion and skewness as well. The `doclus` macro in Program 2.5 will run multiple cluster solutions (from `first` to `last`) and generate a multi-panel display of the cluster means using PROC SGPANEL.

The macro expects arguments for the data set (`data`), list of variables (`varlist`), smallest number of clusters (`first`) and largest number of clusters (`last`). The macro DO loop ranges over the desired cluster solutions, `first` to `last`. For each number of clusters (`numclus`), the macro calls PROC FASTCLUS, saving the cluster assignments in the `clusoutX` data set, where X indicates the number of clusters. PROC FREQ computes a frequency distribution with percentages in addition to counts, because we are often interested in knowing the percentage of cases indicating the relative sizes of the clusters.

Program 2.5 The doclus macro

```
%MACRO doclus(dat, varlist, first, last);          varname = "&varname";
  %DO numclus = &first %TO &last;                   x = &varname;
    PROC FASTCLUS DATA=&dat MAXITER=100             OUTPUT;
        CONVERGE=0 DRIFT MAXC=&numclus              KEEP cluster varname x;
        out=clusout&numclus;                        %LET i = %EVAL(&i+1);
      VAR &varlist;                                 %LET varname = %SCAN(&varlist, &i);
    RUN;                                          %END;
    PROC FREQ DATA=clusout&numclus;               RUN;
      TABLES cluster;
    RUN;                                          PROC SGPANEL DATA=_long;
                                                    PANELBY cluster / LAYOUT=columnlattice;
    DATA _long;                                     DOT varname / RESPONSE=x STAT=mean;
      SET clusout&numclus;                          REFLINE 0 / AXIS=x;
      LENGTH varname $8;                            ROWAXIS DISPLAY=(nolabel);
      %LET i = 1;                                 RUN;
      %LET varname = %SCAN(&varlist, &i);       %END; /* DO numclus */
      %DO %WHILE(%LENGTH(&varname)>0);          %MEND;
```

The `DATA` step transforms the data set for `PROC SGPANEL`, which generates the multi-panel dot plot. There is a loop that steps through the list of variables (`varlist`) one variable at a time. The resulting data set will have one row for each combination of respondent and variable, that is, if there are n observations and p variables then `_long` will have np rows. `Varname` is a string variable that takes the value of the variable name, and `x` is a variable that takes the value of variable `varname`.

In the call to `PROC SGPANEL`, the `DOT` command with the `STAT=mean` option indicates that we want to compute the mean of the variable `x` for each value of `varname` and plot the mean as a dot. The `PANELBY` command tells SAS to create a separate panel for each value of the `cluster` variable. A reference line (`REFLINE` statement) is added at 0, showing the typical (mean) person in the population.

EXAMPLE 2.7:   Theater example continued

Read the theater data set into SAS, standardize the variables, and generate the three-, four- and five-cluster solutions. Interpret the three-cluster solution.

Solution   The following program accomplishes the task:

Program 2.6 K-means solution to theater example

```
DATA theater;
  INFILE "theater.csv" DSD TRUNCOVER FIRSTOBS=2;
  INPUT attitude planning parents goodval getto age educ income cnty$;
RUN;

%LET clusvar = attitude planning parents goodval getto;
PROC STANDARD DATA=theater OUT=Ztheater MEAN=0 STD=1;
  VAR &clusvar;
RUN;
%doclus(Ztheater, &clusvar, 3, 5);
```

The `clusvar` macro variable stores the variables to be used in the cluster analysis and is referenced by both `PROC STANDARD` and the call to the `doclus` macro. It is good practice to use a macro variable to specify the list of variables because if the user decides to change the variables there will be only one change to the program. Specifying the same list of variables in multiple locations often leads to mistakes because the user might forget to change the list in one location. Such redundancy should be avoided.

PROC STANDARD transforms the data so that each variable has a mean of 0 (MEAN=0) and standard deviation of 1 (STD=1). The resulting standardized data set is stored in the new set Ztheater, which is what will be analyzed by PROC FASTCLUS.

Figure 2.9 shows the dot plot for the three-cluster solution. The value 0 therefore indicates the average person in the population. All values greater than 0 are above average and values less than 0 are below average. This mean centering will make the cluster solutions easier to interpret. The vertical line in each panel is plotted at 0 to indicate the average person. Dots to the right of the 0 line show that the cluster is above average, and those to the left of 0 are below average.

Figure 2.9 Dot plot of the cluster means for the theater example

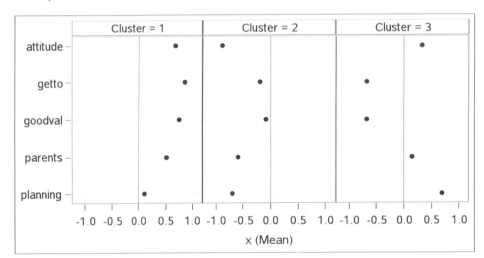

- Cluster 1 is above average on all five dimensions. Members of this cluster have the most positive attitude toward theater, rate it highest on its value for the money, and find it easy to get to. Their parents attended plays more than average, and they are about average on the perceived amount of planning.

- Cluster 2 is below average on all five dimensions. Those in this cluster find it somewhat difficult to get to a play, rate the value for the money below average, and have the most negative overall attitude of the three clusters. Their parents were substantially less likely to attend plays. They rate the amount of planning as quite low (which is not a bad thing).

- Cluster 3 is more mixed. They have a good attitude toward theater and their parents attended more than average, but they believe it requires a lot of planning, is difficult to get to and is not a good value for the money.

Figure 2.10 shows multi-panel box plots comparing the clusters. The _long data set is created by a call to the doclus macro. Notice that the diamonds in each box show the means, which were plotted as dots in Figure 2.9. The box plots show more detail about the within-cluster distributions. We can also assess differences in the within-cluster spread because the length of the boxes equal the interquartile range. The box plots also show skewness and outliers. Of course, sometimes we are not interested in this level of detail, and then the dot plot in Figure 2.9 is sufficient.

The three-cluster solution for the theater example is shown in the first three rows of Table 2.4. In the next section we will discuss the four- and five-cluster solutions as well as

Figure 2.10 Box plot of the clusters for the theater example

```
PROC SGPANEL DATA=_long;
  PANELBY cluster;
  HBOX x / CATEGORY=varname;
  REFLINE 0 / AXIS=x;
  ROWAXIS DISPLAY=(nolabel);
RUN;
```

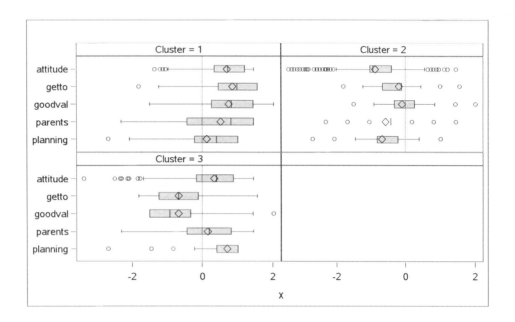

the three-cluster Gaussian mixture solution, which are also provided in this table. Cluster 1 comprises 32% of the population, cluster 2 makes up 37% and cluster 3 makes up the remaining 31%. The clusters are of roughly equal size, which is common with *K*-means.

Table 2.4 *K*-means and Gaussian mixture (GM) solutions to the theater data

Cluster	Cases	Percent	attitude	planning	parents	goodval	getto
3.1	891	32%	0.691	0.117	0.524	0.749	0.852
3.2	1,006	37%	−0.885	−0.690	−0.588	−0.091	−0.181
3.3	850	31%	0.324	0.693	0.147	−0.677	−0.678
4.1	600	22%	0.390	0.581	−0.003	−0.486	0.787
4.2	961	35%	−0.919	−0.704	−0.576	−0.086	−0.260
4.3	625	23%	0.382	0.675	0.409	−0.562	−1.092
4.4	561	20%	0.731	−0.167	0.534	1.293	0.820
5.1	553	20%	−0.182	0.645	−0.738	−0.700	−0.770
5.2	814	30%	−0.942	−0.786	−0.492	−0.022	−0.152
5.3	610	22%	0.599	0.617	0.957	−0.631	−0.006
5.4	229	8%	0.622	−1.771	0.504	0.742	0.737
5.5	541	20%	0.665	0.578	0.202	1.146	0.710
GM3.1		46%	0.567	0.715	0.156	−0.075	−0.002
GM3.2		28%	−0.590	−0.637	−0.309	0.154	−0.074
GM3.3		26%	−0.381	−0.599	0.056	−0.032	0.085

Another way to visualize a cluster solution is to use *principal components analysis* (PCA). Instead of giving a full development of PCA here, we provide only a brief overview.

See Mardia et al. (1979) for a more thorough presentation.

PCA finds a lower-dimensional representation of multivariate data. In this case we have five-dimensional observations. PCA identifies the best two-dimensional plane and projects the five-dimensional points onto the plane. Best has two equivalent meanings: (1) the plane shows as much variation in the original data as possible (that is, the variance of the two-dimensional observations is maximized) and (2) the plane minimizes the amount of information that is lost (that is, the sum of squared orthogonal deviations from the original points to their projections onto the plane is minimized). We can think of PCA as showing the best shadow of the five-dimensional points on a plane.

Figure 2.11 Scatter plot showing the three-cluster solution to the theater data using the first two principal components

```
PROC PRINCOMP DATA=clusout3 OUT=pcout N=2;
  VAR &clusvar;
RUN;

PROC SGPLOT DATA=pcout;
  SCATTER X=prin1 Y=prin2 / GROUP=cluster;
RUN;
```

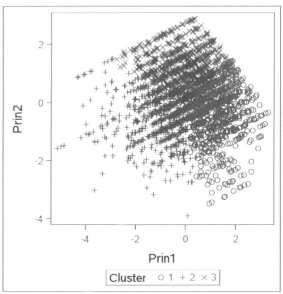

Eigenvectors		
	Prin1	**Prin2**
attitude	0.592557	0.234873
planning	0.216741	0.666284
parents	0.488283	0.236258
goodval	0.407872	−.510177
getto	0.443981	−.429885

Figure 2.11 shows the original points projected onto the first two principal components. The eigenvalues measure the variance explained by each component. By default, PROC PRINCOMP analyzes standardized variables (correlation matrix), so the total variance in the data equals the number of variables, in this example five. The first eigenvalue is 1.71 (1.71/5=34%) and the second is 1.28 (1.28/5=26%). Thus, the first two components account for approximately 60% of the variance in the original data. The remaining 40% of the variance lies in the three dimensions orthogonal to the plane shown in the scatter plot. This two-dimensional shadow shows 60% of the variation in the original five dimensions.

The eigenvectors are shown next to Figure 2.11 and characterize how much weight is assigned to each of original variable. All of the entries of the first eigenvector are positive, indicating that the first principal component is roughly an average of the original five variables. The second component contrasts perceived value and ease of getting to the theater with the other three variables. Those who have positive attitudes, have parents who attended theater, rate planning high, and rate value low and rate getting to the theater low have large values of the second component. The green (×) cluster 3 has high values of component 2, and moderate values of component 1, reinforcing our earlier interpretation. The blue (o) cluster 1 has the largest values of component 1, and the red (+) cluster 2 has the lowest values of component 1.

2.3   A process for building segmentations

The steps for building a segmentation model discussed in the subsections below are as follows:

1. Select variables.
2. Transform variables (if necessary).
3. Find various cluster solutions and profile them.
4. Choose a cluster solution and name it.

Later subsections will discuss some strategies for dealing with a large number of segmentation variables.

2.3.1   Selecting variables and choosing a solution

The first step is to select the variables to be used in estimating the segmentation model. The ultimate objective of a segmentation model is to identify groups of people with different wants and needs, so that the marketer can create more effective marketing programs. Notice that a set of clusters could have different wants and needs, but if the marketer is unable to configure contacts that outperform a one-size-fits-all approach, this set of groups would not be useful. The fact that the quality of a segmentation solution depends on the effectiveness of the contacts that are created from the solution makes choosing a solution difficult.

The nature of the groups identified by a segmentation model depend on the variables included in the analysis. If attitudinal variables are included in the cluster analysis, such as those in the theater example, then segments will be different in terms of their attitudes. If we had used behavioral variables, such as the number of plays a person attended in the past year and the number of different theaters (similar to the newspaper example), the groups would differ in terms of their behaviors, but not necessarily their attitudes. Developing a segmentation is analogous to painting a picture. If the artist uses red paint, the painting will turn out red. The use of blue paint will produce a blue picture. Neither red nor blue are correct in any absolute sense. It all depends on what the artist wants to create.

There is no simple metric that tells the analyst that attitudes are better than behaviors or vice versa. Such a metric would depend on the effectiveness of the marketing programs created from the different cluster solutions. It is therefore essential for the analyst to have a clear understanding of what will be done with the clusters, the business situation and the range of tactics available.

Another example will help clarify the points that there are no right or wrong variables, and the variables you use in cluster depend on what you intend to do with the clusters. From an evolutionary point of view it makes sense to assign whales and mice to the same cluster of mammals, which are characterized by variables such as being endothermic and having hair, three middle-ear bones, and mammary glands. Species that "are high" on all of these characteristics are assigned to the mammal cluster. Now consider the task of a zoo keeper devising transportation means for different animals. With this objective, it is not very useful to group whales and mice together. Grouping whales and sharks together would make more sense based on their size, mass, need for salt water, and so on. When studying evolution, the number of middle-ear bones is an important variable, but this variable is irrelevant when transporting zoo animals.

A heuristic for assessing the usefulness of the various variables available is to ponder the following question: if there were segments that were high on the variable and other segments that were low on the variable, how would the organization market differently to the two groups? If the analyst has difficultly in identifying different actions, then the variable is probably not going to prove useful and should be dropped.

In practice analysts often revisit the question of variable selection. They might find clusters based on certain variables and like some aspect of the solution, but then think of other differences that would be desirable. They would next run new solutions after including the new variables, or re-weighting the variables already included.

Another consideration is whether the segments will be used to target contacts at individuals, which is often called *personalization*. This is in contrast to other uses including *customization*, where the marketer creates configurations for different segments and allows users to self-select the configuration that is right, or *market segmentation*, where the marketer will target (usually) one segment.

If the marketer intends to personalize messages for individual consumers or prospects, then the marketer must know the segment to which each person belongs with reasonable accuracy. This affects the variable selection because the analyst will want to include more variables that are available for all customers rather than those that come from a marketing research survey of a sample of customers. For example, attitudes are typically known only for those who respond to a survey, while behavioral variables such as recency, frequency, monetary value, and previous purchase categories are known for all existing customers.

An alternative use of segmentations is to estimate CLV using the migration model (Chapter 5). For the purpose of estimating the future value of a customer, we will see that recency, frequency and monetary value (RFM) are usually good variables. But these variables are not good for understanding customers' wants and needs. We may use RFM to estimate the value of customer groups, but not for creating more relevant marketing contact points.

2.3.2   Crossing separate segmentations

Firms often have many variables available for defining segments and the task of segmenting customers can be overwhelming. It can be simplified by dividing the variables into groups, developing separate segmentations for each group and crossing the segmentations. This approach was discussed in Elsner et al. (2004).

An example will make the idea clear. Consider a retailer with a loyalty program that tracks (1) all of the items in every shopping basket, including the price paid for each item and whether coupons were used, and (2) promotional history. The retailer has the ability to target personalized messages and incentives to individual customers (for example, sending printed coupons, e-mails or text messages, and printed coupons issued at check out). Two sets of feature variables that could be extracted from this database are as follows:

- *Department.* A segmentation could be developed based on the departments in which a customer normally shops. Suppose, for example, that this is a men's clothing store and there is a segment that buys only suits, but does not buy from complementary departments such as dress shirts, belts, or ties.

- *Promotional response.* A separate segmentation could be developed based on response to promotions. Some customers could be responsive to coupons, while others are not. Some might only shop when there is a sale.

The department segments could determine the objective such as: cross-sell the only suits segment to other departments. The promotional-response segments could be used to determine the type of incentive offered. For example, the store could send a mobile text message with a coupon for a dress shirt to those who are coupon responsive. For customers in the shop-only-when-there's-a-sale segment, a different contact point would be necessary (for example, send the customer advanced notice of a big sale).

Other segmentations could also be created from this database and crossed with the department and promotional-response segments:

- *Loyalty.* Variables such as recency, frequency and monetary are indicators of loyalty. Many other variable can be created from them such as *average order amount*, monetary divided by frequency; *average item amount*, monetary divided by number of items purchased; *purchase rate*, number of shopping occasions divided by tenure (how long).

- *Demographics/firmographics.* The most actionable demographics depend on the nature of the product or service, but some important ones include gender, marital status, presence of children, and income. Some firmographics include the number of employees and the standard industrial classification (SIC) code.

Elsner et al. (2004) illustrate crossing department segments with loyalty segments using a book retailer. This particular retailer focuses on overstock books and specializes in history books, but sells overstocks from other categories (departments) such as utilitarian home-and-garden books, cook books, and so on. The paper proposes content area (department) segments and loyalty segments such as long lapsed, recently lapsed, active customers with a small average item amount, and active customers with a large average item amount. Crossing the two segmentations enables more relevant contact points, which are shown to increase response rates. For example, the company could send different contact points to lapsed customers than to active ones. The split on average item amount indicated whether the customer primarily purchased paperbacks or hardbacks, facilitating relevant recommendations. The department segments determined the types of titles that would be featured. Thus, the company would send a contact point featuring *paperback history* books to a customer in the history-department segment and in the active, low-average-item-amount segment. Lapsed customers who had purchased home-and-garden books in the past received a reactivation offer featuring relevant books.

We will see in Chapter 5 and section 6.2.3 that recency, frequency and average order amount are among the best indicators of future value. Consequently, RFM segments might inform the amount that can be spent on a contact point. As always, is the incremental revenue that bounds the amount that can be spent, but if a contact point will increase revenue by, say, 5%, then 5% of a large number (base amount for good customers) is more than 5% of a smaller number (base amount for weaker customers).

When a firm has a record of previous transactions that records specifically what customers are buying, demographics often add very little extra value to a segmentation system. For example, if we know that a customer is 60 years old then we would likely conclude that this customer is unlikely to buy baby products. If, however, some 60-year-old is buying from the baby department, then the transactional (behavioral) data should supersede the demographic. It is unlikely for a household headed by a 60-year-old to buy baby supplies, but this particular customer may be an exception for any number of reasons. The behaviors (for example, products purchased) *within* demographic segments are usually far more heterogeneous than segments based on the products purchased. Demographics are a proxy for the behavior of interest, and when there is data on the behavior of interest there is no reason to rely on the proxy. Of course, there are situations such as new-customer acquisition when behavioral information is unavailable, and demographics are only data available.

Another virtue of the approach of crossing different segments is that it provides a way of avoiding problems in estimating cluster models with missing values. For example, demographic information is often obtained from third-party, overlay providers, and it is not uncommon for a substantial fraction of customers not to have matches so that the demographics are missing. By segregating demographics from other sets of segmentation variables, we can know, for example, membership in loyalty, promotional-response and department segmentations without knowing demographics. Thus, a contact point could be personalized with information using the first three segmentations, while contact characteristics based on demographics would have to be generic.

2.3.3 Univariate transformations of a variable

Transforming *a single* variable means applying some function to the variable, such as the logarithm, Z-score formula $f(x) = (x - \mu)/\sigma$, or both. The transformed values are then used in the cluster analysis. There are three primary reasons for transforming variables, which will be discussed below: *commensurate units*, *skewed distributions* and *variable weighting*. A fourth reason, which was already discussed in Example 2.7 is to *facilitate interpretation*, which is of secondary importance because it does not affect the substantive interpretation of the cluster solution. In addition to transforming a single variable with a univariate function, the next section discusses how to avoid the effects of multicollinearity with multivariate transformations such as computing factor scores.

K-means clustering is highly sensitive to variable scaling and it is therefore important to have commensurate units. We can see this from the objective function in equation 2.3, which gives equal weight to all variables. The deviation from the center on one variable counts the same as the squared deviations on the others. Suppose, for example, that there are $p = 2$ variables and each is measured in centimeters. If the first variable were rescaled to have millimeter units, then the distances from the center will be 10 times greater on the first variable, and the deviations of the first variable from the centers will contribute 100 times more to the objective function than before. The algorithm will favor this variable more when determining the centers than if the variable were expressed in centimeters (Exercise 2.1). The analyst therefore implicitly controls the weights of different variables in the analysis through the measuring units.

EXAMPLE 2.8:   Bivariate Gaussian mixture with incommensurate units
Both variables in Example 2.3 were expressed in inches. Convert y1 to centimeters and cluster the transformed data.

Solution   To convert inches to centimeters we must multiply y1 by 2.54. Notice how the clusters are now assigned almost entirely on their y1 values, with all observations that have positive y1 values being assigned to the blue (o) cluster, and all with negative y1 values assigned to the red (+) cluster. The squared deviations in the y1 direction dominate those in the x1 direction, and the clusters are determined mostly by y1. Thus, a change in units produces entirely different clusters.

Figure 2.12 Bivariate Gaussian mixture

```
TITLE "Different units";
DATA clus2;
  SET clus;
  y1 = 2.54*y1;
  LABEL y1 = "y (cm)";
RUN;
PROC FASTCLUS DATA=clus2 MAXC=2 out=clusout;
  VAR x1 y1;
RUN;
PROC SGPLOT DATA=clusout;
  SCATTER X=x1 y=y1 / GROUP=cluster;
RUN;
```

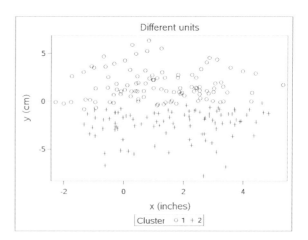

K-means also produces undesirable results when the distributions of the manifest variables are skewed. When a variable is skewed, K-means will often produce a solution in which there are many small clusters describing the tail, and one large cluster for the vast majority of the data. When there are outliers, it is not uncommon for K-means to devote an entire cluster to a single observation.

In situations where the variables were measured with commensurate units (for example, all variables were measured on five-point Likert scales) and the distributions are not highly skewed, there is not a strong need for standardization of any kind, and the analyst might use the raw variables to estimate the cluster model. Otherwise, the analyst will want to transform the variables prior to estimation following one of two approaches.

The first can be called the *symmetrize-and-standardize* approach and involves two separate steps. The first step is to transform skewed variables to be more symmetrical by using the log or square-root transformation. There is no reason to log variables that are already fairly symmetrical. Logging such variables will create problems by making them left skewed. The second step is to standardize all variables used in the analysis to be Z scores with mean 0 and standard deviation 1. The reader will note that the Z-score transformation does not affect skewness (Exercise 2.3), and thus skewness problems must be addressed with a separate transformation in the first step. The unit of measure for Z scores is the standard deviation, and this is one approach to finding commensurate units across variables.

The second approach is called *quantile standardization*. Instead of using raw variables in the analysis, the analyst first finds, for example, the deciles of each variable (for example, using PROC RANK) and then uses the decile number $(1, 2, \ldots, 10)$ in the clustering. Notice how the deciles of all variables are on scales that range from 1 to 10 and the distribution of decile numbers will be uniform (and thus symmetrical) as long as there are not larger numbers of duplicate values in the raw data.

The original newspaper data measured time in minutes and respondents were asked about more than eight content areas. The data set shown Table 2.1 are actually octiles of time and sections. Octiles (and deciles) can be computed in SAS using PROC RANK as follows. Suppose that the original data set contained variables timemin, giving the time in minutes, and nsections, giving the raw count of section areas. The GROUPS=8 option indicates that we want octiles. The names of the original variables are specified in the VAR statement and the names of the new variables containing the octiles are specified in the RANKS statement. The data set specified by the OUT= option contains all of the original variables plus the new variables listed in the RANKS statement.

Program 2.7 Program illustrating how to use PROC RANK to find octiles

```
PROC RANK DATA=raw OUT=octiles GROUPS=8;
  VAR timemin nsections;
  RANKS time sections;
RUN;
```

In practice, I recommend trying both approaches and using the one that gives the most actionable results. The quantile approach introduces measurement error, because all observations in, for example, the top decile are rounded to the same value. Smooth transformations such as the log or square root would also seem to be more desirable than the lumpy discrete bins introduced by the quantiles.

The quantile approach produces transformed variables that have uniform distributions, while log or square root transformations will often produce transformed variables that are approximately normal (see discussion of lognormal distribution in section 6.2.2). The tails of a uniform distribution are substantially thicker than those from a normal distribution,[4] and the effect of thicker tails is to inflate the variance and give more weight to the extremes, after grouping outliers together in the top (or bottom) quantile. This exaggerated variance often makes it easier to interpret clusters, and it is not uncommon for clusters resulting from quantile-scaled variables to be easier to interpret than those from the symmetrize-and-standardize method.

The beginning of this section noted that there are four reasons for transforming a single variable, and we have already discussed skewed distributions and commensurate units. The other reasons are to facilitate interpretation and change the weights of individual variables. Even if the original variables are symmetrical and their units are commensurate, the analyst may wish to mean center the variables to facilitate interpretation. Likewise, it can be easier to interpret mean-centered quantile numbers. As we already mentioned in Example (2.7) and the discussion of Figure 2.9, when variables have been standardized or mean centered, cluster means of 0 indicate an average level on the variable, positive values indicate above-average levels, and negative values indicate below-average levels.

Our discussion of commensurate measuring units noted that the K-means solutions are highly dependent on variable scaling. Changing the units of a single variable from, for example, centimeters to millimeters increases the weight of this variable in the objective function (2.3). The analyst can use this fact to increase or decrease the weight of a variable—multiplying a variable by a constant greater than one will increase the variable's weight. Multiplying by a constant less than one will decrease the weight. Sometimes a variable will dominate an analysis, where the clusters are mainly defined by differences on this variable. One solution is to multiply this variable by, say 0.7, before the analysis and thereby reduce its influence on the objective function.

Readers may be uncomfortable tweaking variable weights in this way, but one must recognize all of the other arbitrary assumptions that affect the cluster solutions, such as the selection of variables and measuring units (including decisions such as five-point or seven-point scales). Keep in mind that, from a marketing point of view, one cluster solution is better than another only if it enables the marketer to create customized contact points that make more money than contact points that could be created for the other solution. This is a highly subjective criterion.

2.3.4 Multivariate transformations and multicollinearity

A univariate transformation applies a function to a single variable to symmetrize its distribution or change the measuring units. A multivariate transformation is a function of multiple variables and is used to avoid the effects *multicollinearity*, where manifest variables are highly correlated with each other.

We begin by discussing the effects of multicollinearity. The effect of multicollinearity on K-means clusters is to increase the weight of the dimensions underlying the correlated variables (see exercise 2.1). To understand why this is the case, consider clustering $p = 3$ variables. Suppose x_1 and x_2 are exactly equal to each other, and thus perfectly correlated, and x_3 is uncorrelated with x_1 and x_2. Recall the objective function in equation 2.3 gives equal weight to every variable included in the analysis. Since x_1 and x_2 are identical, the squared deviations from the cluster centroid along $x_1 = x_2$ are counted twice, but those along the x_3 dimension are counted once. Therefore, the dimension measured by x_1 and x_2 receives twice as much weight as x_3. Thus, another way of increasing the weight of a dimension is simply to include multiple copies of it in the analysis.

EXAMPLE 2.9:   Bivariate Gaussian mixture with multicollinearity

Estimate the two-cluster solution to Example 2.3 using three copies of y1 and one of x1.

Solution   We list y1 three times in the VAR statement. Squared deviations in the y1 direction now count three times in the objective function, and the clusters shown in Figure 2.13 are determined mostly by their y1 value.

Figure 2.13 Bivariate Gaussian mixture with multicollinearity

```
TITLE "Multicollinearity";
PROC FASTCLUS DATA=clus MAXC=2 out=clusout;
  VAR x1 y1 y1 y1;
RUN;
PROC SGPLOT DATA=clusout;
  SCATTER X=x1 y=y1 / GROUP=cluster;
RUN;
```

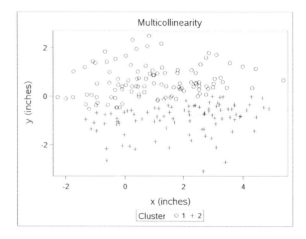

This simple example may seem contrived, but an analyst might unwittingly give more weight to certain dimensions. Consider the Theater attitudes in Example 2.2. Recall that there were 10 highly correlated questions that produced a single factor, which was called `attitude`. Instead of including the `attitude` factor scores in the cluster analysis with the other four variables, we could have used the original ten attitude variables plus the other four. The problem with this approach is that it would implicitly give more weight to the attitude dimension, and the resulting clusters would differ almost entirely on attitude alone. The factor analysis model (Hatcher, 1994) posits that each of the 10 variables is a manifestation of attitude plus some random error. Including the 10 original variables is thus the same thing as including 10 copies of the attitude variable, each measured with error.

These problems with multicollinearity can be avoided by identifying the underlying dimensions in the data with principal components or factor analysis, and then using estimates of the underlying dimensions instead of the observed variables. Two common estimates of the underlying dimensions are the factor scores, which are computed as a weighted average of the observed variables, or by simply averaging the correlated variables for each respondent. With either approach we are evaluating some multivariate function of some variables.

When the distribution of factor scores is highly skewed the analyst will usually want to apply either the symmetrize-and-standardize or quantile approach discussed in section 2.3.3 to the factor scores before clustering. Most of the time factor analysis books discuss applying the technique to survey data, where the variables are measured on, for example, five-point scales, which are fairly well behaved. Often we will be factoring different measures of frequency and monetary value from a data set. These variables tend to be highly right-skewed with outliers. Be sure to log or decile right-skewed variables before factoring Malthouse (2001).

2.3.5   Running and profiling cluster solutions

The analyst usually does not know the exact number of clusters before doing the analysis. Absent a strong reason to find a specific number of customers, it is customary to estimate a variety of cluster solutions by varying the number of clusters extracted, the variables included in the analysis and the weights assigned to the individual variables. The `doclus` macro in Program 2.5 automates running multiple cluster solutions. After studying the various solutions, the one that leads to the best marketing actions is selected. As we discuss later in this section, SAS and other packages provide various statistics measuring how well a particular solution fits the data, but ultimately the solution must be actionable, and the most actionable solution may not always be the one that fits the data best.

The decision maker should first specify a ballpark number of clusters based on what can be supported after the analysis (for example, 3–6, 5–8, and so on). For example, if the purpose of the segmentation model is to configure customized versions of the product and communications, and the organization would never want to support more than, say, seven versions (at least at the present time), then there is little reason[5] to look at solutions beyond seven, and the two- or three-cluster solutions might also be dropped from consideration because they would provide too few options.

Profiling clusters involves studying how they differ on variables not used in defining them. There are often two levels of profiling. When the analyst is considering different cluster solutions, the cluster means are typically supplemented by finding the means of other numerical variables, and running cross tabs with other categorical variables, on the survey or in the database. These supplementary analyses will help the analyst and decision maker understand the different clusters better and assist in choosing a final solution.

The second level of profiling comes after the solution has been chosen. At this time the analyst compares the clusters on a more extensive set of other variables. Sometimes companies commission additional qualitative research, for example, commissioning focus groups on typical members (that is, those with small distances to the cluster centers) of different clusters. Such focus groups could be useful in developing, for example, the creative advertising messages used for each segment. Additional quantitative marketing research from surveys and overlays are also used.

Again, profiling involves finding the means of numerical variables by cluster, and computing crosstabs of categorical variables (reporting percents conditional on segment membership). In addition to the means or percents, it is also useful to perform a one-way analysis of variance on numerical variables and chi-square test of independence on categorical ones. The F statistics and chi-square test statistics provide information about the magnitude of the differences across the clusters and can help the analyst evaluate which variables are interesting. It is not uncommon to profile on hundreds of variables, and the F and chi-squared tests will help guard against type I errors and prioritize which variables to study.

EXAMPLE 2.10:   Theater example continued

Find the three-, four- and five-cluster solutions for the theater example. Compare the three- and four-cluster solutions with a crosstab. Profile the three-cluster solution.

Solution   The call to the `doclus` macro in Program 2.6 ran the different solutions, which are summarized in Table 2.4. The notation "cluster 3.1" indicates cluster 1 from the three-cluster solution. In looking at the means, Cluster 4.2 is similar to 3.2 with below average ratings of all five dimensions. Cluster 4.3 is similar to cluster 3.3, with above-average scores on attitude, planning and parents, but below-average scores on value and getting to the theater. Cluster 4.3, however, is even more negative on getting to the theater and more positive on parents than 3.3. Unlike the three-cluster solution, there is no cluster with all positive means. Instead, cluster 4.1 has above average attitude, planning (requires planning) and get-to scores, about average scores on parents, and a below-average perception of value. Cluster 4.4 has a positive mean on all variables except planning, which is roughly 0. We could speculate that 4.4 comprises the most avid current theater attendees.

The `doclus` macro creates output data sets `clusout3` and `clusout4` with the three- and four-cluster solutions. We can get a better understanding of how the two solutions relate to each other by merging the data sets and crossing the cluster assignments. `PROC FASTCLUS` saves the cluster assignments in the `cluster` variable and we must rename `cluster` before merging the two data sets.

The output is shown in Table 2.5. The crosstab confirms what we suspected from our inspection of the means. Most members of cluster 3.2 are in cluster 4.2 (the negative group). Most members of 3.3 are in 4.3, but a substantial fraction are assigned to 4.1. The positive cluster 4.1 splits between 4.4 and 4.1.

Table 2.5 Crosstab of three- and four-cluster solution, theater example

```
DATA both;
  MERGE clusout3(RENAME=(cluster=clus3))
    clusout4(RENAME=(cluster=clus4));
  BY id;
RUN;
PROC FREQ DATA=both;
  TABLE clus3 * clus4 / NOROW NOCOL NOPERCENT;
RUN;
```

	Table of clus3 by clus4				
clus3	clus4				
	1	2	3	4	Total
1	293	7	40	551	891
2	61	931	4	10	1006
3	246	23	581	0	850
Total	600	961	625	561	2747

The three-cluster solution can be further profiled on age, education, income and their county of residence with the following program. Output is summarized in Table 2.6.

Program 2.8 Profiling the three-cluster theater solution

```
PROC GLM DATA=clusout3;
  CLASS cluster;
  MODEL age educ income = cluster / SS3;
  MEANS cluster / DUNCAN;
RUN;

PROC FREQ DATA=clusout3;
  TABLE cnty * cluster / NOPERCENT NOCOL CHISQ;
RUN;
```

Table 2.6 Profiles of the three-cluster theater solution. The table shows the means of age, income and education by cluster, and gives a crosstab with the county of residence (count/adjusted standardized residuals).

Profile Variable	Cluster			
	3.1	3.2	3.3	F
Age	6.47	6.81	6.47	3.27*
Income	5.15	4.76	5.13	4.93**
Education	5.35	4.69	5.45	55.6***
Chicago	165/5.5	116/−2.2	87/−3.3	
Suburb Cook	355/−0.1	410/0.7	332/−0.6	
DuPage	135/0.8	130/−1.7	130/0.9	
Lake	57/−0.9	60/−1.7	76/2.6	
Other	179/−4.3	290/3.3	225/1.0	

The first row of the table gives the mean age of each cluster along with the F statistic from a one-way ANOVA, testing the null hypothesis that all three clusters have the same mean age, $H_0 : \mu_1 = \mu_2 = \mu_3$. $F = 3.27$ and is significant, indicating that we can reject this null and conclude that the clusters have different mean ages. The differences in mean ages, however, are small, with cluster 3.2 being slightly older than clusters 3.1 and 3.2. The next row gives the means of income, which was measured on a 12-point scale. The differences are highly significant (two stars indicating $P < .01$), with cluster 3.2 having lower income than 3.1 and 3.2.

The third row gives the means for education and the F statistic is much larger ($F = 54.2$) indicating that the clusters vary much more in their education than their age or income. The F statistic is useful in prioritizing which variables to focus on. Education is measured on an eight-point scale. Clusters 3.1 and 3.3 have the highest education levels, with 3.2 having lower education levels.

The bottom portion of the table gives a crosstab of the cluster assignment and the county of residence. The value Chicago indicates a Chicago residence, while Suburb Cook indicates someone living in suburban Cook County (Chicago is also located within Cook County). DuPage County is located to the west of Chicago and comprises many suburbs. Lake County is located to the north of Chicago and also has many suburbs. Other refers to all other counties within the greater Chicago area. The first number in each cell is the observed count in the cell and the second number is the adjusted standardized residual. The chi-square test statistic is 50.6 on 8 degrees of freedom ($P < .0001$), suggesting that there is an association between cluster membership and county of residence. As with the F statistic, the chi-square statistic or the P value[6] can be used to prioritize which categorical variables produce the greatest difference across segments.

Program 2.9 Macro to compute adjusted-standardized residuals from chi-square test of independence

```
%MACRO adjres(data, row, col);          *(1-(col_total/total)));
PROC FREQ DATA=&data;                   adj_resid = (count-expected)/denom;
  TABLES &row*&col / OUTPCT OUTEXPECT   RUN;
    OUT=out1 NOROW NOCOL NOPERCENT
    DEVIATION CHISQ;                     PROC SORT DATA=adj_resid;
RUN;                                       BY descending adj_resid;
                                         RUN;
DATA adj_resid;
  SET out1;                              PROC PRINT DATA=adj_resid NOOBS;
  col_total = (100*count)/pct_col;         VAR &row &col count expected adj_resid;
  row_total = (100*count)/pct_row;         SUM count;
  total = (100*count)/percent;           RUN;
  denom = SQRT(expected                  %MEND;
    *(1-(row_total/total))
```

Under the null hypothesis of independence, adjusted standardized residuals have standard normal distributions (Agresti, 1990, § 7.3.2), and values greater than 2 or less than -2 suggest that independence does not hold for a particular cell. Adjusted residuals can be computed using the macro in Program 2.9. Positive residuals indicate that a cell is over-represented relative to what would be expected under independence, and negative residuals indicate the cell is under-represented. Chicago is over-represented by cluster 3.1, and under-represented by clusters 3.3 and 3.2. Lake County is over represented by those in cluster 3.3, and cluster 3.2 is under-represented by those living in other counties.

Assigning names to clusters is an important task that is often under-appreciated. The analyst must understand that, to the end users of a segmentation, the name will often become the primary description of the segment. The people who are creating contact points may not be willing or able to study all of the cluster profiles (for example, the crosstabs and ANOVAs from the previous section). They should read supporting documentation of the segments, but may not. The cluster name will be the first indication of who is in a segment and should be carefully selected to reflect what is known about the segments.

2.3.6   Fit statistics and model selection

The analyst must usually determine the number of clusters, but there is no easy solution to this task. SAS offers several statistics that quantify how well a set of clusters fit the data, although we will argue below that fit should not be the only criterion. For example, PROC FASTCLUS reports *pseudo F* statistics:

$$F = \frac{\text{SSB}/[p(k-1)]}{\text{SSE}/[p(n-k)]}$$

where SSB is the between-cluster variation and SSE is the within-cluster variation. If clusters fit the data, the between-cluster variation will be large, the within-cluster variation will be small, and the pseudo F will spike. One can compare pseudo F statistics across cluster solutions and select one with a large spike. This process is illustrated in the following example.

EXAMPLE 2.11:   Trimodal Gaussian mixture

Consider a mixture of $K = 3$ normal distributions with means 0, 4 and 8, and a common standard deviation $\sigma = 1$. The following SAS program generates 500 observations from each distribution and plots the distribution.

Figure 2.14 Histogram of trimodal Gaussian mixture.

```
DATA trimodal;
  DO i = 1 TO 500;
    x=RANNOR(12345); OUTPUT;
    x=RANNOR(12345)+4; OUTPUT;
    x=RANNOR(12345)+8; OUTPUT;
  END;
RUN;

PROC SGPLOT DATA=trimodal;
  HISTOGRAM x;
  DENSITY x / TYPE=KERNEL(C=.3);
RUN;
```

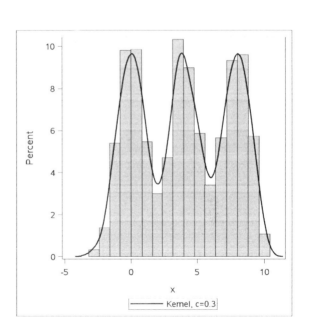

Table 2.7 gives the pseudo F values for the $2, 3, \ldots, 8$ cluster K-means solutions that have been extracted from the output. There is a large spike in F value for $K = 3$ clusters (8645.36), which is surrounded by substantially smaller F values. This shows that the pseudo F statistics can identify the correct number of clusters.

While it is desirable for a cluster solution to fit the data, fit should not be the only criterion. Another guiding principle should be to select a set of clusters that best solves the business problem. Fitting the data and solving the business problem are not the same objective, and solving the problem should have priority over fitting the data. In the case of customization with subsegmentation models, the business problem is to find segments that enable creating contact points that are more effective (and profitable) than a one-size-fits-all contact.

Table 2.7 Pseudo F values from trimodal Gaussian mixture example

```
%MACRO clusters;
%DO i = 2 %TO 8;
  PROC FASTCLUS DATA=trimodal MAXC=&i;
    VAR x;
  RUN;
%END;
%MEND;
%clusters;
```

Number Clusters	Pseudo F
2	4228.72
3	8645.36
4	5544.30
5	8138.17
6	8382.03
7	9568.34
8	11118.92

2.4 The finite mixture model

Equation (2.1) suggested that the K-means model finds clusters that are spherical in that they have equal within-cluster variance in all directions and across all clusters. This model seems restrictive because there is usually no theoretical justification for assuming clusters with equal shapes and sizes. The finite mixture model generalizes equation 2.1 and relaxes these assumptions, as well as accommodating categorical manifest variables.

We begin with the same data as before: x_{ij} is the value of manifest variable $j = 1, \ldots, p$ from subject $i = 1, \ldots, n$. Observation i is assumed to be from one of K classes, labeled $1, 2, \ldots, K$. We will now assume that class membership G is a discrete random variable with $P(G = k) = \eta_k$, that is, the probability that a randomly selected person from the sampled population comes from class k is η_k, a parameter estimated by the model. The values of η_k specify the *prior distribution*. The prior probabilities sum to 1, that is, $\eta_1 + \cdots + \eta_K = 1$. The value η_k indicates the size of class k. The comparable quantity from K-means is the percentage of cases assigned to cluster k (for example, the Percentage row in Table 2.3).

We will also think of vector $\mathbf{x}_i$, assuming we know it is from class k, as being a realization of a random vector $\mathbf{X}$ having *class-conditional distribution* $f_k(\mathbf{x}|\boldsymbol{\theta}_k)$, which describes the distribution of $\mathbf{X}$ for a specific cluster k with parameters $\boldsymbol{\theta}_k$. It is common to assume that the class-conditional distribution is normal and under this assumption the finite mixture model is called the *Gaussian mixture model*. The parameter vector $\boldsymbol{\theta}_k$ consists of the mean and variance for the Gaussian mixture model. Later in this section we will discuss how, when the manifest variables are categorical, the class-conditional distributions are assumed to be a product of multinomials (or Bernoulli trials in the case of dichotomous manifest variables). This is called the *latent class model* and the parameter vector $\boldsymbol{\theta}_k$ consistent of the probabilities.

The *observed distribution* of X is thus a mixture of the class-conditional distributions:

$$f(\mathbf{x}) = \sum_{k=1}^{K} \eta_k f_k(\mathbf{x}|\boldsymbol{\theta}_k).$$

Given an observed vector $\mathbf{x}$, we also need to know from which distribution the observation comes. For example, if we know the values of the manifest variables for a customer, from which segment does the customer come? We answer this question with the *posterior distribution*:

$$P(G = k|\mathbf{x}) = \frac{\eta_k f_k(\mathbf{x}|\boldsymbol{\theta}_k)}{\sum_k \eta_k f_k(\mathbf{x}|\boldsymbol{\theta}_k)} = \frac{\eta_k f_k(\mathbf{x}|\boldsymbol{\theta}_k)}{f(\mathbf{x})}.$$

We illustrate these terms with a mathematical example, where we know the exact distributions.

EXAMPLE 2.12:   Univariate, two-class Gaussian mixture model

Consider a mixture of $K = 2$ normal distributions. The first distribution ($k = 1$) is $\mathcal{N}(0, 0.5^2)$, with a mean $\mu_1 = 0$ and a standard deviation $\sigma_1 = 0.5$, and the second distribution ($k = 2$) is $\mathcal{N}(3, 1)$. One third ($\eta_1 = 1/3$) of the population comes from distribution 1 and $\eta_2 = 2/3$ comes from population 2. Recall that the probability density function (PDF) for a normal distribution $\mathcal{N}(\mu, \sigma^2)$ is

$$f(x|\mu, \sigma^2) = \frac{1}{\sigma\sqrt{2\pi}} \exp\left[-\frac{1}{2}\left(\frac{x - \mu}{\sigma}\right)^2\right],$$

which is the class-conditional distribution in this example.

The observed and class-conditional distributions are illustrated in Figure 2.15. The dashed (red) line shows class-conditional distribution 1 and the dotted (blue) line shows distribution 2. Both *class-conditional* distributions are normal:

$$f_1(x) = \frac{1}{.5\sqrt{2\pi}} \exp\left[-\frac{x^2}{2(.5)^2}\right] \quad \text{and} \quad f_2(x) = \frac{1}{\sqrt{2\pi}} \exp\left[-\frac{(x-3)^2}{2}\right].$$

If we knew that an observation came from distribution 1 then its random variable would have a mean of 0 and standard deviation 0.5. The area under the dashed (blue) curve is twice that of the solid (red) curve. This is because we know from the prior probabilities that $\eta_2 = 2\eta_1$.

Figure 2.15 Univariate, two-class Gaussian mixture

```
DATA gauss;
  DO x=-4 TO 8 BY .02;
    f1 = PDF('NORMAL', x, 0, .5)/3;
    f2 = 2*PDF('NORMAL', x, 3, 1)/3;
    mix = f1+f2;
    OUTPUT;
  END;
  LABEL f1 = "N(0, 0.25)"
    f2 = "N(3, 1)"
    mix = "Mixture";
RUN;
PROC SGPLOT DATA=gauss(WHERE=(x>=-2));
  SERIES X=x Y=mix;
  SERIES X=x Y=f1 / LINEATTRS=(COLOR='red');
  SERIES X=x Y=f2 / LINEATTRS=(COLOR='blue');
  YAXIS LABEL="f(x)";
RUN;
```

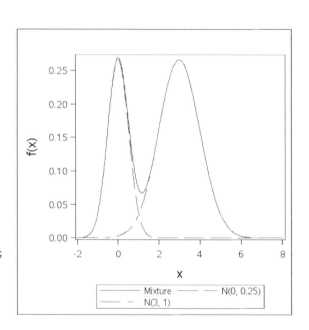

Unfortunately, the observations do not come labeled red or blue, and the analyst observes the black curve representing the mixture of the other two. The model must recover the two class-conditional distributions (means and variances) and mixing proportions η_k. The PDF of the observed mixture distribution is shown by the solid line (black) in Figure 2.15, and its equation is

$$f(x) = \frac{1}{3(.5)\sqrt{2\pi}} \exp\left[-\frac{x}{2(.5)^2}\right] + \frac{2}{3\sqrt{2\pi}} \exp\left[-\frac{(x-3)^2}{2}\right].$$

The posterior probabilities are given by $P(G = k|x) = \eta_k f_k(x)/f(x)$ and are plotted in Figure 2.16 (see Exercise 2.11). Consider the value $x = 4$, where the dashed (blue) line is nearly 1 and the red solid line is nearly 0, indicating that we are nearly certain that an observed value 4 comes from the dashed (blue) distribution ($k = 2$). Likewise, we are nearly certain that an observed value $x = -1$ comes from the red class ($k = 1$) because $P(G = 1|x = -1) \approx 1$.

Figure 2.16 Posterior probabilities for two-class Gaussian mixture

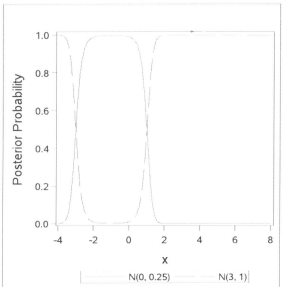

```
DATA gauss;
   SET gauss;
   post1 = f1/mix;
   post2 = f2/mix;
   LABEL
      post1 = "N(0, 0.25)"
      post2 = "N(3, 1)";
RUN;

PROC SGPLOT DATA=gauss;
   SERIES X=x Y=post1/LINEATTRS=(COLOR='red');
   SERIES X=x Y=post2/LINEATTRS=(COLOR='blue');
   YAXIS LABEL="Posterior Probability";
RUN;
```

The task of distinguishing between classes becomes substantially more difficult for x values around 1 because the (prior-weighted) class-conditional PDFs cross at 1 in Figure 2.15. Consequently, the posterior plots also cross at $x = 1$. The value $x = 1.1$ is slightly more likely to have come from the dashed (blue) distribution ($k = 2$), but there is still a substantial probability that it came from the solid (red) distribution ($k = 1$). Such an observation is not typical of either class because it is in a tail of both distributions. In practical marketing terms, it would be difficult to decide whether to send such a customer the contact for class 1 or 2. If the contact points are of equal quality, either would work about the same for customers with $x \approx 1$.

The plot is somewhat surprising because the posterior curves cross twice, once at $x = 1$ and again at $x = -3$ (Exercise 2.11 shows that these are two roots of a quadratic equation). The reason is that the variances of the class-conditional distributions are not equal. The dashed (blue) distribution has a larger variance, and therefore the tails approach 0 more slowly than those of the solid (red) distribution. A value $x < -3$ is very unlikely to occur at all, but if one does it is more likely to have come from the dashed (blue) distribution. Such assignments are perhaps undesirable and illustrate a problem with the finite mixture model.

EXAMPLE 2.13: Univariate Gaussian Mixture Model With Data

We simulate data from the mixture distribution and estimate the model parameters with PROC FMM. The program in Figure 2.17 generates 100 observations from distribution 1 and then 200 observations from distribution 2 so that $\eta_1 = 1/3$. A histogram of the 300 cases is superimposed on the figure to the right of the program. The density estimate (blue, solid line) clearly shows a bimodal distribution, with the left mode smaller than the right one.

The program also uses `PROC FMM` to estimate the component distributions. The `KMIN` and `KMAX` options specify the minimum and maximum number of clusters to find. The posterior distribution is saved in the `ans` data set, with `post1` and `post2` giving the estimated posterior probabilities of coming from classes 1 and 2, respectively. Output from the program is shown below.

Figure 2.17 Generating data for the two-class Gaussian mixture example and estimate with `PROC FMM`

```
DATA gauss2;
  k = 1;
  DO i = 1 TO 100;
    x=0+.5*RANNOR(1234); /* mu=0, sd=.5 */
    OUTPUT;
  END;
  k = 2;
  DO i = 1 TO 200;
    x=3+1*RANNOR(1234); /* mu=3, sd=1 */
    OUTPUT;
  END;
RUN;


PROC FMM DATA=gauss2 GCONV=0;
  MODEL x = / KMIN=2 KMAX=2;
  OUTPUT OUT=ans
    post(COMPONENTS) = post1 post2;
RUN;
```

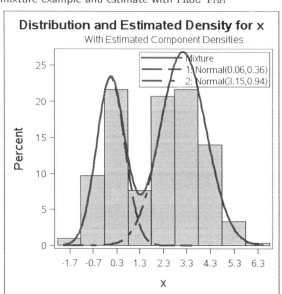

Parameter Estimates for 'Normal' Model					
Component	Parameter	Estimate	Standard Error	z Value	Pr> |z|
1	Intercept	0.05777	0.07074	0.82	0.4141
2	Intercept	3.1505	0.08168	38.57	< .0001
1	Variance	0.3595	0.06356		
2	Variance	0.9428	0.1241		

Parameter Estimates for Mixing Probabilities					
Parameter	Estimate	Standard Error	z Value	Pr > |z|	Probability
Probability	−0.6226	0.1344	−4.63	< .0001	0.3492

The output shows that `PROC FMM` has estimated the true parameters very well. The top part of the output gives the estimates of the means (Intercept) and variances. Component 1 corresponds to the dashed (red) distribution, and has an estimated mean of 0.05777, which is less than one standard error from the true mean of 0. The variance of Component 1 is 0.3595, which is approximating the true parameter $\sigma_1^2 = (.5)^2 = .25$.

Component 2 estimates the green (dash-dot) distribution. The estimated mean is 3.1505 (the true value is 3) and the estimated variance is 0.9428 (the true value is 1).

The bottom part of the output estimates the prior probabilities. The Estimate gives the logit of the probability that a case comes from Component 1. Inverting the logit we find

$$\hat{\eta}_1 = \frac{1}{1 + e^{-(-0.6226)}} = .3492,$$

which is close to the true value 1/3.

EXAMPLE 2.14:   Univariate Gaussian mixture model with K-means

It is instructive to examine the K-means solution to the two-class Gaussian mixture example. This problem should be difficult for K-means because the clusters have unequal sizes (for example, $\eta_1 = 1/3$) and variances. The program and relevant output is summarized below.

```
PROC FASTCLUS DATA=gauss2 MAXC=2;
  VAR x;
RUN;
```

Cluster	Freq	Percent	Mean	Std Dev
1	173	58%	3.357	0.818
2	127	42%	0.318	0.807

We mentioned that K-means has a bias toward producing clusters of equal size. The within-cluster standard deviations are nearly equal (both around 0.8, while the true values are 0.5 and 1) and the mean of the left mode is estimated at 0.32 (rather than 0). Because the left distribution has a mean and standard deviation that are too large, more cases are assigned to this cluster than should be (127 rather than 100). There is a single classification boundary: all cases less than $(3.357 + 0.318)/2 = 1.84$ are closer to the left cluster centroid and are thus assigned to the left class, and cases greater than 1.84 are assigned to the mode on the right. Thus, K-means does a worse job of recovering the generating mixture distribution. From a marketing perspective, however, the K-means solution may be just as good as the Gaussian mixture model because the substantive interpretation of the two is similar and having a single boundary makes more sense from a marketing-execution viewpoint. We would likely want to send those assigned to the blue group having $x < -3$ a contact point developed for the red group.

2.4.1   Bivariate normal distribution

The previous section introduced the finite mixture model with an example where the class-conditional distributions were univariate (that is, $p = 1$) normal distributions. If we have more than $p = 1$ manifest variable, we will need to use some multivariate distribution to characterize the class-conditional distributions that get mixed. One of the most frequently used distributions is the *multivariate normal distribution* (MVN), which generalizes the univariate normal distribution to include multiple random variables. See Johnson and Wichern (2002) or Mardia et al. (1979) for a more complete discussion of the general MVN distribution. This subsection will cover the special case where $p = 2$, called the *bivariate normal distribution*.

The bivariate normal distribution generalizes the univariate normal distribution. Consider $p = 2$ random variables X_1 and X_2. Let μ_j and σ_j $(j = 1, 2)$ be the mean and standard deviation of X_j. The *correlation* between X_1 and X_2 is given by

$$\rho = \frac{\text{Cov}(X_1, X_2)}{\sigma_1 \sigma_2} = \frac{\sigma_{12}}{\sigma_1 \sigma_2},$$

where σ_{12} is called the *covariance* of X_1 and X_2. Note that $\sigma_{12} = \rho \sigma_1 \sigma_2$. Define the *mean vector* of random vector $\mathbf{X} = (X_1, X_2)'$ as

$$\boldsymbol{\mu} = E(\mathbf{X}) = \begin{pmatrix} \mu_1 \\ \mu_2 \end{pmatrix}$$

and the *covariance matrix* as

$$\boldsymbol{\Sigma} = E[(\mathbf{X} - \boldsymbol{\mu})'(\mathbf{X} - \boldsymbol{\mu})] = \begin{pmatrix} \sigma_1^2 & \sigma_{12} \\ \sigma_{12} & \sigma_2^2 \end{pmatrix} = \begin{pmatrix} \sigma_1^2 & \rho \sigma_1 \sigma_2 \\ \rho \sigma_1 \sigma_2 & \sigma_2^2 \end{pmatrix}.$$

The bivariate normal PDF is

$$f(x_1, x_2) = f(\mathbf{x}) = \frac{1}{2\pi\sigma_1\sigma_2\sqrt{1-\rho}} \exp\left[-\frac{1}{2}(\mathbf{x} - \boldsymbol{\mu})'\boldsymbol{\Sigma}^{-1}(\mathbf{x} - \boldsymbol{\mu})\right], \qquad (2.4)$$

where $\boldsymbol{\Sigma}^{-1}$ is the inverse of $\boldsymbol{\Sigma}$

$$\boldsymbol{\Sigma}^{-1} = \frac{1}{\sigma_1^2\sigma_2^2(1-\rho^2)}\begin{pmatrix} \sigma_2^2 & -\rho\sigma_1\sigma_2 \\ -\rho\sigma_1\sigma_2 & \sigma_1^2 \end{pmatrix}.$$

The formulas above might seem intimidating, but one should not let them obscure the main ideas. The bivariate normal distribution concisely summarizes the joint distribution of two normal random variables with 5 parameters: (μ_1, μ_2) give the coordinates of the center of the joint distribution, and variance parameters σ_1^2, σ_2^2 and ρ characterize the dispersion and orientation.

Figure 2.18 below illustrates how the three variance parameters describe the shape of the distribution by showing contours of the PDF, that is, $\{\mathbf{x} : f(x_1, x_2) = 100c\}$ for $c = 1, 3, 6, 10, 15$. When $\rho = 0$ the variables are uncorrelated. The top two graphs have $\rho = 0$ and the contours are perfect circles. (See Exercise 2.13.) We earlier described such distributions as spherical, and K-means assumes clusters with this round shape. A scatter plot from these distributions would resemble a snow ball and show no pattern. The difference between the top two plots is that the one on the left has $\sigma_1 = \sigma_2 = 0.5$ and the one on the right is more dispersed with $\sigma_1 = \sigma_2 = 1$. The contours or more spread out on the right, indicated more dispersion.

The middle left plot in Figure 2.18 illustrates the effect of having $\rho = 0$ but $\sigma_1 \neq \sigma_2$. Because $\rho = 0$ there continues to be no association between the variables. The contours, however, have become elliptical with more spread in the vertical (x_2) direction, because $0.5 = \sigma_1 < \sigma_2 = 1$.

The remaining plots illustrate the effect of $\rho \neq 0$. The middle right plot has equal spread in both directions ($\sigma_1 = \sigma_2 = 1$), but the variables are now correlated with $\rho \neq 0$. The effect is to rotate the elliptical contours. Because the spread is the same in both directions, the major and minor axes of the ellipses have 45-degree angles with the x_1 and x_2 axes.

The lower left plot shows the effect of increasing the correlation ρ between the variables. The ellipse becomes more eccentric with longer contours. Because $\sigma_1 = \sigma_2 = 1$, the major and minor axes are still at 45-degree angles with the coordinate axes. In general, the parameter ρ determines how eccentric (flat) the contours will be. When $\rho = 0$ we have circles. Positive ρ produce a major axis in the first and third quadrants and negative values of ρ would position the major axis in the second and fourth quadrants. As $|\rho|$ approaches 1 the ellipse will approach a line.

The bottom right plot shows the effect of having correlated random variables with unequal spread ($0.5 = \sigma_1 \neq \sigma_2 = 1$). The spread is greater in the x_2 direction, and the axes of the elliptical contours are no longer at 45-degree angles with the coordinate axes.

One point of this discussion is to illustrate the issues involved in generalizing the K-means model. We can think of there being a spectrum of models, with K-means being the simplest and the general Gaussian mixture with five parameters per cluster and $k - 1$ prior probabilities at the other end. Recall that K-means implicitly assumes spherical clusters with equal spread (homoscedastic) and size ($\eta_k = 1/K$, for all k). With $p = 2$ manifest variables and normal distributions,[7] all clusters would look like the top left plot in Figure 2.18. They would all have round contours with a single common variance in both directions. It is useful to count the parameters as a measure of the complexity of this model. With $p = 2$ manifest variables there are two cluster means for each class conditional distribution, giving $2K$ means plus 1 common variance term. For p manifest variables there are pK means, plus 1 common variance term.

At the other extreme is the general bivariate Gaussian mixture model, with 5 parameters $(\mu_1, \mu_2, \sigma_1, \sigma_2, \rho)$ for each class-conditional distribution and $K - 1$ prior

Figure 2.18 Contour plots of four bivariate normal distributions, each with mean (0,0). Contours are shown for when $100 \times$ PDF equals 1, 3, 6, 10 and 15.

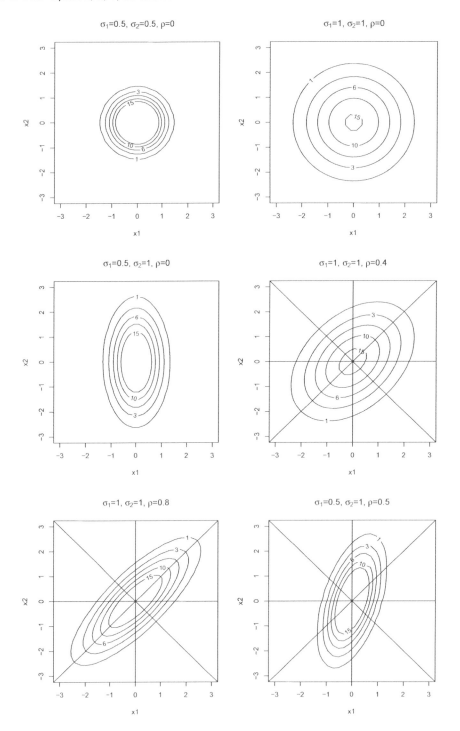

probabilities, giving $6K - 1$ parameters. For p manifest variables there would be Kp mean parameters, $Kp(p + 1)/2$ variance parameters, and $K - 1$ prior probabilities. Thus the complexity of the model grows linearly with K and quadratically with p.

We often seek a compromise, where we relax some of the K-means assumptions without going all the way to the general Gaussian mixture. One simplifying assumption is called *class-conditional independence*, where all variables are assumed to be independent (and therefore uncorrelated with $\rho \equiv 0$) within a cluster. In terms of shape, this means that all clusters look like the first three plots in Figure 2.18. This reduces the complexity substantially by having diagonal covariance matrices with p variance parameters instead of $p(p+1)/2$ per cluster. Model complexity now grows linearly with p. The reduction is not so great when $p = 2$, but it becomes more substantial for larger p.

A stronger constraint would be to assume spherical clusters, where within a cluster the variances are equal in all directions. In this case there would be only one variance parameter per cluster, that is, the covariance matrix is $\sigma_k^2 \mathbf{I}$. This model is more flexible than K-means because the variances can differ across clusters and clusters can be different sizes (prior probabilities).

EXAMPLE 2.15: Bivariate Gaussian mixture with unequal prior probabilities

We return to Example 2.3 with two clusters, $\boldsymbol{\mu}_1 = (0,0)'$, $\boldsymbol{\mu}_2 = (3,0)'$, and common variance is $\sigma^2 = 1$. This example will have unequal prior probabilities, $\eta_1 = 2/3$ and $\eta_2 = 1/3$, by generating $n_1 = 100$ and $n_2 = 50$ observations.

Solution See the SAS code next to Figure 2.19 to generate and data, estimate the K-means model and plot the solution. There are 59 observations assigned to cluster 2, illustrating K-means' bias toward equal-sized clusters. A two-class Gaussian mixture model estimated with software made available by Adrian Raftery (Fraley and Raftery, 2002) estimates the prior probabilities almost exactly, with $\hat{\eta}_1 = 0.6769$ and $\hat{\eta}_2 = 0.3231$.

Figure 2.19 Bivariate Gaussian mixture with unequal prior probabilities

```
TITLE "Unequal cluster sizes";
DATA clus3;
  DO i=1 TO 100;
    x1 = RANNOR(123);
    y1 = RANNOR(123);
    truth=1;
    OUTPUT;
  END;
  DO i=1 TO 50;
    x1 = RANNOR(123)+3;
    y1 = RANNOR(123);
    truth=2;
    OUTPUT;
  END;
RUN;
PROC FASTCLUS DATA=clus3 MAXC=2 out=clusout;
  VAR x1 y1;
RUN;
DATA anno;
  SET clusout;
  IF truth = cluster;
  RETAIN function "oval" height width 3
    x1space y1space "datavalue";
RUN;
```

```
PROC SGPLOT DATA=clusout SGANNO=anno;
  SCATTER X=x1 y=y1 / GROUP=cluster;
RUN;
```

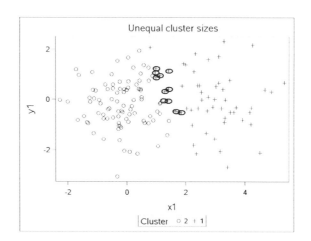

The reader is encouraged to generate other bivariate Gaussian mixtures and then estimate them. For example, assume equal prior probabilities, round clusters, but have one

cluster with more dispersion (for example, $\sigma_1 = 1$ and $\sigma_2 = 1/2$). Examine clusters that are elongated in one direction so that the contours are ellipses rather than circles. There could also be a correlation between the variables within a cluster.

EXAMPLE 2.16:   Newspaper readership (continued)

We illustrate the concepts of prior and class-conditional distributions by returning to the newspaper example. Table 2.8 gives the estimates to the five-class model, assuming bivariate normal class-conditional distributions. The prior distribution is shown in the second row. Nonreaders comprise 26% of the population, ..., and heavy readers make up 23%. These percentages are similar to the K-means estimates reported in Table 2.3, although the Gaussian mixture model assigns substantially more to the nonreader segment and fewer to the light-reader segment than K-means.

Table 2.8 Estimated from a Gaussian mixture model for the newspaper data

Parameter	Nonreader $k = 1$ Triangle Black	Light $k = 2$ Square Red	Skimmer $k = 3$ Circle Green	Selective $k = 4$ × Blue	Heavy $k = 5$ Star Pink
Prior η_k	25.9%	19.4%	19.3%	12.5%	22.9%
Mean time μ_{1k}	0.716	2.554	2.758	5.578	6.377
Mean sections μ_{1k}	0.779	2.603	5.725	2.501	5.547
Variance time σ_{1k}^2	0.872	0.908	1.431	1.070	0.453
Variance sections σ_{2k}^2	1.011	0.975	0.452	0.813	1.430
Covariance σ_{12k}	0.485	−0.489	0.016	−0.472	−0.038
Correlation ρ	0.516	−0.519	0.020	−0.507	−0.048

The next two rows give the means for the class-conditional distributions, which are plotted in Figure 2.20. The model was estimated and the plot was created using software made available by Adrian Raftery (Fraley and Raftery, 2002). The substantive interpretation is also similar to the K-means solution (compare with the cluster means reported in Table 2.3). Again, the means for both nonreaders and light readers are somewhat larger for the Gaussian mixture.

The last three rows give the within-cluster variance, covariance and correlation estimates, and the cluster shapes are shown in Figure 2.20. The correlations are computed from the three variance estimates. For example, for nonreaders, $0.485/\sqrt{0.872 \times 1.011} \approx .516$. Notice how the shapes of the clusters are described by the variances. Consider the skimmer cluster (green circles). The correlation .02 is close to 0 indicating that time and sections are nearly unrelated in this cluster. Accordingly, the axes of the ellipse in Figure 2.20 are aligned with the coordinate axes. The correlation for light readers (red squares) is negative ($-.52$) and the ellipse shows a negative association between time and sections within this cluster. The correlation is positive (.52) for nonreaders, and the ellipse points to the upper right, which indicates a positive association.

The assignments to the clusters are similar, but not identical, between Figure 2.20 and Figure 2.8. Deciding which one is better from a marketing perspective is subjective. There are aspects of the Gaussian mixture model that are undesirable. For example, the point (5,7) is classified as a heavy reader by K-means, but skimmer by the mixture model. Likewise, (7,3), (7,4), and (6,5) are selectives in the K-means solution and heavy reader in the mixture model. Those in (2,1) and (1,2) are light readers in the K-means solution, but nonreaders in the mixture model. The K-means assignments seem easier to defend.

The variance estimates describe the shape of the ellipse. Consider the skimmer segment (green circles) in the upper right. Notice that the within-cluster variance of time (1.43) is

Figure 2.20 Plot showing finite mixture model assignments for the newspaper example

Classification

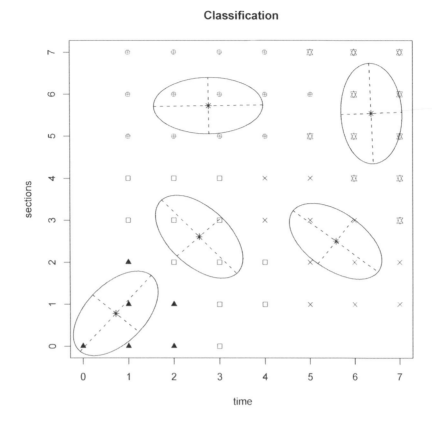

substantially greater than the variance for sections (0.45). Consequently, the ellipse is longer in the time direction than the sections direction, and there are some different (and perhaps undesirable) cluster assignments. The opposite pattern is true for the heavy readers, with more variation in sections than in time. The implicit assumption of K-means is that all the clusters are round with equal variation in all directions.

EXAMPLE 2.17:   Theater Example (continued)

A three-class Gaussian mixture model was estimated for the Theater example, with the estimates of the prior distribution and class-conditional means reported in the last three rows of Table 2.4. The within cluster variances have not been reported. The solution is somewhat different. Cluster GM3.1 has similar means as cluster 3.1 from K-means but is somewhat larger (46% versus 33%). The means from the Gaussian mixture for `getto` and `goodvalue` are nearly 0, but they were somewhat negative for the K-means solution.

GM3.2 is similar to 3.2, in that both are mostly below average on nearly all dimensions. GM3.3 has a substantially different interpretation than 3.3. The question is, which is more actionable?

2.4.2   Binary latent class model

The multivariate normal distribution is often used for mixture distributions of numerical manifest variables. For categorical manifest variables, we will use a product of multinomial distributions to model the class-conditional distributions. We discuss the dichotomous case here, but the model can be easily extended to allow for more than two response categories for each dimension.

Again, we have a sample of n units (indexed by i) and p manifest variables (indexed by j). In this section each manifest variable takes only two values, $x_{ij} \in \{0, 1\}$. Sampling units come from one of K classes, and the probability that a unit from class k has $x_j = 1$ is π_{jk}. Each manifest variable, conditional on being from class k, is thus a Bernoulli trial with $P(X_j = x_j | k) = (1 - \pi_{jk})^{1-x_j} \pi_{jk}^{x_j}$. It is customary to assume class-conditional independence so that the class-conditional distribution is the product of the Bernoulli trials:

$$f_k(\mathbf{x}_i) = \prod_{j=1}^{p} (1 - \pi_{jk})^{1-x_{ij}} \pi_{jk}^{x_{ij}}$$

EXAMPLE 2.18: Macready Mastery Data

We illustrate latent class analysis for binary manifest variables using data from Macready and Dayton (1977), which is also analyzed more completely in Bartholomew and Knott (1999, pp. 142–3). Summarized count data are provided in Table 2.9 from $n = 142$ students. Each student attempted $p = 4$ tasks, and either passed ($x_j = 1$) or failed ($x_j = 0$) each of the tasks. For example, the first five columns of the first row indicate that 41 students failed all four tasks. The next row tells us that 23 students passed tasks x_1, x_2 and x_4, but failed task x_3. The problem is to determine natural groups (or segments) of students based on their performance on these tests.

Table 2.9 Macready mastery data

x1	x2	x3	x4	count	x1	x2	x3	x4	count
0	0	0	0	41	0	1	0	1	5
1	1	0	1	23	0	1	1	1	4
1	1	1	1	15	0	0	1	1	4
1	0	0	0	13	0	0	0	1	4
1	1	1	0	7	1	0	1	0	3
1	1	0	0	7	0	1	1	0	2
1	0	0	1	6	1	0	1	1	1
0	1	0	0	6	0	0	1	0	1

The output below gives the $K = 2$ cluster solution using a program written by the author (Malthouse, 2003b). Estimates of the class-conditional probabilities (π_{jk}) are provided in the $P(X|k)$ column and plotted as a multi-panel bar graph. The prior probability estimates, which sum to 1, are in the $P(k)$ column.

Cluster $k = 1$ comprises $\hat{\eta}_1 = 41.37\%$ of the population and did not do well on any of the tasks. Given that a student is in class 1, the model estimates that there is a $\hat{\pi}_{11} = .2087$ chance that the student passed task 1, a $\hat{\pi}_{21} = .0685$ chance that the student passed task 2, and so on. Because this cluster performed so poorly, it is labeled the novices.

Cluster $k = 2$ is $\hat{\eta}_2 = 58.63\%$ of the population and performed better on the tasks. A member of cluster 2 has a $\hat{\pi}_{12} = .7536$ chance of passing task 1, a $\hat{\pi}_{22} = .7805$ chance of passing task 2, and so on. This cluster is called the experts. It appears that task 3 this the most difficult for both clusters.

We can compute posterior probabilities from these estimates. For example, suppose that a student passes only task 1 ($x_1 = 1$ and $x_2 = x_3 = x_4 = 0$). Is this student a novice or an expert? Recall that posterior probabilities are given by

$$P(G = k | \mathbf{x}) = \frac{\eta_k f_k(\mathbf{x})}{\eta_1 f_1(\mathbf{x}) + \eta_2 f_2(\mathbf{x})}$$

Figure 2.21 Latent class solution of Macready mastery data

```
DATA lca;
  INPUT cluster varname$ p @@;
  LABEL p="Conditional Probability P(X|k)";
DATALINES;
1 x1 0.2087  1 x2 0.0685
1 x3 0.0181  1 x4 0.0524
2 x1 0.7536  2 x2 0.7805
2 x3 0.4317  2 x4 0.7077
RUN;

PROC SGPANEL DATA=lca;
  PANELBY cluster / LAYOUT=columnlattice;
  VBARPARM CATEGORY=varname RESPONSE=p
    / DATALABEL;
  COLAXIS DISPLAY=(nolabel);
RUN;
```

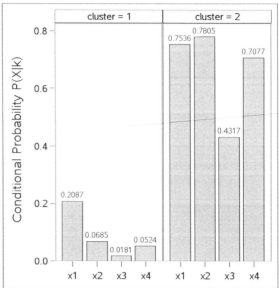

We can compute $f_1(x) = .2087(1 - .0685)(1 - .0181)(1 - .0524) = .1809$ and, similarly, $f_2(x) = .0275$. Thus, the probability that this student is a novice is

$$P(G = 1|\mathbf{x}) = \frac{.4137(.1809)}{.4137(.1809) + .5863(.0275)} \approx .8229.$$

The probability that this student is really an expert (who had a bad day) is $P(G = 2|\mathbf{x}) = 1 - .8229 = .1771$. We would label this student a novice because the largest posterior probability is from cluster $k = 1$.

2.5 Chapter summary

One way to increase CLV is to personalize and customize contact points to smaller groups of customers. The more closely a product or service meets a customer's needs, the customer should stay longer, concentrate share of wallet, and so on. Creating personalized or customized contacts usually begins by segmenting customers, understanding the different needs, and creating appropriate contact points. The ultimate objective of a segmentation model is to identify groups of customers that enable marketing programs that are more profitable than a one-size-fits-all approach (or maximizes profit).

The segmentation models discussed in this chapter assume that each customer i belongs to one of K segments, $g_i \in \{1, \ldots, K\}$. The true segment membership is a *latent variable* in that it cannot be observed directly. Instead, we have measurements of p manifestations of the segment membership $\mathbf{x}_i = (x_{i1}, \ldots, x_{ip})$. The task of the segmentation model is to recover the segment memberships and other information about the segments. The *prior distribution* tells how large each segment is $\eta_k = P(G = k)$, where G is a random variable indicating the segment membership of a randomly selected customer from the population. The *class-conditional distribution* $f_k(\mathbf{x})$ describes the joint distribution of the manifest variables within a segment. The *K-means method* assumes that the class-conditional distributions are spherical, with equal variation in all directions and across all clusters; it also assumes equal-sized clusters ($\eta_k = 1/K, \forall k$). The *Gaussian mixture model* assumes that the class-conditional distributions are multivariate normal.

Assumptions are often made to reduce the number of parameters in each class-conditional distribution. For example, *class-conditional independence* assumes that the manifest variables are independent within a cluster. The *binary latent class model* assumes that the class-conditional distributions are the product of Bernoulli trials for each manifest variable (due to the class-conditional independence assumption). The *observed (mixture) distribution* is

$$f(\mathbf{x}) = \sum_{k=1}^{K} \eta_k f_k(\mathbf{x}).$$

The *posterior distribution* gives the probability that a person comes from cluster k given the manifest variables:

$$P(G = k|\mathbf{x}) = \frac{\eta_k f_k(\mathbf{x})}{f(\mathbf{x})}.$$

As indicated above K-means method makes strict assumptions about the class-conditional distributions. When these assumptions are not true, transforming the data prior to estimation will often improve the solution. Two transformation approaches were discussed. The *symmetrize-and-standardize approach* first applies a transformation, often the log, to symmetrize the distribution of skewed manifest variables, and then standardizes all variables to have mean 0 and variance 1 so that the manifest variables have commensurate units. The *quantile approach* finds quantiles (for example, deciles) of all manifest variables prior to analysis. *Multicollinearity* is when manifest variables are correlated with each other. When a block of manifest variables are correlated, the underlying dimension they measure implicitly receives more weight than other dimensions in a cluster analysis that do not have multiple measures. A solution to the multicollinearity problem is to use a multivariate transformation such as computing factor scores of the correlated variables.

Profiling clusters involves comparing clusters on variables not used in the cluster analysis. Use crosstabs for categorical variables and one-way ANOVAs for numerical variables. Chi-square and F statistics can help prioritize which variables have the greatest differences across clusters.

Notes

[1] The `DISTANCE` variable in a data set created by the `OUT=` option in `PROC FASTCLUS` gives this distance. The `LEAST=` option assigns the exponent, where `LEAST=2` gives Euclidean distances by squaring the differences from the centers.

[2] Different software packages report different monotonic transformations of SSE. For example, the *mean squared error* (MSE) divides SSE by np, or a denominator adjusted for degrees of freedom. The *root means squared error* (RMSE) is the square root of MSE. $R^2 = 1 - \text{SSE/SST}$ gives the fraction of variation explained by the model, where SST is a constant giving the total sum of squared errors. These are all equivalent in the sense that minimizing SSE produces the same solution as minimizing MSE or RMSE, or maximizing R^2.

[3] The specific line can be computed as follows. From the output, the estimated centers are $\bar{\mathbf{x}}_1 = (0.0309, 0.0072)'$ and $\mathbf{x}_2 = (2.882, -0.2289)'$. The midpoint on the segment joining the centers, $(\mathbf{x}_1 + \mathbf{x}_2)/2 = (1.456, -0.111)'$ is clearly an equal distance from each center, and is therefore a point on the boundary line. The slope of the segment joining the centers is $(-0.2289 - 0.0072)/(2.882 - 0.0309) = -0.0828$. The boundary line is orthogonal to this segment and therefore has slope $-1/-0.0828 = 12.08$.

[4] The kurtosis of a normal distribution is 0 and a (continuous) uniform distribution has kurtosis -1.2.

[5] Some practitioners might look beyond the seven-cluster solution and then combine clusters later. The rationale is that some of the clusters identified from the larger solutions can be very actionable. Again, the golden rule is to find clusters that are most actionable.

[6] The test statistic itself does not account for the number of distinct values that that categorical variable can take, but the P-value does.

[7] K-means does not assume normality. If the data came from a non-normal but symmetrical distribution, for example, uniform, then the contours would not have spacing as in Figure 2.18, but they would still be round.

The Simple Retention Model

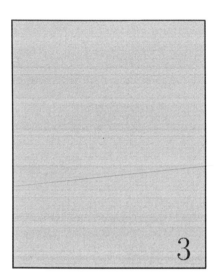

3

Contents

Your company acquires customers, provides them with a product or service, and makes a certain amount of profit each month until they terminate the relationship forever. How much profit do you expect to make from customers during their lifetimes? How would increasing retention rates affect future profit?

These are very common questions. Contractual service providers such as Internet service providers, health clubs, and media content providers (for example, Netflix, digital content subscribers, and so on), are in exactly this situation. For example, subscribers to Netflix pay a certain amount each month until they cancel. Companies that provide cellular phone service receive monthly payments from their customers until they cancel.

One application is determining how much can be spent to acquire a customer. For example, it may cost a cellular phone company $400 to acquire a new customer and provide a handset; even if he only generates $50 in profit each month this would be a good investment as long as the cellular phone company can retain him sufficiently long to recoup the acquisition cost. Likewise, a company that is considering whether to invest marketing resources in retaining customers longer will need to know CLV.

This chapter and the next show how to estimate the value of such customers in contractual situations. We begin with the case in which customers sign a contract for a certain number of periods and are not allowed to cancel. Next, we present the *simple retention model*, which allows customers to cancel, but assumes that the retention rate is constant over time and across customers, and that cash flows are independent of the cancelation time. The next chapter discusses when retention rates change over time, and when payment amounts depend on the time of cancelation.

3.1   The customer annuity model

Suppose for now that new customers sign a contract to make T payments of amount m in the future and are not allowed to cancel the contract. A book-of-the-month club is an example, where customers receive a series of 12 books on different topics, one each month. Customers allow the publisher to debit a credit card for $20 after receiving each book.

Customers in this business situation are annuities. The publisher invests a certain amount of money to acquire a customer and, thus, the promise of T future payments of amount m. It is helpful to illustrate this with a diagram, where each m represents a payment and the subscript the payment number:

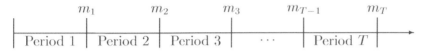

Notice that the payments come at the end of every period. Suppose further that the discount rate is d. The CLV of a customer is given by the formula for the present value of an *ordinary annuity*:

$$\mathrm{PV}_T = \sum_{t=1}^{T} \frac{m}{(1+d)^t} = m\frac{1-(1+d)^{-T}}{d}. \tag{3.1}$$

More generally, the payment m could be a sum of cash inflows and outflows. An example of a negative cash flow is the cost of marketing to a customer each period. We discuss what makes up m in section 3.4. For example, it is often the gross contribution margin per customer—revenues minus the cost of sales.

EXAMPLE 3.1:   Book-of-the-month club

Those who join a monthly book club agree to buy $T = 12$ books, one at the end of each month, each generating a gross margin of $m = \$10$. Find the CLV of a customer, which is the present value of the 12 payments using a monthly discount rate of $d = 1\%$.

Solution

$$\mathrm{CLV} = \mathrm{PV}_{12} = 10\frac{1-(1+.01)^{-12}}{.01} = \$112.55.$$

The Excel function PV also gives the answer: $-\mathrm{PV}(.01,\ 12,\ 10)$.

Companies usually require prepayment for the product or service so that the first payment is received at time 0 rather than at the end of the first period. The T payments are illustrated as follows:

In these situations the formula for an *immediate annuity* is used:

$$\mathrm{PV}_T = \sum_{t=0}^{T-1} \frac{m}{(1+d)^t} = m\frac{(1+d)[1-(1+d)^{-T}]}{d}. \tag{3.2}$$

EXAMPLE 3.2:   Book-of-the-month club (continued)

Suppose the book-of-the-month-club requires prepayment each month for the $T = 12$ books and that each one generates a gross margin of $m = \$10$. Find the present value of the 12 payments, assuming a monthly discount rate of $d = 1\%$.

Solution

$$\mathrm{PV}_{12} = 10\frac{(1+.01)[1-(1+.01)^{-12}]}{.01} = \$113.68$$

or $-\mathrm{PV}(.01, 12, 10,,1)$ in Excel.

To understand where the annuity formulas come from (and other formulas in this chapter), we must remember how to find the sum of a geometric series. A *geometric series* is given by

$$S_T = a + ar + ar^2 + \cdots + ar^{T-1},$$

where $a \neq 0$. This sum can be evaluated by multiplying both sides of the equation by r,

$$S_T r = ar + ar^2 + ar^3 + \cdots + ar^T,$$

subtracting the second expression from the first,

$$S_T - S_T r = S_T(1 - r) = a - ar^T,$$

and solving for S_T

$$S_T = \frac{a(1 - r^T)}{1 - r}. \tag{3.3}$$

The annuity formulas are a special case of this expression, where $a = m$ and $r = 1/(1+d)$ (see Exercise 3.9). When $|r| < 1$,

$$\lim_{T \to \infty} S_T = \frac{a}{1 - r}. \tag{3.4}$$

3.2 The simple retention model

The customer annuity model assumes that customers make a pre-determined number of payments and that they never stop making payments before the end of the contract, but these assumptions are usually not realistic. Instead, some customers discontinue the relationship early and others continue using the product or service long after the initial contract has expired. The *simple retention model* (SRM) estimates CLV assuming the following

- The percentage of customers retained each month (the *retention rate*) r is constant over *time* and across *customers*.
- The period cash flow m is unaffected by the cancelation time.
- The event that a customer cancels in time period t is independent of the event that the customer cancels in any other time period.

These assumptions are relaxed in the next chapter. First, we will show how to estimate CLV using a spreadsheet, and then we will derive formulas.

EXAMPLE 3.3:   Internet service provider (ISP)

An Internet service provider (ISP) acquires 1,000 customers who will pay $50 at the end of each month for the service, with a gross margin of $25. The ISP retains 80% of its customers each month and discontinues service immediately to anyone who fails to make a payment, without attempting to reactivate the customer. Find the CLV of this cohort, assuming a monthly discount rate of 1%.

Solution   The answer can be found using the spreadsheet shown below. Immediately after acquisition (time 0) the ISP has 1,000 customers with a cash flow of $25,000. At the end of the first month (time = 1), 800 (80% of the 1,000) are expected to make payments, generating a total cash flow of $20,000 ($800 × $25) with a present value of $19,802($20,000/1.01). At the end of the second month (time = 2), 640 (80% of the 800) customers are expected to make payments generating a cash flow of $16,000 with a present value of $15,685 ($16,000/1.01^2). The answers for periods 0–5 are shown below. The formulas can be easily programmed in a spreadsheet and then copied. After 100 if you sum the discounted payments the CLV = $120,238. (Readers should reproduce this spreadsheet at this time in software of their choice.)

Time	Expected Number of Customers	Raw Cash Flow	Discounted Cash Flow
0	1000.0	25,000	25,000
1	800.0	20,000	19,802
2	640.0	16,000	15,685
3	512.0	12,800	12,424
4	409.6	10,240	9,840
5	327.7	8,192	7,794
⋮	⋮	⋮	⋮

A virtue of this spreadsheet solution is that it is concrete and intuitive, making the problem easy to understand, but it is somewhat cumbersome, and we have not provided any formal rationale for it. We will develop a convenient, closed-form expression for CLV that enables us to avoid evaluating the sums in a spreadsheet and is based on a probabilistic model. Before doing so, we will briefly review and illustrate the necessary concepts from elementary probability theory.

A *random variable* X assigns a number to the outcome of a random experiment. The *probability mass function* (PMF) of a random variable that takes discrete values gives the probability $f(x) = P(X = x)$ that random variable X will take the value x. Upper-case letters will be used to represent random variables and corresponding lower-case letters indicate a realization of the random variable. We are often interested in knowing the *mean* or *expected value* of X, which describes the location of the middle of the distribution of X:

$$E(X) = \sum_x x P(X = x). \tag{3.5}$$

The mean can be interpreted as a weighted average of the x values, with the weights determined by the probabilities. Sometimes we are more interested in some transformation $g(X)$. For example, X could be the time until cancelation, and $g(X)$ could be the CLV of a customer who cancels at time X. The mean of $g(X)$ is

$$E[g(X)] = \sum_x g(x) P(X = x). \tag{3.6}$$

EXAMPLE 3.4:   Number of orders

Suppose that on any given day a company receives zero orders with probability .2, one order with probability .4, two orders with probability .3, and three orders with probability .1. The company never receives more than three orders in a day. The fixed costs, which are incurred regardless of the number of orders, are five, the marginal cost per order is two and the marginal revenue per order is eight. Find the expected number of orders and the expected profit on a given day. Graph the PMF.

Solution   Let X be a random variable indicating the number of orders on a day and let $g(X) = (8 - 2)X - 5 = 6X - 5$ be the profit on a day when there are X orders. The means are computed by using equations 3.5 and 3.6 above (Malthouse and Mulhern, 2007). It is convenient to evaluate these formulas using a spreadsheet as shown below. The first column enumerates all possible values of X (sample space) and the second records the PMF. The sum of all the probabilities must equal 1, as shown in the last row. The third column computes the product of the first two columns, and its sum is the mean number of orders in a day $E(X) = 1.3$.

x	$P(X = x)$	$xf(x)$	$g(x)$	$g(x)f(x)$
0	.2	0	-5	-1.0
1	.4	0.4	1	0.4
2	.3	0.6	7	2.1
3	.1	0.3	13	1.3
Sum	1	1.3		2.8

The fourth column transforms the number of orders into profit. For example, the probability that profit will equal 13 is the same as the probability of receiving three orders, $P[g(X) = 13] = P(X = 3) = .1$. The last column evaluates equation 3.6 by computing the product of the second and fourth columns; its sum gives the expected daily profit[1] $E[g(X)] = 2.8$.

The graph of the PMF is shown below. The mean, 1.3, is an indication of the center of this distribution.

```
DATA pdf;
   INPUT x p @@;
DATALINES;
0 2     1 4     2 3     3 1
RUN;

PROC SGPLOT DATA=pdf;
   HISTOGRAM X / FREQ=p NBINS=4;
   XAXIS LABEL="Number of Orders (x)";
   YAXIS LABEL="P(X=x) as a percent";
RUN;
```

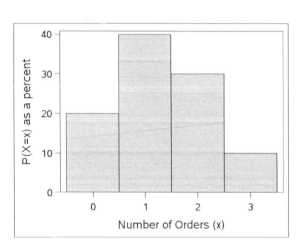

We can now derive a probabilistic model for CLV. Assume that all customers in some group are retained each period with probability r (the retention rate) for all periods and that the event a customer cancels during some period is independent of the event of cancelation during any other period. Let T be a random variable indicating the time of cancelation. Under these assumptions, T has a *geometric distribution*. Probabilities of a geometric distribution are given by PMF

$$f(t) = P(T = t) = r^{t-1}(1 - r). \tag{3.7}$$

The rationale for this formula is that a customer must be retained for $t - 1$ periods and then defect. Because defaulting is assumed to be independent across time periods, the retention probabilities can be multiplied, so that r^{t-1} is the probability of retaining a customer for $t - 1$ periods and $(1 - r)$ is the probability of defaulting (in the last period).

   In addition to knowing the probabilities of certain cancelation times in equation 3.7, we sometimes want to know the probability that a customer has survived until the beginning of period t, which is called the *survival function*,

$$S(t) = P(T \geq t) = r^{t-1}. \tag{3.8}$$

We can equivalently think of the survival function as giving the probability that the customer cancels at time t or later, or that the customer survives the first $t - 1$ periods.

   The survival function can be used to find quantiles of T. The α quantile[2] of random variable T, call it P_α, divides a distribution so that α percent of the distribution has $T \leq P_\alpha$ and $1 - \alpha$ percent of the distribution has $T \geq P_\alpha$, that is, $P(T \leq P_\alpha) = \alpha$ and $P(T \geq P_\alpha) = 1 - \alpha$. We can find the α quantile of the cancelation time under the SRM by solving

$$S(t) = P(T \geq P_\alpha) = r^{P_\alpha - 1} = 1 - \alpha.$$

Taking logs of both sides and solving for P_α we find that

$$P_\alpha = 1 + \frac{\log(1 - \alpha)}{\log r}. \tag{3.9}$$

For example, the *median time until cancelation* is found by substituting $\alpha = .5$ into the equation. Because events occur only at discrete time, the quantile is the greatest integer of equation 3.9.

   The mean of a geometric distribution is given by (see Example 4.2 and Exercise 3.10):

$$E(T) = 1/(1 - r). \tag{3.10}$$

EXAMPLE 3.5:   ISP: distribution of cancelation time

Graph the PMF and survival function of cancelation time for the ISP having a retention rate of 80%. Find and interpret the mean and median time of cancelation. Suppose the ISP implements a new retention campaign and is able to increase the retention rate to 90%. Find the mean and median under this new retention rate.

Solution   The probabilities are computed using $P(t) = .8^{t-1}(1 - .8)$ and plotted in Figure 3.1 (the reader should replicate the probabilities and graph in a spreadsheet program). The distribution is skewed to the right. As we saw in Example 3.3, 20% of the customers are expected to cancel before the payment at time 1 (that is, the customer cancels at $T = 1$) while others will remain much longer. The expected time until attrition is $E(T) = 1/(1 - .8) = 5$ months. This ISP therefore expects 4 payments from each customer if the payments come at the end of a period. The median cancelation time is $P_{.5} = 1 + \log(1 - .5)/\log(.8) = 4.106 \approx 4$. At least half of the customers will survive until period 4.

   The survival function gives the probability that a customer has survived until the beginning of time t. All of the customers (100%) have survived at time 0 and 80% have

Figure 3.1 The geometric distribution $(r = .8)$

```
DATA geo;
  t=0; p=0;  St=1;   OUTPUT;
  t=1; p=.2; St=1-p; OUTPUT;
  DO t = 2 TO 25;
    p=p*.8;
    St=St-p;
    OUTPUT;
  END;
RUN;

PROC SGPLOT DATA=geo;
  STEP X=t Y=p;
  XAXIS LABEL = "Cancelation Time (t)";
  YAXIS LABEL = "Probability P(T=t)";
RUN;

PROC SGPLOT DATA=geo;
  STEP X=t Y=St;
  XAXIS LABEL = "Cancelation Time (t)";
  YAXIS LABEL = "Survival Function S(t)";
RUN;
```

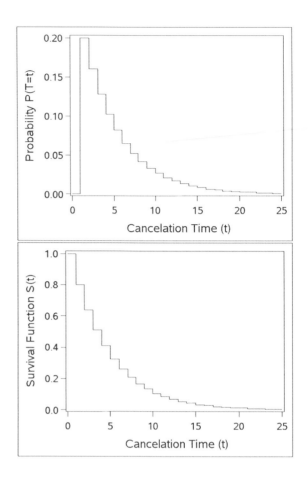

survived at time 1. Only $.8^5 \approx 33\%$ have survived until period 5 and $.8^{10} = 10\%$ have survived until period 10.

After implementing the new retention campaign, the expected time until attrition increases to $E(T) = 1/(1 - .9) = 10$ months. The ISP now expects 9 payments from each customer.

CLV is the sum of the present values of future cash flows. When a customer cancels during period t, there will be t cash flows if they occur at the beginning of a period and $t - 1$ cash flows if they come at the end. For a specific cancelation time, the present value of these cash flows can be found with the annuity formulas (Equation 3.1 or 3.2). But the cancelation time T is random, and CLV will thus have a distribution. Those customers who have larger T have a larger CLV. We can summarize the distribution of CLV with its mean. When cash flows occur at the beginning of the period (immediate annuity) the expected value is

$$E(\text{CLV}) = \frac{m(1 + d)}{1 + d - r}. \tag{3.11}$$

When cash flows come at the end (ordinary),

$$E(\text{CLV}) = \frac{mr}{1 + d - r}. \tag{3.12}$$

Proof   We show the result for ordinary annuities using equation 3.6 with $g(t)$ given by equation 3.1:

$$E(\text{CLV}) = \sum_{t=1}^{\infty} r^{t-1}(1-r)PV_{t-1} = \sum_{t=0}^{\infty} r^t(1-r)PV_t$$

$$= \sum_{t=0}^{\infty} r^t(1-r)m\frac{1-(1+d)^{-t}}{d}$$

$$= \frac{m(1-r)}{d}\left[\sum_{t=0}^{\infty} r^t - \sum_{t=0}^{\infty}\left(\frac{r}{1+d}\right)^t\right]$$

$$= \frac{m}{d} - \frac{m(1-r)}{d}\cdot\frac{1}{1-r/(1+d)}$$

$$= \frac{mr}{1+d-r}.$$

When cash flows come at the beginning of the period the company receives an additional (non-random) payment of m at time 0:

$$E(\text{CLV}) = m + \frac{mr}{1+d-r} = \frac{m+md-mr+mr}{1+d-r} = \frac{m(1+d)}{1+d-r}.$$

EXAMPLE 3.6:   ISP: lifetime value

Find the expected time until attrition and expected CLV of a single ISP customer assuming a monthly discount rate of 1%, monthly cash flows of $25 at the beginning of each month, and retention rates of $70\%, 75\%, \ldots 95\%$, and 98%. Plot CLV against the retention rate.

Solution   We first illustrate using equation 3.11 to compute CLV when $r = .8$, and confirm the answer found with the spreadsheet method in used Example 3.3.

$$E(\text{CLV}) = \frac{\$25(1+.01)}{1+.01-.8} = \$120.24.$$

CLV for the other attrition rates are computed with the same formula and shown in the table below.

The plot illustrates the importance of nurturing long-term relationships with customers. CLV changes at an increasing rate as the retention rate increases. For example, if a company could improve the retention rate from 70% to 75%, CLV would increase from $81 to $97. The same 5% improvement in retention rate from 90% to 95%, however, nearly doubles CLV from $230 to 421$. CLV is doubled again by increasing the retention rate from 95% to 98%. High customer loyalty pays good dividends.

Gupta and Lehmann (2003) calls $r/(1+d-r)$ the *margin multiple*. This multiple tells how the period gross margin for a customer (m) is related to CLV. The margin multiples for different retention rates are computed in Table 3.1. Assuming a 15% discount rate, the period gross margin is multiplied by 3.6 with a 90% retention rate, 4.75 for a 95% retention rate, and so on.

EXAMPLE 3.7:   Insurance company

(Based on by Berger and Nasr, 1998, Case 1) An insurance company wants to estimate CLV. The company pays, on average, $50 per customer yearly on promotional expenses. The yearly retention rate is 75%. The yearly gross contribution per customer is expected to amount to $260. An appropriate annual discount rate is 20%. Find CLV, assuming that

```
DATA clv;
  DO r = .7 to .98 by .01;
    Et = 1/(1-r);
    Eclv = 25*1.01/(1.01-r);
    OUTPUT;
  END;
  FORMAT clv DOLLAR8.2
    r PERCENT5.0 Et 5.2;
  LABEL
    Et = "E(T)"
    Eclv = "E(CLV)";
RUN;

PROC PRINT DATA=clv NOOBS LABEL;
  VAR r Et Eclv;
  WHERE MOD(100*r,5)=0 OR r=.98;
RUN;

PROC SGPLOT DATA=clv;
  SERIES X=r Y=Eclv;
  XAXIS LABEL = "Retention Rate (r)";
RUN;
```

r	$E(T)$	$E(CLV)$
70%	3.33	$81.45
75%	4	$97.12
80%	5	$120.24
85%	6.67	$157.81
90%	10	$229.55
95%	20	$420.83
98%	50	$841.67

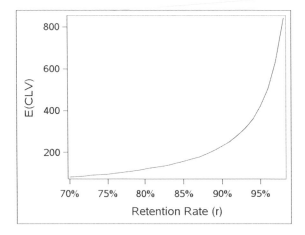

Table 3.1 Margin multiples for different retention and discount rates

Retention Rate (r)	Discount Rate (d)		
	.1	.15	.2
.6	1.20	1.09	1.00
.7	1.75	1.56	1.40
.8	2.67	2.29	2.00
.9	4.50	3.60	3.00
.95	6.33	4.75	3.80
.97	7.46	5.39	4.22
.99	9.00	6.19	4.71

you have just acquired a customer, receive the first payment at time 0 (do not worry about acquisition costs, because you would want to compare your answer with the acquisition costs to evaluate customer profitability), and will incur marketing costs at the end of each year, so that revenues are immediate while costs are ordinary.

Solution   We use equation 3.11 to compute lifetime revenue because the first payment comes at the beginning of the relationship. For costs, equation 3.12 is used because the first costs will not be incurred until the end of the first year.

$$\frac{\$260(1 + .2)}{1 + .2 - .75} - \frac{\$50(.75)}{1 + .2 - .75} = \$610.$$

3.3   Estimating retention rates

The previous section assumed that the retention rate r was known, but in practice it usually must be estimated from data. An organization observes when customers are acquired and can trace the history of payments. Some but not all of these customers will cancel. A customer who has not yet canceled is said to be *censored* and the organization will not have observed this customer's cancelation time yet. This section shows how to estimate retention rates from such data, allowing for some customers to be censored.

We want to estimate the retention rate for some group of $n_0 + n_1$ customers that were acquired in the past, where n_1 of the customers have already canceled (so that defection time t has been observed), while n_0 others are still active (censored). Let T denote a random variable and t be an observed cancelation time, that is, a realization of T. If customer i has already canceled, let t_i be the observed times of defection, so that customer i has been active $t_i - 1$ periods and cancels at time t_i. For those still active, let c_i be the time of censoring so that customer i has been active c_i periods and the company knows that the time of cancelation for this customer is $T_i > c_i$.

EXAMPLE 3.8:   Educational service provider

A company provides a supplementary educational service to junior high-school students in Asia. Those who enroll in the service may cancel at any time. Each month the company sends the student a booklet of reading materials and exercises to supplement their lessons at school. During the month, the student completes the exercise book and returns the materials to the company for grading and feedback. This example illustrates the type of data that such an organization has.

The table below shows one year of transaction history for eight customers who were acquired during the year. An R indicates that the customer was retained and a C indicates that the customer canceled. Customers enroll and make their first payment during the period before the first R. Customers do not make a payment during the period in which they cancel. Customer id $= 1$ subscribed to the service in month 4, continued to use the service during month 7, and then canceled in month 8, so that $t_1 = 3$ indicates a cancelation during the third month of life.

Id	Month number												t	c
	1	2	3	4	5	6	7	8	9	10	11	12		
1						R	R	C					3	
2		R	R	R	R	R	R	R	R	R	R	C	11	
3	R	R	R	R	R	R	R	R	R	R	R	R		12
4						R	R	R	R	C			5	
5	R	R	R	R	R	R	R	R	R	R	R	R		12
6						R	R	R	R	R	R	R		8
7						R	R	R	R	R	R	C	8	
8	R	R	C										3	

Customer 2 joined during month 1 and canceled during month 12, which was month $t_2 = 11$ of life. Customer 3 is *censored*, having joined during month 1 and never canceled. The company only knows that the time of cancelation for this customer is greater than 12. Estimates that do not account for censoring underestimate the true retention rate. Customers 5 and 6 are also censored. Note that there are $n_1 = 5$ customers who have canceled in this study and $n_0 = 3$ customers who are censored.

We now derive the maximum likelihood estimate for the retention rate (r). Using equations 3.7 and 3.8, the likelihood function for r is

$$L(r) = \prod_{i=1}^{n_1} P(T = t_i) \prod_{i=1}^{n_0} S(c_i + 1) = \prod_{i=1}^{n_1} (1 - r) r^{t_i - 1} \prod_{i=1}^{n_0} r^{c_i}. \qquad (3.13)$$

This is maximized by taking logs, differentiating with respect to r, equating the derivative to 0, and solving for r:

$$\hat{r} = \frac{\sum t_t + \sum c_t - n_1}{\sum t_t + \sum c_t} = 1 - \frac{n_1}{\sum t_t + \sum c_t}. \tag{3.14}$$

The caret or hat over the $\hat{r}$ indicates that it is an estimate of parameter r. This equation has an intuitive interpretation. The denominator of the second term gives the total number of periods in which customers can cancel (opportunities to cancel) and numerator is number of cancelations. Thus, the second term estimates the default rate.

EXAMPLE 3.9:   Educational service provider (continued)

Estimate the retention rate for the educational service provider using the eight customers discussed in Example 3.8.

Solution   The cancelation time was observed for $n_1 = 5$ customers and $n_0 = 3$ were censored. The sum of defection times is $\sum t_i = 3 + 11 + 5 + 8 + 3 = 30$ and the sum of censoring times is $\sum c_i = 12 + 12 + 8 = 32$. The retention rate is estimated as

$$\hat{r} = 1 - \frac{5}{30 + 32} \approx 92\%.$$

We can think of this as a series of coin flips. Each period the customer flips a coin, where heads indicates canceling, and tails indicates not canceling. Each customer flips the coin until heads comes up, at then stops flipping the coin. In total, these eight customers have flipped the coin 62 times, and only five heads were observed (cancelations). We estimate the defection rate as $5/62$.

EXAMPLE 3.10:   Educational service provider: one-year

The educational service provider in Example 3.8 acquired more than just eight customers. This problem examines a larger random sample of 671 customers who joined for the first time during this year. The table below gives a crosstab of customer status at the end of the study period (censored or canceled) versus the time of cancelation. For example, four customers canceled during their second month, 16 canceled during their third month, and three customers were censored at during month 1. There were $n_1 = 245$ customers who canceled the service during this year (and thus have observed cancelation times) and $n_0 = 426$ censored cases. Estimate the retention rate.

Table 3.2 Data for the one-year educational service provider example

Status	\multicolumn{12}{c}{Time of Cancelation/Censoring}	Total
	1	2	3	4	5	6	7	8	9	10	11	12	Total
Canceled	0	4	16	20	37	28	61	24	19	13	10	13	245
Censored	3	0	2	1	7	33	49	63	30	16	34	188	426
Total	3	4	18	21	44	61	110	87	49	29	44	201	671

Solution   Using equation 3.14 requires computing the sum of cancelation and censoring times. For the three customers censored at time 1 the sum is three. The four customers who canceled or censored at time 2 have a sum of $4 \times 2 = 8$. The 18 who canceled or were censored at time 3 have a sum of $3 \times 18 = 54$, and so on. The sums are therefore $\sum t_i + \sum c_i = 1(3) + 2(4) + 3(18) + \cdots + 12(201) = 5,828$ and the estimated retention rate is

$$\hat{r} = 1 - \frac{245}{5828} = 95.8\%.$$

The numbers substituted into this equation can be produced using PROC MEANS. Here is the SAS program to read the data in and compute the numbers. The bigT variable gives the time of cancelation or censoring, cancel is a dummy variable that equals 1 for canceling and 0 for censoring, and count is the number of customers.

Program 3.1 Reading data for one-year educational service provider

```
DATA service1yr;
  INPUT bigT cancel count @@;
  LABEL bigT = "Cancelation Time (T)"
    cancel = "Dummy 1=cancel, 0=censored";
DATALINES;
2 1 4      3 1 16     4 1 20     5 1 37     6 1 28     7 1 61     8 1 24     9 1 19
10 1 13    11 1 10    12 1 13    1 0 3      3 0 2      4 0 1      5 0 7      6 0 33
7 0 49     8 0 63     9 0 30     10 0 16    11 0 34    12 0 188
RUN;
```

```
PROC MEANS DATA=service1yr SUM MAXDEC=0;
  VAR cancel bigT;
  WEIGHT count;
  OUTPUT OUT=answer SUM=;
RUN;
```

Variable	Label	Sum
cancel	Dummy 1=cancel, 0=censored	245
bigT	Cancelation Time (T)	5828

We can have SAS compute the retention rate and both the expected and median time until cancelation (ET) with a single SQL statement:

Program 3.2 PROC SQL program computing retention rates

```
PROC SQL;
  SELECT
    cancels LABEL="Number Cancels",
    flips LABEL="Opportunities to Cancel",
    Rhat LABEL="Retention Rate (r)" FORMAT=6.4,
    1/(1-Rhat) AS ET LABEL="E(T)" FORMAT=5.1,
    1+LOG(.5)/LOG(Rhat) AS median LABEL="Median(T)" FORMAT=3.0
  FROM (SELECT SUM(cancel) AS cancels,
      SUM(bigT) as flips,
      1-SUM(cancel)/SUM(bigT) AS Rhat
    FROM answer);
```

Number Cancels	Opportunities to Cancel	Retention Rate (r)	E(T)	Median(T)
245	5828	0.9580	23.8	17

3.4 Per-period cash flows m

The formulas for estimating CLV in Equations (3.12) and (3.11) depend on knowing m, the cash flows realized each period. This section addresses two sets of issues around m: which cash flows should be included, and whether m is constant over time and customers.

3.4.1   Deciding which cash flows to include

Our goal is to arrive at a period contribution for each customer, which is revenues less variable costs, but deciding which cash flows to include in m can be complicated. Following Pfeifer et al. (2005), our definitions of both CP and CLV do not specify exactly which costs and revenues are included, and there can be different implementations depending on the decision being made (Roberts and Berger, 1999; Blattberg et al., 2008). A simple example of how this can become complicated is acquisition costs. If we are deciding whether to spend marketing resources to acquire a customer, then clearly the cost of acquiring the customer should be considered. If a customer has already been acquired and we are deciding, for example, whether to increase the retention marketing efforts (for example, by increasing the number of sales calls), then acquisition and other sunk costs are not relevant.

Roberts and Berger (1999, p. 184) give two general guidelines for making decisions about which costs to include:

- All relevant costs of servicing the customer should be included.
- Exclude fixed costs as appropriate.

In addition, Blattberg et al. (2009, p. 164) emphasize the importance of making cost assumptions explicit and justifying which are included or excluded.

Which costs are relevant depend on the nature of the business and decision being made. Shepard (1999) gives examples of different profit-and-loss statements for various businesses. For example, in the case of a direct-to-consumer retailer the revenues would include gross sales and other fees such as shipping and handling. Deducting returns gives *net sales*. Relevant costs of sales can include the cost of goods sold, costs of lost or damaged items, bad debt, order processing costs, shipping costs, and return processing costs. Promotional expenses can include components such as creative development, media (for example, paying a search engine for keywords, paying a web site to display a banner, list rentals, postage, and so on), paper and printing. For some applications a contribution to overhead is also deducted.

We have stressed the importance of quantifying the effect of marketing actions on *incremental* CLV—what is the *difference* in CLV between when the organization takes the marketing action and when it does not? When incremental CLV is the relevant outcome, decisions about which costs to include are somewhat simpler. Because incremental CLV is the *difference* between CLV with and without the contact or action, fixed costs cancel out. For example, if the decision is whether or not to increase the number of marketing contact points, fixed costs such as executive salaries, rent and depreciation are the same whether or not the number of contacts is increased and therefore have no impact on incremental CLV. All costs associated with the increase in marketing contact points are relevant, such as the cost of developing additional creative content, and purchasing additional media, paper, printing, and so on.

EXAMPLE 3.11:   Full or marginal costing

This example is based on Blattberg et al. (2009, Issue 16). Suppose, for the sake of simplicity, that a firm has only two customers. Customer 1 generates net revenues (net of variable costs) of $500 and Customer 2 generates only $150. The company has fixed costs of $400, regardless of the number of customers. These fixed costs pay for executive salaries, a call center, and so on. Averaging these fixed costs between both customers assigns $200 to each. CLV for the two customers is computed the table below.

Customer	Marginal Costing	Full Costing
1	CLV = $500	CLV = $500 − $200 = $300
2	CLV = $150	CLV = $150 − $200 = −$50

ing_ f

Under marginal costing both customers have positive CLV, while under full costing Customer 2 has a negative CLV. It seems that the firm would be better of without this customer, and the firm should allow Customer 2 to churn. The company would then be left with the following profits:

	With Customer 1	With Customers 1 and 2
Net Revenues	$500	$500 + $150 = $650
Fixed Costs	$400	$400
Total Profits	$100	$250

Clearly the firm is better off retaining Customer 2. Again, we should exclude fixed costs as appropriate. See Roberts and Berger (1999, pp. 184–6) for a similar example.

Sometimes costs are semi-variable, where they are constant within a given range, but then jump once a threshold is crossed Blattberg et al. (2009, p. 164). For example, existing call centers, web services, and fulfillment centers can service some range of customers. If the decision is whether to acquire customers, the fixed costs are not relevant as long as acquiring customers does not necessitate adding additional capacity. At some point, however, a threshold will be crossed and the existing infrastructure will be incapable of serving the customer base in an efficient way. At this point the cost of, for example, an additional fulfillment center becomes relevant.

3.4.2 The constant cash-flow assumption

The SRM assumes that m is constant over time and customers. In some situations this is a reasonable assumption. For example, the amount of revenue that an ISP receives from its customers each month is usually constant and, if we can assume the marginal costs of serving the customer are also constant over time and customers, then profit is also constant. We now give several examples of when profits are not constant and show how to estimate CLV in these situations.

EXAMPLE 3.12:   Educational service provider

All subscribers to the educational service provider in Example 3.8 pay the same monthly fee, so revenue is constant over time and customers. Costs, however, vary. All customers receive the same materials, which have marginal costs for the paper, printing and postage. Some students will return the materials for grading, generating additional marginal costs for return postage, labor for grading, and an additional postage for returning the materials to the student. Thus, there are two possible costs, depending on whether the materials are returned.

EXAMPLE 3.13:   Movie service

Consider a company such as Netflix that mails movies to its members. Suppose a family pays m per month for a service where the company mails the family a single movie, the family watches the movie and mails it back, the company sends another movie, and so on. Each time the family receives and returns a movie the company encounters marginal costs selecting the movie, packaging it, mailing it to the customer, paying the return postage, and placing the movie back into inventory. While the marginal revenue per month is constant over time, the marginal costs are proportional to the number of movies.

EXAMPLE 3.14:   Electronic coupon company

An Internet coupon company acquires members who give their e-mail address and agree to receive coupons for products that interest them. The company sends coupons to their members until they opt out. Each time a member clicks on a coupon the company receives a payment from the coupon sponsor. The marginal revenue depends on the number of coupons that a member decides to click on and thus is not constant over time.

EXAMPLE 3.15:   Cell phone provider

Cellular phone customers often have contracts where they pay some (constant) monthly fee for a certain number of minutes that can be used within a certain territory. Customers who use more than this number of minutes or roam outside the territory, however, pay a penalty, so revenue is not constant over time.

When the period payment fluctuates over time we represent it as a random variable M. We use the lower-case m when it is an observed value or a constant. We can conveniently substitute an average into equation 3.12 or 3.11 whenever M and T are statistically *independent*; otherwise, the problem is more complicated, and we have to use the methods discussed in the next chapter.

Before proving this, we review what it means to be independent and when this condition is or is not satisfied. Estimating CLV when M is not constant requires averaging over two sources of randomness, the time until cancelation T and the payment amount M. Loosely speaking, M and T are independent if one does not affect the other, that is, if information about the defection time reveals nothing about the likely payment amounts. For example, if customers must pay a penalty fee for canceling before a contract has ended, cancelation time and payment amount are dependent because a customer who does not cancel generates the normal cash flow, whereas one who does generates the normal cash flow plus the penalty. Information about the cancelation time thus changes the payment amount. This will be discussed further in Example 4.2.

We now discuss the rationale for needing independence. Suppose that the discount rate is 0 and T and M are independent. Recall from probability theory that the covariance between T and M is $\mathrm{Cov}(T, M) = E(TM) - E(T)E(M)$, so that under independence the covariance is 0, $E(TM) = E(T)E(M)$, and

$$E(\mathrm{CLV}) = E((T - 1)M) = E(TM - M) = E(T)E(M) - E(M).$$

One can estimate the average monthly payment $E(M)$ and *separately* estimate the mean time of attrition $E(T)$. The same is true when the discount factor is positive, because discounting amounts to computing a function of random variable T, and the expectation of product of functions of random variables equals the product of the expectations of the functions.

EXAMPLE 3.16:   Educational service provider: different costs

Suppose that the profit for a customer who returns the materials for grading is $20 per month, the profit is $28 per month for a customer who does *not* return the materials, and that 60% of customers return. Payments occur at the beginning of a period. Find CLV using a monthly discount rate of 1% and a retention rate of 95.8%.

Solution   The profit is $20 for 60% of the customers and $28 for the remaining 40%, so the average profit per customer is

$$E(M) = \$20(.6) + \$28(.4) = \$23.20.$$

We can substitute this into equation 3.11:

$$E(\mathrm{CLV}) = \frac{\$23.20(1 + .01)}{1 + .01 - .958} \approx \$451.$$

3.5 Chapter summary

The retention model can be used by organizations that acquire customers who generate some cash flow m (the payment), each period until the customer cancels the service in period T (the cancelation time). After canceling, customers do not return. Each period the organization retains some percentage r, called the *retention rate*, of its remaining customers. The retention rate is assumed to be constant over time and customers.

The cancelation time T is a random variable with a *geometric distribution*. The probability that a customer is retained for $t-1$ periods and then cancels at time t is $P(T=t) = r^{t-1}(1-r)$. The *survival function*, which is the probability that a customer survives at least until the beginning of period t, is $P(T \geq t) = r^{t-1}$. The expected time of cancelation is $E(T) = 1/(1-r)$. The α quantile is given by $[P_\alpha = 1 + \log(1-\alpha)/\log r]$, where $[\cdot]$ is the greatest integer function.

CLV is the expected sum of discounted future cash flows from a customer. Suppose the discount rate is d. When customers agree to make n payments in the future and are not allowed to cancel (that is, $r = 100\%$), CLV is computed using the formulas for *annuities*, PV_n, given in the table below. *Ordinary annuities* assume that payments are come at the end of a period while *immediate annuities* assume payments come at the beginning of a period. When customers are allowed to cancel ($r < 100\%$), the formulas for expected CLV are also provided below.

Quantity	Cash Flow Comes At	
	End of Period	Beginning of Period
PV_n	$\sum_{t=1}^{n} \frac{m}{(1+d)^t} = m\frac{1-(1+d)^{-n}}{d}$	$\sum_{t=0}^{n-1} \frac{m}{(1+d)^t} = m\frac{(1+d)[1-(1+d)^{-n}]}{d}$
$E(\text{CLV})$	$\frac{mr}{1+d-r}$	$\frac{m(1+d)}{1+d-r}$

Estimating r in practice is complicated by the fact not all customers have canceled. Those who have not canceled are said to be *censored*. To estimate retention rate r from a group of customers, suppose that n_1 have canceled with cancelation times $t_1, \ldots, t_{n_1}$, and n_0 have not yet canceled with censoring times $c_1, \ldots, c_{n_0}$. Then the retention rate can be estimated by

$$\hat{r} = 1 - \frac{n_1}{\sum d_t + \sum c_t}.$$

In deciding which revenues and costs to include the per-period cash flows, all relevant costs of servicing the customer should be included and fixed costs should be excluded as appropriate. When the period payment M fluctuates, the average of M can be substituted into the above formulas provided that M is independent of T.

Notes

[1]Some readers may recall that there is a special formula for evaluating the expected value of a *linear transformation*, $E(aX + b) = aE(X) + b$. For this problem, $E(6X - 2) = 6 \times 1.3 - 5 = 2.8$, which matches the answer given in the table above. We will, however, be evaluating the expected value of *nonlinear* functions of a random variable where this formula will not work. For this reason, we illustrate how to evaluate equation 3.6 directly from the definition in this example.

[2]This definition of a quantile is for continuous distributions and serves our purpose. Discrete random variables are more complicated. See Hyndman and Fan (1996) for discussion.

The General Retention Model

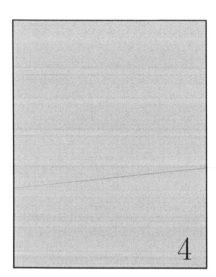

4

Contents

The simple retention model (SRM) discussed in the previous chapter assumes that the retention rate is constant over time, as illustrated in the left side of Figure 4.1. But retention rates are not always constant. For example, companies in many different industries offer products or services at a lower rate for the first few periods. Credit cards commonly offer a low rate of interest for balance transfers during the first few months and then increase the rate. Cable, Internet service, and telephone companies commonly offer one monthly fee for the first few months and then increase it. In such cases, the retention rate often begins high and then drops after the rate increase, as shown in the right side of Figure 4.1. The last section shows how to account for unobserved heterogeneity in the retention rates with the beta-geometric model.

The first section of this chapter develops the General Retention Model (GRM), which extends the SRM by allowing retention rates and cash flows to vary over time, and cash flows to depend on the time of cancelation. It also shows how to find the expected value of CLV in such situations. The next three sections show how to estimate retention rates with a class of statistical models commonly called *survival analysis*. section 4.5 discusses an important strategy for increasing CLV, which is detecting *trigger events*.

4.1 The general retention model

An organization acquires customers who generate cash flows at times $t = 0, 1, 2, \ldots$, until canceling during period T, which is is a random variable. Customers might cancel during any period, perhaps with a penalty, and never return. If customers do return after

Figure 4.1 Example retention rates over time

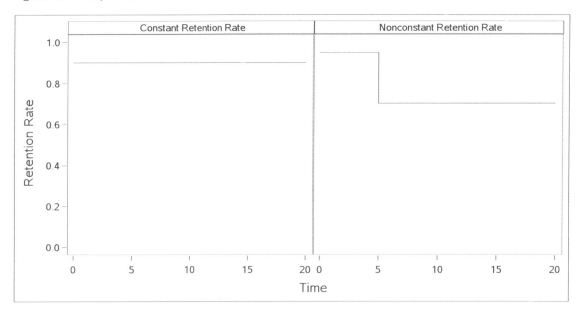

canceling, the migration model in Chapter 5 is more suitable. Let r_t be the probability of retaining a customer at time t. The SRM assumed $r_t = r$ for all t while the GRM relaxes this assumption. Assume further that the event a customer cancels at time t is independent of canceling at time $t' \neq t$.

The *survival function*[1] gives the chance that the customer cancels at time t or later, or equivalently, that the customer is retained for the first $t - 1$ periods:

$$S(t) = P(T \geq t) = \prod_{i=1}^{t-1} r_i. \tag{4.1}$$

This formula generalizes the survival function for the SRM, which was $S(t) = r^{t-1}$. To understand the rationale for this formula, let R_t be the event that the customer is retained in period t. Using independence,

$$P(R_1 \cap R_2) = P(R_1) \times P(R_2) = r_1 r_2.$$

By extending this reasoning for the first $t - 1$ periods, we get the survival function above.

The *probability mass function* (PMF) gives the probability that a customer is retained during the first $t - 1$ periods and cancels during period t:

$$f(t) = P(T = t) = S(t)(1 - r_t) = S(t) - S(t + 1). \tag{4.2}$$

Henceforth, we refer to $f(t)$ as a *probability density function* (PDF). (Note that PMF is usually used for discrete random variables and PDF for continuous variables. While we consider only discrete time periods in this book, it is far more common in survival analysis contexts to study continuous variables. Survival software, including SAS, uses the continuous vocabulary. For example, the keyword that requests a PDF/PMF plot in PROC LIFETEST is PLOT=PDF, and PMF is not even recognized. For this reason, we use PDF even though mathematicians would find this usage to be sloppy.)

Let $\pi_t = 1 - r_t$ be the *hazard rate*, which is the conditional probability of canceling at time t given that the customer has not already canceled:

$$\pi_t = P(T = t | T \geq t) = \frac{P(T = t)}{S(t)} = 1 - r_t. \tag{4.3}$$

Hazard rates are not always probabilities, but in the case of this discrete GRM, they are. It is important to note the relationships between the retention rates, PDF, and survival function. In particular, if we know any one of the three, then we can compute the other two.

Let m_t be the discounted cash flow at time t. The diagram below illustrates our notation. Time is indicated below the tick marks. A customer is acquired at time 0, at which time cash flow m_0 occurs. Period 1 refers to the time between time 0 and 1, so if a customer cancels in Period 1 the company receives only 1 payment, m_0.

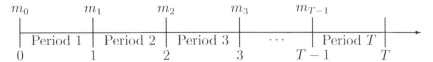

For a customer who cancels at in time period $T = t$ lifetime value is

$$\mathrm{CLV}(t) = \sum_{i=0}^{t-1} m_i,$$

assuming that no cash flow occurs during the period of cancelation t.

We would like to find the expected value of $\mathrm{CLV}(T)$, which could be computed directly from the definition given in equation 3.6:

$$E[\mathrm{CLV}(T)] = \sum_{t=1}^{\infty} f(t)\mathrm{CLV}(t) = \sum_{t=1}^{\infty} f(t) \sum_{i=0}^{t-1} m_i.$$

Alternatively, it is sometimes easier to compute the expected value from the survival function. We can rearrange the terms in the expression above by writing the sum over t horizontally and the sum over i vertically (DeGroot, 1975, p. 155):

$$
\begin{aligned}
E[\mathrm{CLV}(T)] = & f(1)m_0 + f(2)m_0 + f(3)m_0 + f(4)m_0 + \dots \\
& + f(2)m_1 + f(3)m_1 + f(4)m_1 + \dots \\
& + f(3)m_2 + f(4)m_2 + \dots \\
& + f(4)m_3 + \dots \\
& + \ddots
\end{aligned}
$$

The first row is recognized as $m_0 P(T \geq 1) = m_0 S(1)$, the second row $m_0 P(T \geq 2) = m_1 S(2), \dots$. Thus, $E[\mathrm{CLV}(T)]$ can be evaluated either directly from the definition with the PDF or with the survival function:

$$E[\mathrm{CLV}(T)] = \sum_{t=1}^{\infty} m_{t-1} S(t). \tag{4.4}$$

The survival function approach was used in Example 3.3 and is often easier, but there are also situations where it is easier to compute $E(\mathrm{CLV})$ directly from the definition.

As a corollary, we can find the mean time of cancelation by setting $m_t \equiv 1$ so that

$$E(T) = \sum_{t=1}^{\infty} S(t). \tag{4.5}$$

EXAMPLE 4.1:   Hypothetical cell phone

A hypothetical cell phone provider offers only six-month contracts, where customers pay $50 at the beginning of each month. Suppose that 80% are retained in the first month, 90% in the second month, and 95% thereafter except at the times of contract renewal (months 6, 12, 18, ...), when the retention rate is 50%. Find the expected lifetime revenue, assuming a monthly discount rate of 1%. Graph the PDF, survival, and hazard functions.

Solution   This problem is most easily solved using a spreadsheet as shown in the table below.

Row	A	B	C	D	E	F	G
1	t	$m_t =$ $50/1.01^t$	r_t	$S(t) = P(T \geq t)$ $= S(t-1)r_{t-1}$	$f(t) =$ $S(t) - S(t+1)$	m_{t-1} $\times S(t)$	$f(t)$ $\times PV_t$
2	0	50					
3	1	$50/1.01$	.8	1	$1 - .8 = .2$	50.00	10.00
4	2	$50/1.01^2$	.9	$.8S(1) = .8$	$.8 - .72 = .08$	39.60	7.96
5	3	$50/1.01^3$	.95	$.9S(2) = .72$	$.72 - .684 = .036$	35.29	5.35
6	4	48.05	.95	$.95S(3) = .684$	.0342	33.19	6.74
7	5	47.57	.95	$.95S(4) = .6498$	.0325	31.22	7.96
8	6	47.10	.5	$.95S(5) = .6173$	.3087	29.37	90.33
9	7	46.64	.95	$.5S(6) = .3087$	.0154	14.54	5.24
10	8	46.17	.95	$.95S(7) = .2932$	.0147	13.67	5.67
	⋮	⋮	⋮	⋮	⋮		
92	90	20.42	.5	.0000	.0000	0.00	0.00
	⋮	⋮	⋮	⋮	⋮	⋮	
Sum					1	337.09	337.09

Column A enumerates all possible cancelation times, column B computes the discounted cash flow that will occur at a given time if the customer is still active. Column C gives the retention probabilities r_t. Column D computes the survival function using equation 4.1 and E computes the PDF using equation 4.2. To check our work, notice how the values of the PDF sum to 1 in the last row. $E(\text{CLV})$ is computed two different ways in columns F and G. Column F implements the result in equation 4.4 by multiplying the proportion surviving $S(t)$ and the cash flows m_t. The sum of this column gives the expected value of CLV, $337.09.

Column G illustrates the alternative method of evaluating the expected value of CLV, using the definition in equation 3.6. The probability of canceling at time t is multiplied by the total value of a customer who cancels at time t in equation 3.2. In Excel, this can be computed by entering the following formula in cell G3 and copying it down: $=-$E3*PV(.01, A3, 50,, 1). The sum of column G equals the sum of column F, confirming the result in equation 4.4.

Graphs of the hazard, survival, and probability density functions are shown in Figure 4.2. The large spikes in the hazard plot all have a height of .5, while the corresponding spikes in the PDF diminish in magnitude over time because $f(t) = S(t)(1 - r_t)$ and $S(t)$ decreases over time. The spikes appear as large drops in the survival plot.

We now illustrate how the GRM can be used when cash flows depend on the cancelation time.

EXAMPLE 4.2:   Hypothetical cell phone with cancelation fee

Suppose that customers may cancel the cell phone service without any penalty in months $6, 12, 18, \ldots$, but must pay a cancelation fee of $100 if they want to cancel during other

Figure 4.2 PDF, survival, and hazard functions for cell phone example

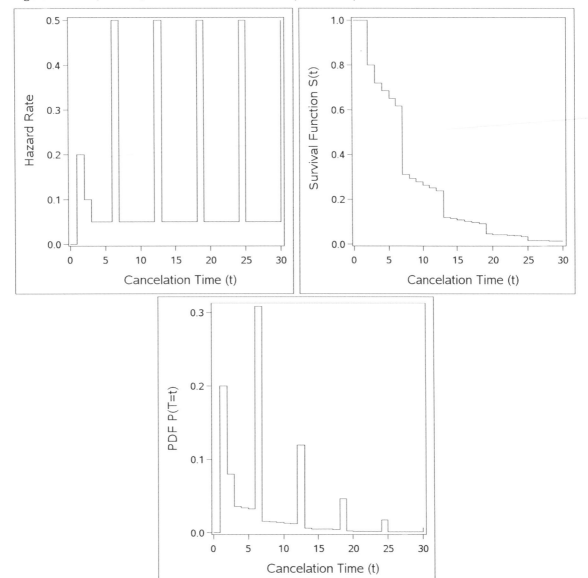

months. Notice that the payments are now dependent on the cancelation time, so even if retention rates were constant the SRM could not be used. For example, a customer who does not cancel at time 5 generates a cash flow of $50, whereas a customer who cancels at time 5 generates a cash flow of $50+$100. What is the expected lifetime revenue of each?

Solution   In this example, it is easier to use the PDF and definition of expected value than the survival function and equation 4.4. The lifetime revenue of a customer who cancels at time t is

$$\text{LTR}_t = \begin{cases} PV_t & \text{for } t = 6, 12, 18, \ldots \\ PV_t + 100/1.01^t & \text{otherwise} \end{cases}$$

Expected LTR can be computed by summing the products $f(t)\text{LTR}_t$. This can be done in Excel by adding a column H to the table above by entering this formula into cell H3 and copying it down in the spreadsheet:
=E3*(−PV(.01,A3,50,,1)+IF(MOD(A3,6)=0,0,100/1.01^A3))

The sum of column H gives the answer: $384.67.

EXAMPLE 4.3:   The simple retention model

Find the expected value of CLV with immediate payments and a constant retention rate.

Solution   Let $m_t = m/(1 + d)^t$ and $r_t = r$. Then,

$$E[\text{CLV}(T)] = \sum_{t=1}^{\infty} m_{t-1} S(t) = \sum_{t=1}^{\infty} m \left(\frac{r}{1+d} \right)^{t-1} = m \sum_{t=0}^{\infty} \left(\frac{r}{1+d} \right)^{t}$$

$$= \frac{m}{1 - r/(1+d)} = \frac{m(1+d)}{1+d-r}.$$

4.2 Introduction to survival analysis

The GRM shows us how to find expected CLV when retention rates vary over time periods, but requires knowing the retention rates or survival function. We estimate them using a class of statistical methods called *survival analysis*.

Survival analysis is a set of methods for understanding the following questions about the time when some *event* such as cancelation occurs:

1. What is the *distribution of the event times*? The geometric distribution is one example, but others are possible. By knowing the distribution, we can answer questions such as: are there times when the event is more or less likely to happen (for example, certain times of the year)? What is the expected time until the event (mean)? At what point in time will the event have occurred for 99% of the customers?

2. How do *static* characteristics of customers such as the acquisition source, demographics, and the length of the initial contract affect the distribution of the event? For example, are customers acquired from one channel (for example, e-mail) systematically more likely to cancel than those from another (such as direct mail)? Are young people more likely to cancel than old? Are those who initially sign two-year contracts less likely to churn than those who sign one-year contracts? These questions will be answered by allowing static covariates to increase or decrease the hazard of events.

3. How do things that happen during the course of a relationship—*time-dependent covariates*—affect the hazard of T? For example, if a customer calls to complain about something, does the hazard of the event change? Suppose that an ISP has technical problems and delivers service that is slower than promised in the contract to certain customers for two days. Are these customers more likely to cancel? We will answer such questions by allowing time-dependent covariates to increase or decrease the hazard of events temporarily.

The shape of the distribution is characterized by the hazard function (or equivalently the PDF or survival function). For example, the solid line in the left plot in Figure 4.3 shows a hazard function that increases over time. We shall often call this the *baseline hazard function*.

Static covariates are variables that do not change over time such as the length of the initial contract, gender, or acquisition source. Returning to the left side of Figure 4.3, suppose that customers are acquired from multiple acquisition sources, the static covariate. Sources vary in quality, which increases or decreases the hazard of canceling. For example, suppose that Source A has lower quality, so that customers acquired from this source are systematically more likely to cancel. The hazard function for those from Source A is the

Figure 4.3 Example retention rates over time

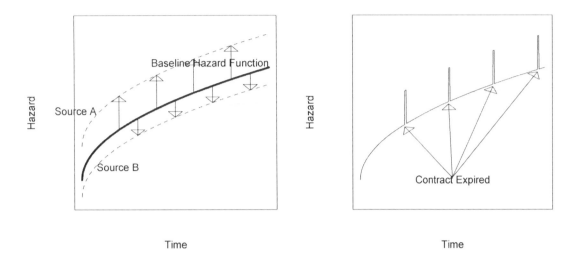

baseline hazard function shifted upward (dashed line above the baseline hazard). Likewise, Source B, which is of higher quality, has a hazard function that is the baseline function shifted downward.

Time-dependent covariates change over time. For example, the contract for a particular customer might be expiring in the current period, or the customer might complain during the current period. The right-side plot in Figure 4.3 shows how the baseline hazard could be affected by a time-dependent covariate indicating whether the contract has expired.

Most survival analysis methods can accommodate *censoring*, where data for part of a customer's life is unavailable. *Right censoring* is where information about a customer's life is unavailable after some point in time and *left censoring* is where information is unavailable before some point. In database marketing, right censoring arises for all customers who have not yet canceled the relationship. This type of censoring was introduced in section 3.3. Left censoring often occurs when data about the early stages of a customer's life are no longer available. For example, perhaps a company adopts a new data warehouse on some date, but is unable to import data on customers from former legacy systems.

There are many excellent books on survival analysis [for example, see Allison (2010) or Therneau and Grambsch (2010)] and the intent of this chapter is not to duplicate these texts. We hope to introduce the survival models that are most useful in estimating retention rates and show how they can be used to estimate CLV.

4.3 Product-moment estimates of retention rates

Survival analysis methods enable us to estimate retention rates so that we can find CLV using the GRM. There are many different survival analysis methods. This section summarizes product-moment estimates (Kaplan-Meier and Life-table methods), which are especially good for exploring the shapes of the hazard and survival functions. These methods serve a similar role as histograms in that they describe the shape of a distribution without making strong assumptions about its shape. The difference is that histograms do not accommodate censoring. The previous section described three questions answered by survival analysis: (1) what is the shape of the distribution of event times, (2) how is the shape affected by static covariates, and (3) how is it shaped by time-dependent covariates? The methods discussed in this section will answer the first of these questions, but are not as well suited for answering the other two as other survival models.

Suppose customers can cancel at times $1, 2, 3, \ldots$. There are n_t customers at risk of canceling at time t and of these d_t cancel (default). The fraction of cases that cancel during period t is d_t/n_t and the retention rate is estimated by $1 - d_t/n_t$. Just as equation 4.1 computed the survival function by multiplying the period retention rates, the product-moment method multiplies the estimated retention rates:

$$\hat{S}(t) = \prod_{i=1}^{t} \left(1 - \frac{d_i}{n_i} \right) = \hat{S}(t-1) \left(1 - \frac{d_t}{n_t} \right). \tag{4.6}$$

Two product-moment estimates are commonly offered in commercial software, the *Kaplan-Meier* (KM) and the *life-table method*. The methods treat censored cases slightly differently, but in practice usually give similar conclusions. Let c_t be the number of customers censored at time t. The KM method considers all people who are censored at t as being at risk, so the number of people at risk in the next period is the number at risk in the previous period less those who defaulted or were censored:

$$n_{t+1} = n_t - d_t - c_t,$$

where n_0 is the number of customers at the beginning of the study, $c_0 = d_0 = 0$, and $t = 0, 1, 2, \ldots$. The life-table method, in contrast, assumes that only half of those censored at $t+1$ are at risk

$$n_{t+1} = n_t - d_t - \frac{c_t + c_{t+1}}{2}.$$

The difference between these methods is illustrated and discussed in the example below. Statistical software commonly gives plots of the hazard function for the life-table method but not for the KM method.

EXAMPLE 4.4:   Educational service provider—product moment estimates

Estimate the survival functions for the one-year educational service data given in Example 3.10 using both the KM and life-table methods.

Table 4.1 Kaplan-Meier and life-table estimates of the one-year educational service example

	A	B	C	D	E	F	G	H
					Kaplan-Meier		Life Table	
		Num. Cancel	Num. Censor	Num. at Risk	Retention Rate	Survival Function	Number at Risk	Survival Function
	t	d_t	c_t	n_t	$1 - d_t/n_t$	$S(t)$	n_t	$S(t)$
	1	0	3	671	1.0000	1.0000	669.5	1.0000
	2	4	0	668	0.9940	0.9940	668	0.9940
	3	16	2	664	0.9759	0.9701	663	0.9700
Solution	4	20	1	646	0.9690	0.9400	645.5	0.9400
	5	37	7	625	0.9408	0.8844	621.5	0.8840
	6	28	33	581	0.9518	0.8418	564.5	0.8402
	7	61	49	520	0.8827	0.7430	495.5	0.7367
	8	24	63	410	0.9415	0.6995	378.5	0.6900
	9	19	30	323	0.9412	0.6584	308	0.6474
	10	13	16	274	0.9526	0.6271	266	0.6158
	11	10	34	245	0.9592	0.6015	228	0.5888
	12	13	188	201	0.9353	0.5626	107	0.5173

See the spreadsheet above. Columns A–C were given by the problem. Column D gives the number of customers who could cancel during the time period under the KM model.

During period 1, all 671 are eligible to cancel, but none do so. The retention rate and survival functions therefore are both 100%. Three cases are censored during the first period and so there are $671 - 0 - 3 = 668$ customers who are at risk during period 2. Four customers cancel during period 2 and the retention rate for period 2 is estimated as $1 - 4/668 = 99.4\%$. No cases are censored during period 2, so there are $668 - 4 - 0 = 664$ remaining customers who can fail in period 3, of whom 16 cancel and two are censored. The period 3 retention rate is estimated as $1 - 16/664 = 97.59\%$. At the beginning of period 4 there are $664 - 16 - 2$ customers still in the study. Column F estimates the survival function using equation 4.6.

The life-table method assumes that cancelation and censoring can occur at any time, instead of only at discrete time points $1, 2, \ldots$. Assuming that censoring times are uniformly distributed throughout the interval, only half of the cases censored during an interval were eligible to cancel. During time period 1, $671 - 0 - 3/2 = 669.5$ cases could fail. In period 2, the remaining $3/2$ cases that were censored in period 1 are out of the study and no longer eligible to cancel, so $n_2 = 669.5 - 0 - 3/2 = 668$. The estimated survival function is computed in the same way as for KM, using the life-table numbers of at-risk customers.

Graphs of the functions are shown in Figure 4.4. The SAS code used to create these graphs is discussed in Example 4.9, after stratification has been introduced. In the upper left the estimated hazard rates are plotted against time. The life-table estimates show that the hazard rate is not constant. Hazard rates are very low after acquisition, but steadily increase over the first few months. There is a large spike during month 7, which is probably due to some of the customers being on six-month contracts. Contract length will be explored further in subsequent examples.

The horizontal red line displayed with plus signs $(+)$ shows the SRM estimate $(1 - \hat{r} = 1 - .958 = .0442$ from Example 3.10) for comparison. The SRM overestimates the hazard rate before month 7 and underestimates it afterward. The upper right plot shows the hazard probabilities. The bottom two plots show the survival function and the lower plot the PDF.

EXAMPLE 4.5:   Educational service provider—estimating retention rates in SAS

Estimate the survival and hazard functions using SAS.

Solution   The `service1yr` data set was created in Program 3.1. The data set has three variables: `bigT` is the time of canceling or censoring, `cancel` is a dummy variable indicating whether the customer canceled (1) or was censored (0) during the current period, and `count` will be used to weight the cases. The following program produces the KM and life-table estimates:

Program 4.1 KM and life-table estimates

```
PROC LIFETEST DATA=service1yr PLOTS=S;
  TIME bigT*cancel(0);
  FREQ count;
RUN;

PROC LIFETEST DATA=service1yr METHOD=LIFE INTERVALS=1 to 12 by 1 PLOTS=(S, H, P);
  TIME bigT*cancel(0);
  FREQ count;
RUN;
```

The `cancel(0)` statement tells SAS that censored cases are indicated by the value 0. The reader should try this code out in SAS and see how the output matches Table 4.1. Code and data sets are available for download at the author's web site.[2] In particular column F gives the Survival column in the LIFETEST output. By default, LIFETEST produces KM estimates, but the METHOD=LIFE requires life-table estimates instead. The PLOTS=S option produces a survival plot. The life-table method will also generate hazard

Figure 4.4 Life-table estimates of the PDF, survival, and hazard functions for the one-year educational service example

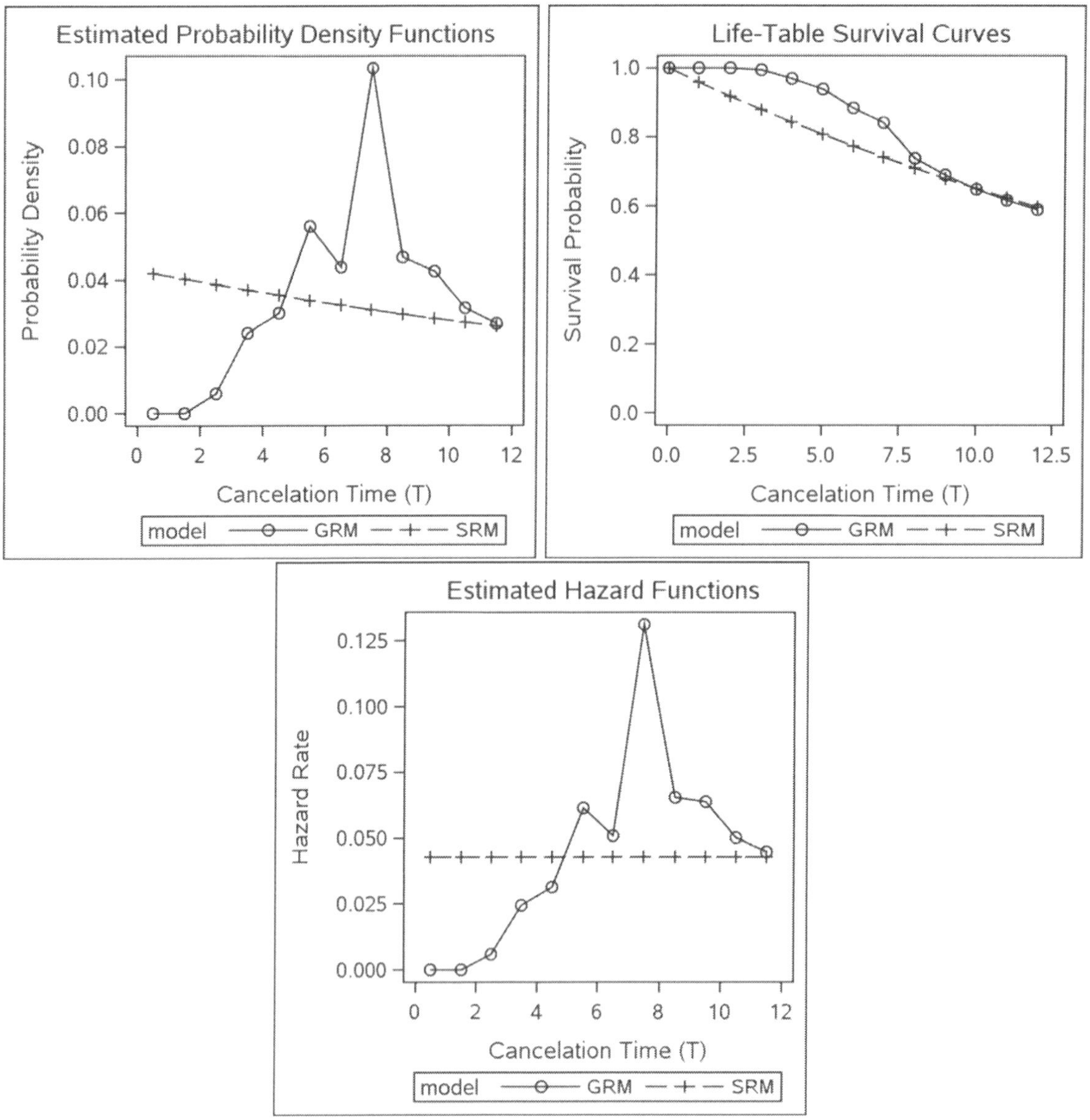

(H) and PDF (P) plots. The `LIFE` method also accepts an `INTERVALS` statement defining the bins; here the life table will range from period 1 through 12 with a bin width of 1 period. The `FREQ` statement specifies that the `count` variable indicates the number of customers represented by each row. Note that no `FREQ` statement is necessary when each row represents a single customer.

4.3.1   Estimating long-term value from product-moment estimates

We now show how to estimate *long-term value* from life-table estimates. This estimates customer value over an extended future window rather than CLV, which would estimate future value in perpetuity. There are ways to extend the approach to give CLV estimates, as outlined in Exercises 4.11–4.14.

The GRM model in equation 4.4 shows how the expected value of CLV is related to the survival function, which was assumed to be known. The product-moment estimates from this section provide estimates of the survival function. We will show how to substitute the product-moment estimates into the GRM formula with an example.

EXAMPLE 4.6:   Educational service provider—five years

The data set `service5yr.sas7bdat` gives a larger sample from the service organization over a five-year period. Estimate the survival, hazard, and probability distribution functions. Estimate five-year long-term value assuming a monthly discount rate of 1%. Recall that the company makes $m = \$23.20$ profit per customer at the beginning of each period. Compare the estimate of long-term value with those from the SRM.

Solution   The PDF, hazard, and survival functions are plotted in Figure 4.5. (These were produced with `METHOD=LIFE`, `INTERVALS` and `PLOTS` options as shown by the code in the lower left corner. See Example 4.9 to see how the SRM estimates are superimposed.)

Figure 4.5 Life-table estimate of PDF, hazard, and survival functions for five-year educational service example

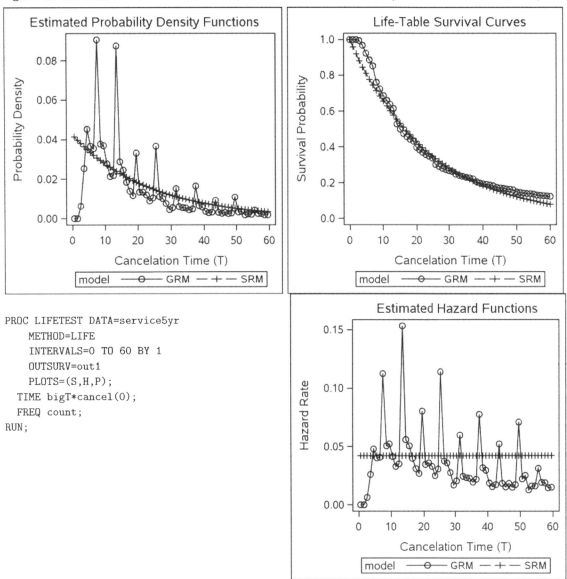

```
PROC LIFETEST DATA=service5yr
    METHOD=LIFE
    INTERVALS=0 TO 60 BY 1
    OUTSURV=out1
    PLOTS=(S,H,P);
  TIME bigT*cancel(0);
  FREQ count;
RUN;
```

The hazard function shows a periodic pattern with large spikes at months 13, 25, 37 and 49, and smaller spikes at months 7, 19, 31, 43 and 55. The cause of this pattern is that people sign up for one-, six-, or twelve-month contracts. It goes without saying that the company should investigate retention programs at these times of high risk. The horizontal dashed line shows the estimate from the SRM, which assumes a constant hazard rate and does not capture the periodic pattern. The graph of the PDF also shows how poorly the SRM fits.

It appears that the hazard of defecting decreases over time. This is likely due to the *sorting effect* described by Fader and Hardie (2007). Suppose an organization acquires customers who have different retention rates. For example, some "loyalists" have high retention rates while other "non-loyalists" have a smaller one. Over time, those with a lower retention rate will be more likely to churn, and the average retention rate across all remaining customers will increase over time as the customer base becomes over-represented by loyalists. See Exercise 3.11 for a simple illustration. Such *unobserved heterogeneity* motivates the need for the beta-geometric distribution discussed in section 4.6.

While both the hazard function and PDF show a poor SRM fit, the survival functions from the life table and SRM are similar. The survival function will be used to estimate CLV. Therefore, the two models may well give similar estimates of CLV despite the poor fit.

We now show how to compute long-term value estimates in SAS using the KM method. The code is nearly identical to that used in Program 4.1, but we add the `OUTSURV=` option to create a data set with the survival probabilities. The `survSRM` column gives the survival function for the SRM, which can be easily compared with that from the GRM in the `survival` column.

```
PROC LIFETEST DATA=service5yr OUTSURV=out1;
  TIME bigT*cancel(0);
  FREQ count;
RUN;

DATA out1;
  SET out1;
  BY bigT;
  IF bigT>0 AND FIRST.bigT;
  rhat = 1-44367/1073935;
  clv = survival*23.20/(1.01**(bigT-1));
  survSRM = (rhat)**(bigT-1);
  clvSRM = 23.20*(rhat/1.01)**(bigT-1);
RUN;

PROC PRINT DATA=out1 NOOBS;
  VAR bigT survival survSRM clv clvSRM;
  SUM clv clvSRM;
  FORMAT clv clvSRM DOLLAR8.2;
RUN;
```

bigT	survival	survSRM	clv	clvSRM
1	1.00000	1.00000	$23.20	$23.20
2	0.99359	0.95869	$22.82	$22.02
3	0.96815	0.91908	$22.02	$20.90
4	0.92296	0.88111	$20.78	$19.84
5	0.88644	0.84471	$19.76	$18.83
6	0.85110	0.80981	$18.79	$17.88
7	0.76073	0.77636	$16.63	$16.97
⋮	⋮	⋮	⋮	⋮
54	0.14022	0.10688	$1.92	$1.46
55	0.13597	0.10246	$1.84	$1.39
56	0.13356	0.09823	$1.79	$1.32
57	0.13111	0.09417	$1.74	$1.25
58	0.12929	0.09028	$1.70	$1.19
59	0.12754	0.08655	$1.66	$1.13
60	0.12563	0.08297	$1.62	$1.07
			$424.11	$436.66

The two long-term value estimates are given at the bottom of the table. They are computed in the `DATA` step and `PROC PRINT` using equation 4.4:

$$E(\text{CLV}) = \sum_{t=1}^{60} S(t)\frac{23.20}{1.01^{t-1}} = \$424.11.$$

The SRM retention rate can be estimated using equation 3.14:

$$\hat{r} = 1 - 44367/1073935 = .9587.$$

The expected long-term value (using Equations 3.3 and 3.8) is computed as follows, and shows that despite the poor fit of the SRM, the expected CLV estimates are relatively equal.[3]

$$E(\text{CLV}) = \sum_{t=1}^{60} \hat{r}^{t-1} \frac{23.20}{1.01^{t-1}} = 23.20 \frac{1 - (.9587/1.01)^{60}}{1 - (.9587/1.01)} = \$436.66.$$

Because the two numbers are so close to each other, if one is seeking a ballpark estimate of CLV, then the extra effort required to use the GRM might not be justified. This should not be construed as questioning the value of survival analysis. The remainder of the chapter will give several additional important applications of survival analysis in customer management.

4.3.2   Comparing subgroups with stratification

Sometimes we will want to compare survival functions across subgroups defined by some discrete, static characteristic. For example, does the survival function—and hence CLV—differ between customers in different age groups? Do men and women have different survival functions? Are the survival functions different for customers acquired from source A than from source B?

The `STRATA` statement in `PROC LIFETEST` enables the user to specify a variable defining subgroups. It also provides a significance test of the null hypothesis that the survival functions are the same.[4] We will illustrate stratification with the service provider example, breaking out the survival function by starting contract length. This is only one static customer characteristic, and in practice, you might have many such variables, including age, gender, acquisition source, and so on. You will want to inspect each stratification variable separately when exploring the data, and perhaps build a discrete-time or proportional hazard model that incorporates multiple covariates. The cell phone case at the end of the chapter will give you practice.

EXAMPLE 4.7:   Educational service provider—stratifying on contract length
The `startlen` variable gives the length in months of the starting contract. Compare the survival, hazard, and probability density functions across starting contract lengths for the service provider. Also compare the expected long-term value estimates.

Solution   The following SAS code generates the survival functions and CLV estimates, and Figures 4.6 and 4.7 show the plots.

Program 4.2 KM estimates with stratification and computing long-term value

```
PROC LIFETEST DATA=service5yr OUTSURV=out2;     PROC PRINT DATA=out2 NOOBS;
  STRATA startlen;                                BY startlen;
  TIME bigT*cancel(0);                            VAR bigT survival clv;
  FREQ count;                                     SUM clv;
RUN;                                              FORMAT clv DOLLAR8.2;
                                                RUN;
DATA out2;
  SET out2;
  BY startlen bigT;
  IF bigT>0 AND FIRST.bigT;
  clv = survival*23.20/(1.01**(bigT-1));
RUN;
```

- One-month contracts (solid line, left side of Figure 4.7). The probability of canceling increases over the first few months before reaching a maximum value of 7.4% during month 4, and slowly decreases thereafter. The decrease could be due to the sorting effect.

Figure 4.6 Life-table estimate of hazard and survival functions for five-year educational service example, stratified by starting contract length

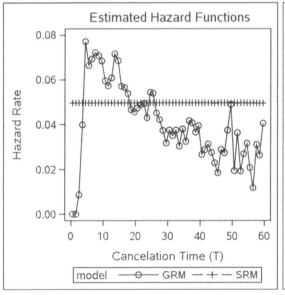

- Six-month contracts (short dashed line). There are spikes in the retention rate at months 7, 13, 19, ..., 55.
- Twelve-month contracts (long dashed line, right side of Figure 4.7). Those on twelve-month contracts have large spikes at months 13, 25, 37, and 49; smaller spikes begin to emerge six months after the large spikes, presumably because some customers switch to shorter contracts over time.

Figure 4.7 Separate hazard plots for one-month (left) and twelve-month (right) contracts for the five-year educational service example

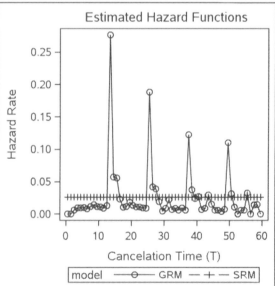

Long-term value estimates are compared in Table 4.2. Those who sign up for twelve-month contracts initially are worth substantially more than those who sign up for shorter initial contracts. The table also gives five-year SRM estimates for the three groups, and again, there is little difference between them. The computations are left as an exercise (4.9).

Table 4.2 Comparing SRM and the five-year GRM CLV estimates

Stratum	SRM $\hat{r}$	SRM CLV	GRM CLV
All	$1 - 44,367/1,073,935 = 95.87\%$	\$436.66	\$424.11
One-month	$1 - 26,136/539,288 = 95.15\%$	389.60	376.43
Six-month	$1 - 14,130/376,527 = 96.25\%$	442.48	430.79
Twelve-month	$1 - 4101/158,120 = 97.41\%$	554.67	541.70

EXAMPLE 4.8: Educational service provider—incentives to enroll with longer contracts

Table 4.2 showed that the difference in CLV between those who initially enroll with twelve-month versus one-month contracts is $541.70 - \$376.43 = \$165.27$. True or false: it would be profitable for the company to spend up to \$165.27 to provide incentives to those considering one-month initial contracts to enroll with twelve-month contracts instead?

Solution   New customers self-select an initial contract length and those who enrolled with one-month contracts are likely systematically different from those who enrolled on twelve-month contracts. For example, those who select the twelve-month contract could be more certain that the service will meet their needs, while those who enroll on a month-by-month basis might want to try the service before making a longer commitment. Extending the initial contract length of this latter group will not change this extraneous factor and those converted to the longer initial contract might have CLV that is less than \$541.70. We would not be able to say that the above statement is true unless people had been randomly assigned to initial contract lengths so that the groups would have been comparable at the start.

EXAMPLE 4.9: Comparing SRM and life-table estimates

Use the one-year data educational service data to compare the SRM estimates from Example 3.2 with the life-table estimates from Example 4.5. Plot both solutions on the same survival, hazard, and PDF plots.

Program 4.3 Comparing SRM and life-table estimates

Solution

```
PROC FORMAT;                              DATA both;
  VALUE model                               SET srm service1yr;
    1 = "SRM"                               IF model=. THEN model=2;
    2 = "GRM";                              FORMAT model model.;
RUN;                                      RUN;

DATA srm;                                 PROC LIFETEST DATA=both
  model=1;                                    METHOD=LIFE
  h_t=245/5828;                               INTERVALS=0 to 12 by 1
  S_t=100000;                                 OUTSURV=out1
  cancel=1;                                   PLOTS=(S,H,P);
  DO bigT = .5 to 12.5 BY 1;                TIME bigT*cancel(0);
    count=S_t * h_t;                        FREQ count;
    OUTPUT;                                 STRATA model;
    S_t=S_t - count;                      RUN;
  END;
  count=S_t; cancel=0; OUTPUT;
RUN;
```

Program 4.3 gives the solution. We can use **PROC LIFETEST** with stratification to accomplish this goal. The idea is to create data set **srm** with a constant percentage, $245/5825 = 4.2\%$ based on the results from Example 3.2, of customers canceling each month. This data set also has stratification variable `model` equal to 1 for all cases, indicating the SRM, which is labeled using `PROC FORMAT`. After creating the `srm` data set, the `both` data set concatenates `srm` with the original `service1yr` data sets. Recall that there is no `model` variable in `service1yr`, so the IF statement that assigns `model=2` whenever `model` is missing is assigning the value 2 to set up the life-table GRM estimates. The call to `PROC LIFETEST` is the same as in Example 4.5 except that we are now stratifying by `model`.

4.4   The discrete-time survival model

The product-moment estimates discussed in the previous section estimate the shape of the distribution, but they are not well suited for understanding the effects of covariates. The discrete-time model will estimate the shape of the hazard function and the effects of covariates. Although the notation in this section might seem intimidating, the method is easy to use and understand by anyone who is comfortable with logistic regression and `DATA` step programming with `DO` loops. We will see that the estimates of a constant retention rate in equation 3.14 and the KM estimate in section 4.3 are special cases of this approach. It will also be easy to incorporate both static and time-dependent covariates.

Assume discrete, equal-sized time intervals $t = 1, 2, \ldots$ and let $\pi_{it} = P(T = t | T > t - 1)$ be the probability that customer i cancels during period t, given the customer has survived $t - 1$ periods. We use logistic regression to model π_{it} as a function of covariates:

$$\log\left(\frac{\pi_{it}}{1 - \pi_{it}}\right) = \alpha_t + x_{i1t}\beta_1 + \cdots + x_{ipt}\beta_p, \tag{4.7}$$

where x_{ijt} is the value of covariate j at time t for customer i. We explore this equation and how it can be used to model CLV in the subsections that follow.

4.4.1   Discrete-time model without covariates

We begin by showing how the SRM can be estimated with the discrete-time model. Consider the following logistic model having only an intercept, which is a special case of equation 4.7:

$$\log\left(\frac{\pi_{it}}{1 - \pi_{it}}\right) = \alpha.$$

This model assumes that the hazard π_{it} is constant for all customers and across all time periods.

To implement this model in SAS, we will create one observation for each period that a customer could cancel. Thus, different customers could have a different number of observations. Define the following dependent variable:

$$y_{it} = \begin{cases} 1 & \text{customer } i \text{ cancels in period } t \\ 0 & \text{otherwise} \end{cases}$$

A customer who cancels in period 3 would have 3 observations ($y_{i1} = 0$, $y_{i2} = 0$, $y_{i3} = 1$). A customer who never cancels has $y_{it} = 0$ for all t during the study period. We will demonstrate how to set up the data in SAS to estimate this model in the following example.

EXAMPLE 4.10:   Educational service provider—SRM with logistic regression
Revisit Example 3.10 and use the discrete-time survival model to estimate the retention rate, assuming it is constant over all months and customers (SRM).

Solution   We must first transform Table 3.2 into the following data set with three variables so that logistic regression can be used. The variable `t` is the time period in the customer's life, and `cancelnow` is a dummy variable that equals 1 if the customer canceled during a certain period. The `count` variable will be used to weight the cases.

| Row | Resulting Data Set | | | |
Number	t	cancelnow	count	Remarks
1	1	0	3	$T = 1$, censored
2	1	0	4	$T = 2$, not censored
3	2	1	4	
4	1	0	16	
5	2	0	16	$T = 3$, censored
6	3	1	16	
7	1	0	2	
8	2	0	2	$T = 3$, not censored
9	3	0	2	
10	1	0	20	
11	2	0	20	
12	3	0	20	$T = 4$, censored
13	4	1	20	
14	1	0	1	
15	2	0	1	
16	3	0	1	$T = 4$, not censored
17	4	0	1	
⋮	⋮	⋮	⋮	

Row 1 is for the three customers who were censored at time 1. The value of `cancelnow` is 0 because they did not cancel. The next two rows are for the four customers who canceled during month 2. This group receives two observations. They were retained during period `t` = 1, so `cancelnow` = 0 for row 2. They canceled during `t` = 2, and therefore `cancelnow` = 1 in Row 3. Rows 4–6 are for the 16 customers who canceled during period 16. They were retained during the first two periods, and so `cancelnow` = 0 for their first two rows, and is then set equal to 1 in their third. SAS code to create this data set and estimate the model is as follows, assuming that Program 3.1 has already been run to read in the `service1yr` data set:

Program 4.4 Create data set for discrete-time survival model

```
DATA long;                          PROC LOGISTIC DATA=long DESCENDING;
  SET service1yr;                     MODEL cancelnow = ;
  DO t = 1 to bigT;                   FREQ count;
    cancelnow = cancel*(t=bigT);    RUN;
    OUTPUT;
  END;
RUN;
```

Analysis of Maximum Likelihood Estimates

Parameter	DF	Estimate	Standard Error	Wald Chi-Square	Pr>ChiSq
Intercept	1	−3.1262	0.0653	2293.7927	<.0001

The reader will note from the SAS log that `service1yr` has 22 observations while the output data set `long` has 153. The data sets used by the discrete-time model can have many rows, which is one reason for using weights to improve computational efficiency. SAS includes only an intercept because there are no variables listed on the right side of the equals sign in the `MODEL` statement. The `DESCENDING` option indicates that SAS should model the probability of the larger value of the dependent variable, which in this case is 1 = cancel. Again, the `FREQ` statement specifies that the `count` variable indicates the number of customers represented by each row.

The estimated regression equation is

$$\log \left(\frac{\pi_{it}}{1 - \pi_{it}} \right) = -3.1262.$$

Solving for π gives the estimated probability of canceling

$$\hat{\pi} = \frac{1}{1 + e^{-(-3.1262)}} = .0420$$

for all customers. Using equation 3.14, we found $\hat{r} = .958 = 1 - .0420$, which matches this exactly. The formula for estimating the retention rate of the SRM is just a special case of the discrete-time logistic regression model.

Next, we add parameters to allow for different retention rates for different values of t:

$$\log \left(\frac{\pi_{it}}{1 - \pi_{it}} \right) = \alpha_t.$$

The intercept at time t is α_t. Plotting α_t against t gives the baseline hazard function.[5] The estimates from this model should match those from the KM model, because both are maximum likelihood estimates. This model can be estimated using the same data as the previous model, but we must create dummy variables for individual time periods and use the dummies as predictor variables. This is illustrated below.

EXAMPLE 4.11:   Educational service provider—estimating different retention rates with logistic regression

Revisit Example 4.4 and use the discrete-time survival model to estimate retention rates, which accommodates rates that vary over months.

Solution   We now estimate a logistic regression predicting `cancelnow` from `t` as a categorical variable so that each month can have a different retention rate. SAS estimates a model equivalent to the one above, but with a different parameterization:

$$\log \left(\frac{\pi_{it}}{1 - \pi_{it}} \right) = \alpha + \alpha_t,$$

where α is the intercept for the baseline month (12) and $\alpha_t (t = 1, \ldots 11)$ measures how the intercept for month t differs from the baseline month 12. For example, the intercept for month 1 is $\alpha + \alpha_1$. If $\alpha_1 = 0$ then months 1 and 12 have the same retention rate. If all of the month effects are 0 (that is, $\alpha_1 = \cdots = \alpha_{11} = 0$), then the retention rate is the constant $1/(1 + e^{-\alpha})$ and the SRM is adequate. When $\alpha_t \neq 0$, month t has a different retention rate than month 12 and the SRM is inadequate. We can estimate the model and display the predicted probabilities for each month with the following SAS code:

Program 4.5 PROC LOGISTIC used to estimate life table

```
PROC LOGISTIC DATA=long DESCENDING;        PROC SQL;
  CLASS t / PARAM=REF;                       SELECT
  MODEL cancelnow = t;                          DISTINCT t,
  FREQ count;                                   1-phat AS rhat FORMAT=7.4
  OUTPUT OUT=probs PREDICTED=phat;           FROM probs;
RUN;
```

Model Fit Statistics		
Criterion	Intercept Only	Intercept and Covariates
AIC	2034.447	1895.360
-2 Log L	2032.447	1871.360

Testing Global Null Hypothesis: BETA=0			
Test	Chi-Square	DF	Pr > ChiSq
Likelihood Ratio	161.0865	11	< .0001

Table 4.3 shows the parameter estimates from `PROC LOGISTIC` and the estimated probabilities from `PROC SQL`. We begin by evaluating whether the overall model is significant by testing

$$H_0 : \alpha_1 = \cdots = \alpha_{11} = 0 \quad \text{versus} \quad H_1 : \alpha_t \neq 0 \text{ for some } t.$$

If the null hypothesis is true, then all months have the same retention rate and we can use estimates from the intercept model above (SRM). The first row gives the results of a likelihood ratio test with 11 degrees of freedom. The P-value is less than .0001, so we reject H_0 and conclude that at least one month has a different retention rate. The chi-square statistic is computed as the difference between deviances (`-2 Log L` for -2 times the log likelihood value) provided in the output: $2032.447 - 1871.360 = 161.0865$. The intercept-only column gives the fit statistics (deviance) of the SRM, while the intercept-and-covariates column is for the GRM. Thus, deviance is reduced by 161 by adding the 11 degrees of freedom, which allows for different retention rates in different months. Rejecting this hypothesis indicates that the SRM is inadequate because the retention rate changes over time.

Table 4.3 Parameter estimates for Example 4.11

Analysis of Maximum Likelihood Estimates							$\hat{r}_t$
Parameter		DF	Estimate	Standard Error	Wald Chi-Square	Pr>ChiSq	
Intercept		1	−2.6715	0.2868	86.7787	< .0001	
t	1	1	15.5229	344.7	0.0020	0.9641	1
t	2	1	−2.4405	0.5777	17.8458	< .0001	.9940
t	3	1	−1.0298	0.3825	7.2496	0.0071	.9759
t	4	1	−0.7721	0.3658	4.4544	0.0348	.9690
t	5	1	−0.0943	0.3331	0.0802	0.7771	.9408
t	6	1	−0.3117	0.3461	0.8110	0.3678	.9518
t	7	1	0.6533	0.3175	4.2337	0.0396	.8827
t	8	1	−0.1063	0.3557	0.0893	0.7651	.9415
t	9	1	−0.1011	0.3717	0.0740	0.7856	.9412
t	10	1	−0.3281	0.4037	0.6604	0.4164	.9526
t	11	1	−0.4855	0.4319	1.2639	0.2609	.9592
t	12						.9353

Having concluded that retention rates are significantly different, the parameter estimates tell us which months have higher or lower retention rates. The parameter estimates from the SAS output have been entered into Table 4.3, and an additional column has been added giving the estimated retention rates ($\hat{r}_t$) from the `SQL` statement in the program above. The intercept row gives the log-odds ratio for the month 12 default rate, -2.6715. The default rate is thus $1/(1 + e^{2.6715}) = .0647$ and the retention rate is $1 - .0647 = .9353$. The retention rate for month 11 is estimated as follows:

$$\hat{r}_{11} = 1 - \frac{1}{1 + e^{-(-2.6715 - 0.4855)}} = .9592.$$

Likewise, for the other months. The estimated retention rates equal those made by the KM estimate in Table 4.1, just as the estimate from the intercept model equals the SRM estimate. Both these methods are making maximum likelihood estimates, so we expect them to be identical.

One could also model the baseline hazard function with a parametric function of time (for example, $\sqrt{t}$) or a nonparametric functional form such as a spline. In the previous example, however, any functional form that assumes a continuous function, including splines and power functions of time, would not be advisable because the baseline hazard function has a discontinuity at $t = 7$. Whenever there are contracts, beware of imposing continuity constraints. Another issue with spline models is that extrapolation is difficult.

Thus, the discrete-time logistic regression model can be used to estimate both a constant retention rate (intercept model) as well as a model that allows retention rates to vary over time (intercept and covariate model). In the next section we will learn about static covariates and how they systematically change the hazard.

4.4.2 Static covariates

The previous section showed how to estimate the retention rates for different values of t assuming that the retention rates were the same across all customers. This section will show how to adjust the estimates for customer-level characteristics. Let x_i be some numerical or categorical measurement on customer i that does not change over time (static). The examples cited earlier include variables such as gender, acquisition source, age, credit rating, and so on. This static covariate can be included as follows:

$$\log\left(\frac{\pi_{it}}{1 - \pi_{it}}\right) = \alpha_t + \beta x_i.$$

The effect of x_i is therefore to shift the entire (logit) baseline hazard function (α_t) up or down as depicted in the left panel of Figure 4.1. When $\beta = 0$ then covariate x has no effect on retention rates. Positive values of β indicate that the hazard function shifts upward as x increases. We can, of course, include more than one static covariate in the same model.

EXAMPLE 4.12:   Educational service provider—including a static covariate
Create a SAS data set to include a static covariate for the starting contract length in the one-year service provider example. Estimate and interpret the model.

Solution   We will return to the raw data, which is available in the `ex4_30.sas7bdat` data set. This data set has a larger random sample of 4,721 observations that are all joined during the same month. By using customers who start in the same month we will avoid having to worry about seasonal effects in this example, which would complicate our models.[6] The first 15 observations are as follows:

Program 4.6 Display service database for selected customers

```
PROC PRINT DATA=curr.ex4_30;
  VAR pay0-pay11 test0-test11;
  id custid;
  WHERE custid IN (137, 143, 160, 163, 165, 5993, 6030, 6610, 6623);
RUN;
```

There is one row for each customer. The `custid` variable uniquely identifies a customer. Variables `pay0-pay11` give the contract length for each of the 12 months, where a value 0 indicates that the customer is no longer a member. The variables `test0-test11` will be analyzed in the next section and give the number of tests submitted by a student during the particular month. These variables are indexed by time and not period number, so the 0 in `pay0` refers to the time at which the payment was made. This is consistent with our indexing of the m_t variable earlier in the chapter. Note that m_t is actually payment number $t + 1$.

custid	pay0	pay1	pay2	pay3	pay4	pay5	pay6	pay7	pay8	pay9	pay10	pay11
137	6	6	6	6	6	6	6	6	6	6	6	6
143	6	6	6	6	6	6	0	0	0	0	0	0
160	6	6	6	6	6	6	0	0	0	0	0	0
163	1	1	1	1	1	0	0	1	1	1	1	1
165	1	1	1	1	1	0	0	0	0	0	0	0
5993	1	0	0	0	0	0	0	0	0	0	0	0
6030	12	12	12	0	0	0	0	0	0	0	0	0
6610	1	1	1	1	6	6	6	6	6	6	6	6
6623	1	1	1	12	12	0	0	0	0	0	0	0

Customers 137–142, 144–150, 161, and 162 never canceled during the study period. Customer 137 had two six-month contracts while customer 139 and one twelve-month contract. Customer 143 canceled during period 6, after completing one six-month contract. Customer 163 canceled during month 5 and then rejoined in month 7. This is an example of a *repeated event*, where the customer has come back to life (so to speak) and we must study the time until the second cancelation. We will not discuss methods for analyzing repeated events; see Allison (2010, pp. 236–247) or Malthouse (2007) for further discussion.

custid	test0	test1	test2	test3	test4	test5	test6	test7	test8	test9	test10	test11
137	4	4	4	4	4	4	0	4	4	4	4	0
143	4	4	4	4	4	0	0	0	0	0	0	0
160	4	4	4	4	4	4	0	0	0	0	0	0
163	4	4	4	4	4	0	0	4	4	4	4	4
165	0	0	0	0	0	0	0	0	0	0	0	0
5993	0	0	0	0	0	0	0	0	0	0	0	0
6030	4	4	4	0	0	0	0	0	0	0	0	0
6610	4	4	4	4	4	4	4	4	1	3	4	4
6623	4	4	4	0	0	0	0	0	0	0	0	0

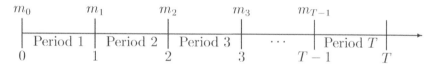

We need to prepare the long data set so that we can use `PROC LOGISTIC`. Program 4.7 accomplishes the task. There should be one record for every opportunity to cancel. Because nobody cancels at time 0, the loop starts at 1.

Program 4.7 Prepare data for discrete-time survival model with time-dependent covariates

```
DATA long;
  SET curr.ex4_30;
  ARRAY pay{0:11} pay0-pay11;
  ARRAY test{0:11} test0-test11;
  startlen = pay0;
  cancelnow = 0;
  DO t = 1 TO 11 UNTIL(pay{t}=0);
    lagnotest = (test{t-1}=0);
    cancelnow = (pay{t}=0);
    OUTPUT;
  END;
  KEEP custid startlen t cancelnow lagnotest;
RUN;

PROC PRINT DATA=long NOOBS;
  BY custid;
  VAR t startlen cancelnow lagnotest;
  WHERE custid IN (137,143,160,163,5993);
RUN;
```

Customer 137 was retained all eleven periods and is therefore censored. Consequently there are eleven records, all with `cancelnow` = 0. This customer had an initial contract length of six months, so all records have `startlen` = 6. The `lagnotest` variable will be discussed in the next section on time-dependent covariates and indicates whether the customer did not submit any tests during the previous month.

custid=137			
T	startlen	cancelnow	lagnotest
1	6	0	0
2	6	0	0
3	6	0	0
4	6	0	0
5	6	0	0
6	6	0	0
7	6	0	1
8	6	0	0
9	6	0	0
10	6	0	0
11	6	0	0

Customer 143 signed up for a six-month contract, made payments $m_0, \ldots, m_5$, and then canceled during period during period 6. This customer has six opportunities to cancel and therefore there are six observations, each with `startlen` = 6. The first five have `cancelnow` = 0 and the last (t = 6) with `cancelnow` = 1 because the customer cancels during this period. This student did not submit any tests during the month before canceling (`pay5` = 0) and therefore `notestlag` = 1 for t = 6.

custid=143			
T	startlen	cancelnow	lagnotest
1	6	0	0
2	6	0	0
3	6	0	0
4	6	0	0
5	6	0	0
6	6	1	1

Customer 5993 cancels during the first period of his life (`pay1` = 0). He has one opportunity to cancel and does. Only one record is created.

custid=5993			
T	startlen	cancelnow	lagnotest
1	1	1	1

The SAS code for estimating the model is nearly identical to the previous example, except that the static covariate `startlen` has been added to both the CLASS and MODEL lines. Listing it under CLASS causes SAS to create dummy variables for the different levels of `startlen`; if we had not listed it there, it would have been included as a numerical variable and been given one degree of freedom. This would have assumed that the change in the logit of canceling was constant across all starting lengths, and this assumption might not be true.

Program 4.8 Logistic regression program

```
PROC LOGISTIC DATA=long DESCENDING;
  CLASS t startlen / PARAM=REF;
  MODEL cancelnow = t startlen;
  ESTIMATE "1 vs 6 month" startlen 1 -1;
RUN;
```

The specific model being estimated is:

$$\log \left(\frac{\pi_{it}}{1 - \pi_{it}} \right) = \alpha + \alpha_t + \beta_1 x_{1i} + \beta_6 x_{6i},$$

where $x_{1i} = 1$ if customer i has a starting contract length of one month and 0 otherwise, x_{6i} is a similar dummy for six-month initial contracts, and $\alpha_t (t = 1, \ldots 10)$ estimates the baseline hazard function.

Parts of the output are provided below. We begin with the Type 3 Analysis of Effects table. The first line for T tests $H_0 : \alpha_1 = \cdots = \alpha_{10}$ against the alternative that at least one of the months has a different retention rate. If we cannot reject this H_0, then we can assume a constant retention rate and use the SRM, possibly stratified by starting length. The `startlen` line tests $H_0 : \beta_1 = \beta_6 = 0$. If we cannot reject this, then we could drop `startlen` from the model and conclude that the starting length of the contrast has no effect on retention rates. In this example both are highly significant. It is a good idea to examine such a test before looking at the parameter estimated to avoid type I errors when you are testing individual parameters.

Type 3 Analysis of Effects			
Effect	DF	Wald Chi-Square	Pr > ChiSq
T	10	840.4289	< .0001
startlen	2	259.5015	< .0001

The parameter estimates are shown below. The baseline hazard function shows a similar pattern as the KM analysis earlier. There is a spike at T = 6, presumably because many people go out of contract at the end of the previous month. The two lines for `startlen` indicate how much greater the hazard of canceling is for those on initial one- or six-month contracts. The base category is a twelve-month contract, and $\hat{\beta}_6 = 1.2425$ indicates that, regardless of the month, the log-odds of a customer on a six-month canceling are 1.2425 greater than those on twelve-month contracts. The odds ratio (omitted here, but provided in the SAS output) is computed as $e^{1.2425} = 3.464$ and indicates that the odds of someone on a six-month contract canceling are 3.464 *times* greater than those of someone on a twelve-month contract. The last column gives the P-value testing $H_0 : \beta_6 = 0$ versus a two-sided alternative, and if we cannot reject this hypothesis, then we do not have evidence to say that six-month contracts differ from twelve-month ones. In this case we reject H_0 with $P < .0001$.

Analysis of Maximum Likelihood Estimates						
Parameter		DF	Estimate	Standard Error	Wald Chi-Square	Pr>ChiSq
Intercept		1	−5.2925	0.1763	901.3097	< .0001
T	1	1	−1.2946	0.2291	31.9253	< .0001
T	2	1	0.0134	0.1634	0.0067	0.9346
T	3	1	0.7282	0.1480	24.2168	< .0001
T	4	1	0.4031	0.1554	6.7275	0.0095
T	5	1	0.5110	0.1540	11.0121	0.0009
T	6	1	1.9101	0.1373	193.5766	< .0001
T	7	1	0.9913	0.1486	44.4983	< .0001
T	8	1	0.6325	0.1572	16.1967	< .0001
T	9	1	0.3515	0.1663	4.4667	0.0346
T	10	1	0.0503	0.1784	0.0794	0.7781
startlen	1	1	1.7922	0.1284	194.8925	< .0001
startlen	6	1	1.2425	0.1316	89.1693	< .0001

The effect for one-month contracts is also highly significantly different from twelve-month contracts ($H_0 : \beta_1 = 0$). The odds of those on one-month contracts defaulting are $e^{1.7922} = 6.003$ times those of someone on a twelve-month contract.

One might also want to test whether those on one-month contracts have different hazard rates than those on six-month contract ($H_0 : \beta_1 = \beta_6$). The `ESTIMATE` command estimates the difference between the coefficients. A difference of 0 indicates that the two are equal. The 1 -1 part of the statement specifies the precise linear combination of the `startlen` parameters, summing the estimate for one-month contracts times 1 and the estimate for six-month contracts times -1. The relevant output is shown below, with $1.7922 - 1.2425 = 0.5497$ and $P < .0001$ indicating that we can reject the null hypothesis. We conclude that the log-odds of canceling are greater for those on one-month contracts than for those on six-month ones.

Estimate				
Label	Estimate	Standard Error	z Value	Pr > |z|
1 vs 6 month	0.5497	0.05454	10.08	< .0001

There is an important problem with the above model: it is most likely misspecified. Figure 4.6 suggested that the shape of the baseline hazard function depended on the length of the initial contract. Those who started out on six-month contracts have a spike at month seven. Those on other contracts do not. This implies that there is an interaction between `t` and `startlen`. This model can also be estimated with `PROC LOGISTIC` by adding a vertical bond symbol (|) between them in the `MODEL` statement:

Program 4.9 Logistic regression program with interaction

```
PROC LOGISTIC DATA=long DESCENDING;
  CLASS t startlen / PARAM=REF;
  MODEL cancelnow = t|startlen;
RUN;
```

The Type 3 analysis will tell us whether we need different baseline hazard functions (α_t) for each value of `startlen`. The interaction row `T*startlen` is highly significant ($P < .0001$) with a large chi-square statistic and indicates that we should include the interaction, which has 20 degrees of freedom. The 10 degrees of freedom for `T` are for those on twelve-month contracts. The interaction includes an additional 11 parameters for each of the other two lengths. The test evaluates whether all 20 of them are 0, in which case no interaction would be necessary. The test statistic indicates that the deviance is reduced by 407 after adding the 20 dummies for the interaction. The P value indicates that we can reject the null hypothesis in that are all 20 of them are 0, suggesting we should keep the interaction.[7]

Type 3 Analysis of Effects			
Effect	DF	Chi-Square	Pr>ChiSq
T	10	11.2428	0.3389
startlen	2	31.9133	< .0001
T*startlen	20	407.0410	< .0001

4.4.3 Time-dependent covariates

The static covariates in the previous section remain constant for each customer during the study period. Time-dependent covariates can change their value for the customer over time. In the case of the educational service provider example there are two obvious examples. Those enrolled in the program are to submit completed test materials each month. Most of the time students submit their materials, but sometimes they do not. It is of interest to know whether those who do not submit their materials have a higher risk of canceling. If so, failing to submit materials should be considered as an early warning that the relationship is at risk. Failing to return materials could indicate that the student is not perceiving sufficient value in the materials or does not like them. Perhaps the company can create a contact point for such students that would "save" them before they canceled. We created a dummy variable `lagnotest` in Example 4.7 that indicates whether the customer did not submit any materials during the previous month.

A second example of a time-dependent covariate is whether the customer is out of contract during a particular month. The difference in the baseline hazard functions shown in Figure 4.6 might be due to the customer being out of contract. We will show how to create a dummy variable `contactup` indicating whether the customer is out of contract.

The values of both `lagnotest` and `contractup` change over time. The general discrete-time hazard model, which allows for time-dependent covariates, is as follows:

$$\log \left(\frac{\pi_{it}}{1 - \pi_{it}} \right) = \lambda(t) + x_{i1t}\beta_1 + \cdots + x_{ipt}\beta_p,$$

where $t = 1, 2, \ldots, \alpha_t$ describe the shape of the (logit) *baseline hazard function*, x_{ijt} is the value of covariate j at time t for customer i. If covariate j is static, then $x_{ij1} = x_{ij2} = \cdots = x_{ij}$. Notice that the effect of the covariate is to shift the entire (logit of the) baseline hazard function up or down.

EXAMPLE 4.13:   Educational service provider—time-dependent covariates

Add a time-dependent covariate that indicates whether a student submitted a test during the previous month (`lagnotest`).

Solution   We already prepared the data set in Program 4.7. We can include the time-dependent covariate simply by adding lagnotest to the `MODEL` statement:

Program 4.10 Logistic regression program with interaction and time-dependent covariate

```
PROC LOGISTIC DATA=long DESCENDING;
  CLASS t startlen / PARAM=REF;
  MODEL cancelnow = t|startlen lagnotest;
RUN;
```

The parameter estimates, with some middle lines omitted, are shown below. The line for `lagnotest` indicates that the logit of canceling is 3.4065 greater for those who did not submit a test in the previous period than those who did. We can also say that the *odds* of canceling in the next period are $e^{3.4065} \approx 30$ times greater when a student fails to submit materials. The P-value is less than .0001, indicating that the difference is highly significant. Not submitting materials is an indication that there is something wrong in the relationship and that the customer is at risk of canceling.

Analysis of Maximum Likelihood Estimates							
Parameter			DF	Estimate	Standard Error	Wald Chi-Square	Pr>ChiSq
Intercept			1	−7.1953	0.4618	242.7366	< .0001
T	1		1	0.8132	0.6424	1.6024	0.2056
T	2		1	0.9871	0.5954	2.7484	0.0974
T	3		1	1.2989	0.5493	5.5909	0.0181
T	4		1	0.2222	0.6399	0.1206	0.7284
⋮							
T*startlen	10	6	1	−0.4725	0.8980	0.2768	0.5988
lagnotest			1	3.4065	0.1009	1139.9417	< .0001

Odds Ratio Estimates		
Effect	Point Estimate	95% Wald Confidence Limits
lagnotest	30.160	24.748 36.754

Returning to the process discussed in Figure 1.1, this analysis indicates that CLV can be changed by reducing the hazard of canceling among the segment of those who do not submit tests. Reducing this hazard becomes the objective, and the company should test contacts.

We will now show how to include a time-dependent covariate for whether the contract is up. Figure 4.5 showed that there is a large spike in the hazard of canceling during the seventh month for those on six-month contracts, but not for those on contracts of other lengths. This suggests that the spike is due to the customer being out of contract rather than there being something unusual about the seventh month. A more proximate cause of the higher attrition rate is that the customer is out of contract, rather than the starting length of the contract, which can be thought of as a measure of commitment at the time of acquisition. As we extend the length of the study period (for example, using the full five years of data) and the acquisition becomes further in the past, one would expect this initial contract length to have less explanatory power. For example, if someone who has been a member for four years is considering canceling, it is more plausible that her parents would consider whether they are in contract rather than their starting contract length. It is better to have the actual cause (being out of contract) as a covariate than a proxy for the cause.

EXAMPLE 4.14:   Educational service provider—time-dependent covariate for being in contract

Add a time-dependent covariate for being in contract to the service example.

Solution   We want to create a variable `contractup` indicating whether the contract was up in the current period. We did not create the variable earlier because the programming logic is more complicated. The trick is to define a variable `timeleft` indicating the number of payments that the customer has left on the current contract.

Program 4.11 Program to create data set for time-dependent covariates

```
DATA long;
  SET curr.ex4_30;
  ARRAY pay{0:11} pay0-pay11;
  ARRAY test{0:11} test0-test11;
  payleft = pay0-1; /* they've made one payment already at t=0 */
  cancelnow = 0;
  DO t = 1 TO 11 UNTIL(pay{t}=0);
    lagnotest = (test{t-1}=0);
    cancelnow = (pay{t}=0);
    contractup = (payleft <= 0);
    OUTPUT;
    IF payleft=0 THEN payleft = pay{t}-1;
    ELSE payleft = payleft-1;
  END;
  KEEP custid t cancelnow lagnotest payleft contractup;
RUN;

PROC PRINT DATA=long NOOBS;
  BY custid;
  VAR T lagnotest payleft contractup cancelnow;
  WHERE custid IN (137, 6030, 6610, 6623);
RUN;
```

Consider customer 137. The `payleft` variable gives the number of payments left on the contract. The customer starts out on a six-month contract and when in period 6 the customer is out of contract, as indicated by `contractup = 1`. The customer signs up for another six-month contract, which extends to the end of the study period.

custid=137				
T	lagnotest	payleft	contractup	cancelnow
1	0	5	0	0
2	0	4	0	0
3	0	3	0	0
4	0	2	0	0
5	0	1	0	0
6	0	0	1	0
7	1	5	0	0
8	0	4	0	0
9	0	3	0	0
10	0	2	0	0
11	0	1	0	0

Customer 6030 signs up for a twelve-month contract and cancels prematurely at T = 3. Notice how `contractup` = 0 for all periods because this customer is never out of contract.

custid=6030				
T	lagnotest	payleft	contractup	cancelnow
1	0	11	0	0
2	0	10	0	0
3	0	9	0	1

Customer 6610 is more difficult because he changes contract lengths. He initially signs up for a one-month contract and continues on one-year contracts until T = 4, when he switches to a six-month contract.

custid=6610				
T	lagnotest	payleft	contractup	cancelnow
1	0	0	1	0
2	0	0	1	0
3	0	0	1	0
4	0	0	1	0
5	0	5	0	0
6	0	4	0	0
7	0	3	0	0
8	0	2	0	0
9	0	1	0	0
10	0	0	1	0
11	0	5	0	0

The model is estimated as follows. The `startlen` variable has been dropped because we are capturing the effect of being out of contract with the `contractup` variable. See Exercise 4.15 for a possible refinement.

Program 4.12 Logistic regression program including time-dependent covariate for being out of contract

```
PROC LOGISTIC DATA=long DESCENDING;
  CLASS t / PARAM=REF;
  MODEL cancelnow = t lagnotest contractup;
RUN;
```

The parameter estimates are shown below. The `contractup` variable is highly significant. The odds of canceling when the contract is up are $e^{1.3957} = 4.038$ times greater than the odds of canceling when in contract. This is a substantial difference, although the difference between those who submit materials and those who do not is even larger ($e^{2.4866} = 12.008$ times).

Analysis of Maximum Likelihood Estimates						
Parameter		DF	Estimate	Standard Error	Wald Chi-Square	Pr>ChiSq
Intercept		1	-7.0025	0.1681	1734.3027	$< .0001$
T	1	1	-0.9404	0.2327	16.3254	$< .0001$
T	2	1	0.1755	0.1678	1.0937	0.2957
T	3	1	0.8656	0.1527	32.1167	$< .0001$
T	4	1	0.3236	0.1595	4.1164	0.0425
T	5	1	0.3740	0.1579	5.6069	0.0179
T	6	1	1.5584	0.1428	119.0668	$< .0001$
T	7	1	0.9710	0.1534	40.0542	$< .0001$
T	8	1	0.6143	0.1618	14.4144	0.0001
T	9	1	0.3036	0.1706	3.1662	0.0752
T	10	1	0.1540	0.1829	0.7083	0.4000
lagnotest		1	3.3226	0.1000	1103.7570	$< .0001$
contractup		1	1.3456	0.0715	354.0110	$< .0001$

4.5 Application: trigger events

Marketing communications has historically focused on pushing messages at consumers in TV, print, banner, radio, and outdoor ads, and also direct marketing mailings and phone calls. In addition to creating and sending outbound messages, marketers must learn to listen to their customers. A dissatisfied customer will sometimes communicate directly with the firm through an e-mail, letter, or call, but not always. Too often, the customer simply stops purchasing. There are, however, sometimes more subtle indications that the relationship is at risk, such as reduced purchase activity. Firms that detect these cues early and make things right can save the relationship and, in doing so, earn higher levels of customer loyalty.

Other cues might signal opportunities. For example, someone who has flown infrequently in the past could start a different job and suddenly begin to travel more often. This sudden spike in purchases indicates that this customer has become a bigger fish. The airline that earns its loyalty will enjoy attractive cash flows in the future. This section discusses how to identify and prioritize such trigger events.

4.5.1 Definition of trigger event

A *trigger event* is something that happens during a customer's lifecycle that (1) the company can detect and (2) affects the customer's CLV (Malthouse, 2007). A *trigger contact* is a targeted intervention that is made in response to the trigger event and is designed to either accelerate or avoid the behavior in the future. Some examples are as follows:

- Suppose that a credit card holder has been using the card several times a week for routine transactions such as gasoline, groceries, restaurants, retail purchases, entertainment, and the like. The customer has been a frequent "transactor" for several years. Suppose that the frequency of transactions suddenly decreases. This sudden decrease is likely a trigger event because it could indicate that the customer will not be using the card as much in the future. The credit card should have reactive contacts in place designed to save this customer.

- Consider an Internet service provider (ISP) who enrolls customers for an initial one-year contract. New customers are allowed to try the service over a 30-day grace period and cancel without penalty, but after the first 30 days customers pay a substantial penalty. Suppose a customer enrolls, but does not log in at all for the first 10 days. This event, inactivity, could indicate that the customer cannot get the service to work and needs help. A customer who cannot get the system to work is likely to cancel the service during the grace period. The ISP should have a reactive contact in place, such as a technical-support call.

- A retail web site accepts an order for some item two weeks before Christmas and sends the customer a confirmation e-mail. The company then learns that the item will be out of stock until after Christmas, and sends the customer an e-mail apologizing for the problem and offers an incentive toward future purchases as compensation for the inconvenience. The trigger event is the company being unable to fulfill the item before Christmas, and the reactive contact is the e-mail.

Trigger events are not useful to a company unless they give rise to effective trigger contacts. Some trigger event could have a substantial effect on CLV for many customers, but if there is no way to respond to the trigger event then the event is not interesting to the firm. For example, if a frequent flyer of airline A moves to a different city where A does not have a hub, but competing airline B does, airline A will find it difficult to retain the customer. If A does not offer direct flights to the places where the customer must travel, the customer will likely switch to an airline that offers such flights.

In addition to giving rise to effective contacts, trigger events should also affect CLV for a substantial number of customers. Some event could cause customers to leave, but if only a small number of customers ever experience the trigger event, the company might be better off investing its resources in fixing other problems. Conversely, an event that has a small effect on CLV for a large number of customers could be very important.

Our definition requires that trigger events affect CLV, but the word affect should not be taken too literally because the event that a company observes might not be the direct cause of the change in future behavior. In the credit card example above, the decreased transaction activity is a manifestation of some more fundamental cause, such as the customer being dissatisfied with the card's rewards. It is this dissatisfaction that causes the customer to accept the competitor's offer and reduce usage of the first company's card. The company can only observe a symptom—the decrease in transaction volume—and we shall therefore focus on it in our analyses. Supplementary market research may be necessary to identify fundamental causes and develop effective trigger contacts.

4.5.2   Prioritizing trigger events

Managers can identify many events that might require a reactive contact. The examples discussed above seem like obvious situations where some response from the company is necessary, but not all events are so obvious. If a catalog customer returns some merchandise, should the company initiate any corrective action? It could be that the customer is dissatisfied with, for example, the quality of the merchandise, and will never buy again. Alternatively, the reason for the return could be that the item did not fit the customer; the customer could be delighted by the return policy and feel a greater sense of loyalty toward the company. In that case, the catalog company should give the customer more opportunities to buy (provided the customer is profitable). A third possibility is that the return does not indicate anything about the future behavior of the customer, in which case no reactive contact is necessary.

What is needed is some way to prioritize which trigger events are important. Because trigger events must affect CLV for a substantial number of customers, the basic idea will be to build a statistical model for CLV that includes as covariates the potential trigger events. The coefficient for a trigger event measures the effect of the event on CLV. An event that has no effect on CLV has low priority while those with a large effect on CLV (and that impact many customers) have a high priority.

It is often too hard to build one grand model for CLV, and we are often better off focusing on one component of CLV. This aligns nicely with the strategies for increasing CLV discussed in section 1.2.2. When the objective is to increase the retention rate of some customer segment, then the survival models discussed in the previous section are a natural choice. They are also well suited when the objective is to increase the purchase rate; in this case the dependent variable is the next purchase occasion rather than canceling. When the objective is to increase CLV another way, the regression models discussed in Chapter 6 are more suitable.

EXAMPLE 4.15: Educational service provider—trigger events

This example builds on Example 4.14, but will use all 60 months of data. Build a trigger event model for the educational service provider assessing the following possible trigger events:

1. The student does not submit exercises during a particular month.

2. The student performs poorly on exercises, indicating that the student is either struggling with the material or not committing sufficient energy to the materials (low involvement). Define a poor score to be one in the bottom quartile of all submitted tests.

3. The student's current contract is expiring.

4. The month itself. It could be that defections are seasonal, with more cancelations occurring, for example, at the beginning of vacation.

Solution   For this analysis the universe is all students who enrolled for the first time at the beginning of the school year five years ago. This gives a universe of size $n = 4,721$. Let π_{it} be the probability that customer i defaults at time t, modeled as

$$\log\left(\frac{\pi_{it}}{1-\pi_{it}}\right) = \alpha_{\text{mod }(t,12)} + \sum_{j=1}^{p} \beta_j x_{ijt},$$

where the α_k models the baseline hazard function giving the intercept for month number $k = 0, 1, \ldots 11$, and x_{ijt} is the value of predictor variable j for customer i at time t. Predictor variable $j = 1$ indicates whether the student did not submit a test during period $t - 1$, variable $j = 2$ indicates whether the student did poorly on exercises submitted during period $t - 1$, and variable $j = 3$ indicates whether the student's contract expired during period $t - 1$.

Table 4.4 Parameter estimates from logistic regression models of educational service company

| | Model 1 | | Model 2 | |
| | y=First Defection | | y=First Defection | |
Parameter	Estimate	Std Err	Estimate	Std Err
Intercept	−5.9145	0.0628	−5.8451	0.0629
Month0	1.1934	0.0393	1.2559	0.0399
Month1	0.1481	0.0582	0.0801	0.0587
Month2	−0.1820	0.0639	−0.2669	0.0644
Month3	0.0836	0.0573	0.0104	0.0578
Month4	−0.2899	0.0641	−0.3711	0.0645
Month5	−0.3615	0.0640	−0.4403	0.0644
Month6	0.7396	0.0410	0.7360	0.0414
Month7	0.1273	0.0588	0.1421	0.0592
Month8	−0.0803	0.0648	−0.0321	0.0651
Month9	−0.2868	0.0701	−0.2318	0.0704
Month10	−0.6038	0.0839	−0.4972	0.0843
Lag No Test	2.1560	0.1049	2.3618	0.1081
Lag Poor Score	0.3531	0.1157	0.5288	0.1185
Contract up	1.3435	0.0454	1.3222	0.0456
Cum No Test			−0.0165	.006455
Cum Poor Score			−0.0251	.005966

Parameter estimates from three models are shown in Table 4.4. First consider the estimates from Model 1. The coefficient for not submitting a test during the previous month is 2.156, indicating that the odds of defecting of someone who does not submit any tests are $\exp(2.156) \approx 8.5$ times greater than those of someone who does submit tests. The coefficient for doing poorly on tests during the previous period is 0.3531, indicating that the odds of defecting of someone who scores poorly on a test are $\exp(0.3531) = 1.4$ times greater than those of someone who does not do poorly. The coefficient for the contract expiring is 1.3435, so that the odds of someone defecting whose contract is expiring are $\exp(1.3435) = 3.83$. Thus, students who do not submit a test or do poorly are at risk. This conclusion is not surprising, but this analysis enables the decision maker to quantify how much students are at risk after various events, and incorporate this information when allocating resources to customer retention activities.

The intercept and month variables describe the baseline hazard function. `Month0 = 1` if the month is beginning of the school year and 0 otherwise; `Month1 = 1` for the next month and 0 otherwise, and so on. The value of the intercept thus gives the baseline hazard function for the month before the school year starts. The value for `Month0` is $-5.9145 + 1.1934 = -3.7211$, indicating that students are more likely to defect during Month 0 than the month before. The intercept and `MONTH*` estimates are plotted against the month number in Figure 4.8. The baseline hazard function is periodic, with defections most likely to occur at the beginning of the school year and after break (month 6).

Figure 4.8 Baseline hazard function for educational service company as estimated by logistic regression in model 1

```
DATA hazard;
  INPUT b @@;
  m = _N_-1;
  est = -5.9145 + b;
DATALINES;
1.1934 .1481 -.1820 .0836 -.2899 -.3615
.7396 .1273 -.0803 -.2868 -.6038 0
RUN;

PROC SGPLOT DATA=hazard NOAUTOLEGEND;
  SERIES X=m Y=est;
  SCATTER X=m Y=est;
  XAXIS LABEL="Month Number";
  YAXIS LABEL="Baseline Hazard Function";
RUN;
```

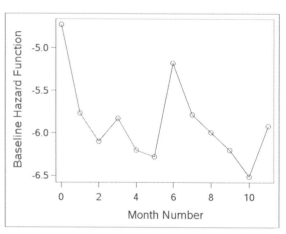

The data for the plot comes from the output. Copying data from the output into a `DATA` statement enables us to accomplish the goal of producing the plot, but it not very elegant. An alternative approach is to save the estimated regression coefficients to a SAS data set by adding an `OUTEST` option to the `PROC LOGISTIC` line. The relevant lines can then be extracted within a `DATA` statement. This would be a good exercise for the reader.

This analysis suggests that students who do not submit materials are at great risk. It should trigger some retention contact, such as mailing a brochure to the parents documenting how the materials improve performance in school and giving suggestions on how to motivate the child to complete the materials. Market research might be necessary to develop an effective reactive contact. Students who submit materials, but perform poorly on them are also at risk, although the risk is lower than for those who do not submit materials at all.

The goal of Model 2 is to evaluate whether recent or chronic undesirable activity is the problem. Are students who have a history of not submitting tests more likely to defect?

Two additional covariates have been added that measure the cumulative number of times a student has not submitted a test ($j = 4$) and the number of poor tests ($j = 5$), that is,

$$x_{ijt} = \sum_{k=1}^{t-1} x_{k,j-3,k}, \qquad (j = 4, 5).$$

Both parameter estimates for the cumulative variables are close to zero, indicating that recent inactivity is a much greater problem than not having submitted many tests in the past.[8]

Survival models can help us prioritize which trigger events are likely to be important, but the ultimate proof of an event's importance comes from a randomized controlled experiment: the firm must create a trigger contact, assign customers who experience the trigger event to treatment and control groups at random, track long-term behavior (or at least a proxy for long-term behavior), and compare the groups.

4.6   The beta-geometric model

The SRM assumes a single retention rate r that is constant across customers and over time. The general retention model allows for the retention rate r_t to vary over time. The discrete-time survival model enables us to have r_t be a function of observed, possibly time-dependent, covariates (for example, $\text{logit}(\pi_{it}) = -\text{logit}(r_{it}) = a + bx_{it}$ where $\pi_{it} = 1 - r_{it}$ is the hazard of canceling and x_{it} is the value of the covariate for customer i at time t).

The beta-geometric (BG) model (Fader and Hardie, 2007, 2010) developed in this section also allows retention rates to vary, but instead of modeling them be a function of observed covariates, it allows them vary randomly over customers. In doing so, it accounts for *unobserved* heterogeneity. A possible limitation of this model is that one cannot account for observed heterogeneity with static or time-dependent covariates. It therefore might not be suitable when there are observed covariates that have strong predictors such as contract status. In the case of static, categorical covariates, one can stratify just as we did with the KM model.

The next section derives maximum likelihood estimates of the beta-geometric model and shows how to implement the model using `PROC IML`. This section requires a solid understanding of undergraduate-level, calculus-based probability theory, and can be skimmed by those without this background. The next section shows how to interpret the parameter estimates and gives examples.

We will continue to work with the hazard of canceling $\pi = 1 - r$. If we know π, then the PMF and survival functions, restated in terms of π, from Equations 3.7 and 3.8 are given by

$$P(T = t|\pi) = (1 - \pi)^{t-1}\pi \quad \text{and} \quad S(t|\pi) = P(T \geq t) = (1 - \pi)^{t-1}.$$

Up to this point, we have assumed that π is a fixed constant, but we will now assume that it varies according to a beta distribution with parameters $\alpha > 0$ and $\beta > 0$:

$$f(\pi|\alpha, \beta) = \frac{\pi^{\alpha-1}(1 - \pi)^{\beta-1}}{B(\alpha, \beta)} \quad \text{for } (0 \leq \pi \leq 1)$$

where $B(\alpha, \beta) = \Gamma(\alpha)\Gamma(\beta)/\Gamma(\alpha + \beta)$ is the beta function and $\Gamma(\cdot)$ is the gamma function.

The beta and gamma distributions and functions are discussed in textbooks covering probability theory (for example, see DeGroot, 1975, §6.8–9). We briefly summarize some of their properties that will be used below. The recursive property of the gamma function is that $\Gamma(\alpha + 1) = \alpha\Gamma(\alpha)$. The shape of the beta distribution is determined by parameters α

and β. The moments can help us understand how the parameters affect the shape. A beta random variable X has a mean, variance, and skewness as follows:

$$E(X) = \frac{\alpha}{\alpha + \beta}, \quad V(X) = \frac{\alpha\beta}{(\alpha + \beta)^2(\alpha + \beta + 1)}, \quad \text{and} \quad \text{skew} = \frac{2(\beta - \alpha)\sqrt{\alpha + \beta + 1}}{(\alpha + \beta + 2)\sqrt{\alpha + \beta}}.$$

When $\alpha > 1$ and $\beta > 1$, it has a single mode located at $(\alpha - 1)/(\alpha + \beta - 2)$. When $\alpha = \beta$ the mode is located at $1/2$.

Program 4.13 SAS program used to generate Figure 4.9 showing different beta distributions

```
ODS ESCAPECHAR='^';
ODS GRAPHICS ON / RESET=index HEIGHT=5in WIDTH=5in IMAGENAME="pdf" IMAGEFMT=ps;
ODS LATEX FILE="beta.tex";
%LET alpha = ^{UNICODE '03B1'x};
%LET beta = ^{UNICODE '03B2'x};

DATA pdf;
  DO x = .01 TO .99 BY .01;
    y88 = PDF('BETA', x, 8, 8);         y44 = PDF('BETA', x, 4, 4);
    y22 = PDF('BETA', x, 2, 2);         y11 = PDF('BETA', x, 1, 1);
    yp5p5 = PDF('BETA', x, .5, .5);     yp54 = PDF('BETA', x, .5, 4);
    y62 = PDF('BETA', x, 6, 2);
    OUTPUT;
  END;
RUN;

DATA anno;
  LENGTH label $45;
  function='text'; x1space="datavalue"; y1space="datavalue"; width=30;
  x1=.5; y1=2.8; label="&alpha=&beta=8"; OUTPUT;
  x1=.5; y1=2.0; label="&alpha=&beta=4"; OUTPUT;
  x1=.5; y1=1.4; label="&alpha=&beta=2"; OUTPUT;
  x1=.5; y1=0.9; label="&alpha=&beta=1"; OUTPUT;
  x1=.5; y1=0.55; label="&alpha=&beta=0.5"; OUTPUT;
  x1=.8; y1=2.8; label="&alpha=6, &beta=2"; OUTPUT;
  x1=.2; y1=3.0; label="&alpha=0.5, &beta=4"; OUTPUT;
RUN;

PROC SGPLOT DATA=pdf SGANNO=anno NOAUTOLEGEND;
  SERIES X=x Y=y88;         SERIES X=x Y=y44;         SERIES X=x Y=y22;
  SERIES X=x Y=y11;         SERIES X=x Y=yp5p5;       SERIES X=x Y=yp54;
  SERIES X=x Y=y62;         YAXIS MAX=3.5 LABEL="PDF";
RUN;

ODS LATEX CLOSE;
ODS GRAPHICS OFF;
```

Beta distributions with different shape parameters are shown in Figure 4.9. All of the terms that are multiplied in the skewness formula are strictly positive except for $(\beta - \alpha)$. This tells us that when $\beta > \alpha$ the distribution will have positive (right) skewness, when $\beta < \alpha$ it will have negative (left) skewness, and when $\alpha = \beta$ it will be symmetrical. Figure 4.9 shows a series of symmetrical distributions where $\alpha = \beta \in \{0.5, 1, 2, 4, 8\}$. When $0 < \alpha = \beta < 1$ the distribution is U-shaped. The distribution is uniform for $\alpha = \beta = 1$. When $\alpha = \beta > 1$ the variance of the distribution decreases as $\alpha = \beta$ increase. Two skewed distributions are also shown. For $\alpha = 6$ and $\beta = 2$ the mode is located at

$(6-1)/(6+2-2) = 5/6 \approx .83$. The plot has Greek letters. See the discussion about Program 4.15 for how to include Greek letters on a SAS plot.

Figure 4.9 Beta distribution with different shape parameters

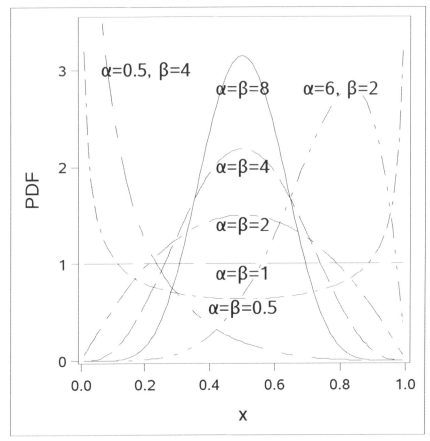

We now show how to estimate the parameters from data. We have observed the cancelation times (realizations of T) for a sample of customers and need to estimate parameters α and β. We will use maximum likelihood estimation, which requires knowing how likely it is to observe the data we have conditional on parameters α and β. At this point, our only expression for $P(T)$ requires knowing π, which has not been observed. We therefore need to find the marginal distribution of T that is not conditional on π. We can do this by integrating the joint distribution of T and π over π. The definition of conditional probability tells us that $P(T|\pi) = P(T \cap \pi)/P(\pi)$, and therefore the joint distribution is $P(T \cap \pi) = P(T|\pi)P(\pi)$, that is, the geometric distribution given π times the beta distribution. The marginal distribution is

$$
\begin{aligned}
P(T = t|\alpha, \beta) &= \int_0^1 P(T = t|\pi)f(\pi|\alpha, \beta)d\pi \\
&= \int_0^1 (1-\pi)^{t-1}\pi \cdot \frac{\pi^{\alpha-1}(1-\pi)^{\beta-1}}{B(\alpha, \beta)}d\pi \\
&= \frac{1}{B(\alpha, \beta)} \int_0^1 \pi^{\alpha}(1-\pi)^{\beta+t-2}d\pi \\
&= \frac{B(\alpha+1, \beta+t-1)}{B(\alpha, \beta)}.
\end{aligned}
$$

Following a similar approach (Exercise 4.16) we can find the survival function:[9]

$$S(t|\alpha, \beta) = \frac{B(\alpha, \beta + t - 1)}{B(\alpha, \beta)}$$

This requires evaluating the beta function, and it is desirable to simplify this expression. Fader and Hardie (2007) derive a recursive formula that is computationally simpler. They begin evaluating the expression for $t = 1$ by substituting gamma functions:

$$P(T = 1|\alpha, \beta) = \frac{B(\alpha + 1, \beta)}{B(\alpha, \beta)} = \frac{\Gamma(\alpha + 1)\Gamma(\beta)}{\Gamma(\alpha + 1 + \beta)} \Big/ \frac{\Gamma(\alpha)\Gamma(\beta)}{\Gamma(\alpha + \beta)} = \frac{\alpha}{\alpha + \beta}.$$

The $\Gamma(\beta)$ values cancel out and, using the recursive property of the gamma function, $\Gamma(\alpha + 1)/\Gamma(\alpha) = \alpha$. To find the successive probabilities ($t = 2, 3, \ldots$), note that

$$P(T = t) = \frac{P(T = t)}{P(T = t - 1)} \cdot P(T = t - 1),$$

so we can, for example, find $P(T = 2)$ by multiplying $P(T = 1)$ by the ratio $P(T = t)/P(T = t - 1)$. We therefore need to find a simple expression for the ratio. Substituting gamma functions and using the recursive property (Exercise 4.16),

$$\frac{P(T = t)}{P(T = t - 1)} = \frac{\beta + t - 2}{\alpha + \beta + t - 1}.$$

The PMF of the beta-geometric distribution is as follows:

$$P(T = t) = \frac{B(\alpha + 1, \beta + t - 1)}{B(\alpha, \beta)} = \begin{cases} \frac{\alpha}{\alpha + \beta} & t = 1 \\ \frac{\beta + t - 2}{\alpha + \beta + t - 1} \cdot P(T = t - 1) & t = 2, 3, \ldots \end{cases} \tag{4.8}$$

A similar recursive relationship for the survival function is $S(t + 1) = S(t)r_t$, where $S(1) = 1$ and retention rates are (Exercise 4.16)

$$r_t = \frac{\beta + t - 1}{\alpha + \beta + t - 1}.$$

We can now state the likelihood function. Assume a sample of n customers. Let d_t be the number of customers who default (cancel) at time t, and let c_t be the number of customers censored at time t (so that we know $T > t$). Just as we did when deriving the MLEs for the SRM in equation 3.13, the likelihood function is

$$L(\alpha, \beta) = \prod_t P(T = t)^{d_t} S(t + 1)^{c_t}$$

and the log-likelihood is

$$l(\alpha, \beta) = \sum_t [d_t \log P(T = t) + c_t \log S(t + 1)]. \tag{4.9}$$

The log likelihood can be maximized using a nonlinear optimization package. There are no known starting values that guarantee convergence. A reasonable set of starting values in many cases would be to fix $\alpha > 1$ (for example, $\alpha = 2$), set the mean equal to the SRM estimates, and solve for β.

EXAMPLE 4.16:   Fader-Hardie example of beta-geometric distribution

We illustrate estimating and interpreting the beta-geometric parameters using the same example presented in Fader and Hardie (2007). Their Appendix B shows how to estimate the model parameters using the solver function in Excel. We will show how to estimate the parameters using PROC IML, the *interactive matrix language*. Table 4.5 gives the survival percentages for a group of high-end customers. We have also computed the percentage of customers who defected in each one-year period.

Table 4.5 Data from Fader-Hardie example

Year (t)	Percent surviving	Percent defaulting $S(t) - S(t-1)$
0	100	
1	86.9	13.1
2	74.3	12.6
3	65.3	9.0
4	59.3	6.0
5	55.1	4.2
6	51.7	3.4
7	49.1	2.6

We must maximize the log-likelihood function in equation 4.9 over values of α and β. The equation can be simplified in this example because censoring only occurs at the end of year 7. Thus, the likelihood and log-likelihood functions are

$$L(\alpha, \beta) = \left[\prod_{t=1}^{6} P(T = t)^{d_t} \right] S(7)^{c_7} \quad \text{and} \quad l(\alpha, \beta) = \left[\sum_{t=1}^{6} d_t \log P(T = t) \right] + c_7 \log S(7).$$

These functions involve four vectors: d_t, c_t, $\log P(T = t)$, and $\log S(t + 1)$. The values of the second two (log-PMF and log-survival function) depend on α and β and are computed from equation 4.8. Vectors d_t and c_t are the observed data, which are given in Table 4.5. We are not told the total number of customers, but this number does not change the optimal values of α and β. The Fader-Hardie appendix assumes 1,000 customers, but we will simply use the percentages, so that the third column gives the values c_t and $c_7 = .491$. Again, one could multiply these numbers by any constant giving the total number of customers, but the optimal values of α and β will remain unchanged.

Program 4.14 gives SAS/IML code. See Program 5.8 for another example of using PROC IML to find MLEs. SAS/IML offers the NLPNRA function for doing nonlinear optimization with the Newton-Raphson method. Before calling NLPNRA, we must (1) assign the data, (2) define the log-likelihood function, and (3) set optimization parameters. These steps are discussed below:

1. The program begins by assigning the data, taken directly from Table 4.5, to matrix x. Rows are separated by commas and columns by spaces in SAS/IML.

2. The next step is to define a function loglik to compute the value of the log-likelihood function, which is the function to be maximized. It is customary to call the parameter vector theta when finding MLEs, and the function loglik accepts an argument theta, which will have the two components α and β. Matrix x is identified as a GLOBAL variable so that we can reference the data values specified earlier from within the function.

3. We define three matrices that are passed to NLPNRA. Starting values are stored in theta0 and we follow Fader and Hardie in using $\alpha = \beta = 1$. The con matrix gives bounds for the parameters, constraining both α and β to be positive. The opt vector indicates that we want to minimize the objective function and controls the amount of output.

Program 4.14 IML program for beta-geometric example

```
PROC IML;
x = {0.869 0.131,
     0.743 0.126,
     0.653 0.090,
     0.593 0.060,
     0.551 0.042,
     0.517 0.034,
     0.491 0.026};
START loglik(theta) GLOBAL (x);
  /* theta[1] = alpha and theta[2] = beta */
  n = NROW(x);    /* number of observations */
  Pt = J(n,1);    /* PMF P(T=t) */
  St = J(n,1);    /* survival function S(t) */
  /* initialize P(T=1) = alpha/(alpha+beta) */
  Pt[1] = theta[1]/(theta[1]+theta[2]);
  St[1] = 1 - Pt[1]; /* init survival function S(1) = 1-P(T=1) */
  DO t = 2 TO n;
    Pt[t] = (theta[2]+t-2)/(SUM(theta)+t-1)*Pt[t-1];
    St[t] = St[t-1] - Pt[t];
  END;
  ll = x[,2]'*(LOG(Pt)) + x[n,1]*LOG(St[n]);
  RETURN(ll);
FINISH;

theta0 = {1 1};    /* starting values for alpha and beta */
con = {0 0,    /* lower bounds for alpha and beta */
       . .};   /* upper bounds for alpha and beta */
opt = {1,      /* find maximum */
       4};     /* print a lot of output */
CALL NLPNRA(rc, result, "loglik", theta0, opt, con);
```

The call to `NLPNRA` produces the output below. The `rc` argument is the return code, where positive values indicate the optimization was successful. Negative values indicate unsuccessful termination. The optimal values of $\hat{\alpha} = 0.668$ and $\hat{\beta} = 3.806$ are stored in `result`. The name of the objective function, `loglik`, must be specified in quotation marks.

Optimization Results			
Parameter Estimates			
N	Parameter	Estimate	Gradient Objective Function
1	X1	0.668089	$-3.57323E - 8$
2	X2	3.806098	0

Value of Objective Function $= -1.611158147$

A graph of the estimated prior distribution is shown in Figure 4.10. The distribution is right skewed without a mode. We can compute the average defection rate across customers $0.668 /(0.668+ 3.806) = 14.9\%$, but some customers have a smaller defection rate and others have a higher one. The graph illustrates the use of the `INSET` command to add comments to a plot. It also shows how to include Greek letter on a plot. One must load appropriate fonts using Program 4.15. The hex number `'03B1'x` (note that the x indicates that a numeric constant is specified in hexadecimal) is the unicode for the Greek letter α.

Figure 4.10 Beta distribution with $\alpha = 0.67$ and $\beta = 3.8$ from Fader-Hardie example

```
DATA pdf;
  DO x = .01 to 1 by .01;
    pdf = PDF('BETA', x, .67, 3.8);
    OUTPUT;
  END;
RUN;


ODS ESCAPECHAR='^';
%LET alpha=^{UNICODE '03B1'x};
%LET beta=^{UNICODE '03B2'x};
PROC SGPLOT DATA=pdf;
  SERIES X=x Y=pdf;
  INSET "  &alpha=.67, &beta=3.8" /
    POSITION=TOPLEFT;
  YAXIS MAX=8 LABEL="PDF";
RUN;
```

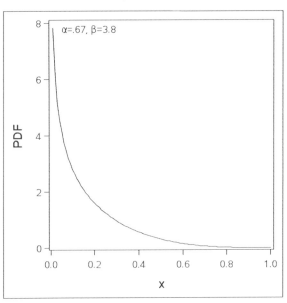

Program 4.15 Load Unicode fonts so that Greek letters can be used

```
PROC TEMPLATE;
  define style unifonts;
  parent=Styles.Default;
  style Graphfonts from GraphFonts /
    'GraphValueFont'=("Monotype San WT J",12pt)
    'GraphLabelFont'=("Monotype San WT J",14pt)
    'GraphDataFont'=("Monotype San WT J",12pt)
    'GraphTitleFont'=("Monotype San WT J",12pt);
  END;
RUN;
```

4.7   Chapter summary

This chapter discusses the GRM, which extends the SRM by allowing retention rates that vary either over time, across customers through static and time-dependent covariates, or as a random effect. If r_t is the retention rate in period t, then the *survival function* gives the chance that the customer cancels at time t or later

$$S(t) = P(T \geq t) = \prod_{i=1}^{t-1} r_i = r_{t-1}S(t-1).$$

The *probability mass function* gives the probability that a customer is retained during the first $t - 1$ periods and cancels during period t:

$$f(t) = P(T = t) = S(t)(1 - r_t) = S(t) - S(t + 1).$$

The *hazard rate* is the conditional probability of canceling at time t given the customer has not yet canceled:

$$\pi_t = P(T = t | T \geq t) = \frac{P(T = t)}{S(t)} = 1 - r_t.$$

CLV can be computed from the survival or probability mass function. If m_t is the net cash flow at time t, then

$$E[\text{CLV}(T)] = \sum_{t=1}^{\infty} f(t)\text{CLV}(t) = \sum_{t=1}^{\infty} m_{t-1}S(t) \quad \text{and} \quad E(T) = \sum_{t=1}^{\infty} S(t).$$

The statistical methods known as *survival analysis* enable us to estimate the functions in the previous paragraph. They will also accommodate retention rates that vary across customers by making them a function of observed customer-level covariates, both static and time-dependent. The *Kaplan-Meier* and *life-table* methods estimate retention rates over time. Retention rates over time can be compared across segments by estimating these models separately for each segment, which is sometimes called *stratification*. The *discrete-time survival model* also estimates retention rates over time and across segments, but also enables the retention rates to be a function of static customer characteristics such as demographics or the acquisition source or *time-dependent covariates*.

Trigger events happen during a customer's lifecycle and indicate some change in CLV and the relationship with the company. If detected early, the company can respond to the problem and retain the customer; otherwise, the customer might switch to another company. Survival analysis can be used to quantify the importance of addressing various trigger events and prioritize which to tackle first.

The beta-geometric model allows retention rates (or equivalently hazard probabilities) to vary randomly over customers according to a beta distribution, but it does not allow for covariates.

Notes

[1] Note that some authors define $S(t) = P(T > t) = 1 - F(t)$, where $F(t)$ is the cumulative distribution function.

[2] See http://support.sas.com/publishing/authors/malthouse.html.

[3] The SRM is $(436.66 - 424.11)/424.11 \approx 3\%$ higher than the GRM, which is in the ballpark. Other sources of bias are probably more important, such as the truncated future period and ignoring heterogeneity in retention rates across customers.

[4] These tests are not illustrated in the example below, but see the TEST statement under PROC LIFETEST.

[5] More precisely, α_t describe the logit of the baseline hazard function. We shall refer to it as the baseline hazard function.

[6] There could be, for example, a seasonal effect for the beginning of summer vacation, and so on. In this example the month of the year is confounded with the month of the customer's life.

[7] All tests discussed in the previous model assume a correctly specified model. Because the previous model was mis-specified, the parameter estimates could be biased and the P-values might not be exactly right. In the next section we will find a better model. The discussion above was intended to illustrate the mechanics of the various tests. The issue of model specification is difficult, requiring knowledge of the context and careful thought.

[8] These cumulative variables are potentially problematic because they are correlated with the lagged variables, which introduces multicollinearity. It is not unusual to observe large changes in the magnitude of the coefficients or even sign flips when such cumulative variables are introduced. The reason for the correlation is likely that they are measuring the same basic dimension. For example, a student who is not very diligent is more likely not to submit materials last month and also more likely to have missed many previous months. Both the lag and cum "no test" variables are measures of the student's diligence.

[9] This expression does not match the one given in Fader and Hardie (2007, Eq. (6)) because they define the survival function as $P(T > t)$ instead of $P(T \geq t)$.

The Migration Model

5

Contents

This chapter discusses one model for estimating CLV when an organization does not have contractual relationships with its customers. We assume that such organizations acquire customers who might or might not generate profit during discrete, equal-length *periods* of time such as a month or a year. In contrast, the *retention model* from the previous two chapters assumes that inactivity indicates the end of the relationship. The *migration model* covered in this chapter assumes that inactivity does not necessarily signal the end of the relationship.

This migration model is appropriate for organizations in many industries, including travel, most traditional and online retailers (clothing, supermarkets, electronics, appliances), automotive, financial services, and nonprofit organizations. For example, a customer who does not fly with an airline during some month might or might not fly again in the next month. Inactivity does not indicate that the customer is gone for good.

We would like to forecast the future value of customers and answer related questions such as:

1. What is the CLV of a customer? (The answer to this question informs a marketing decision such as whether to acquire or retain the customer.)

2. How many active customers will we have after n periods in the future and how much profit will we make?

3. If we invest more in customer retention (and could therefore increase retention rates), how would the size and profitability of our customer base change?

4. Assuming some level of retention marketing, how many customers do we need to acquire to achieve some strategic goal such as maintaining current levels of profitability or increasing the number of active customers by 20% over the next two years?

5. Organizations having contractual relationships with their customers often re-acquire customers who have previously canceled. For example, a cell-phone customer could cancel, switch to a competitor, and return later (after learning that the competitor is even worse). The retention models in the previous two chapters do not account for customers who reactivate. How can such firms correctly account for such reactivated customers?

We will develop models to answer these questions by assuming that a customer is in some *state* during each time period. An example state might be defined by having bought in the previous period. Customers generate cash flows depending on their state, and migrate between states over successive periods with certain *transition probabilities*. This chapter first considers different ways of defining states and shows how to forecast future customer value using two equivalent approaches. The first approach, called the *spreadsheet approach*, is intuitive and easy to understand, but it is also a bit cumbersome. The *matrix approach* is a little more abstract and difficult to understand at first, but it is less cumbersome, and we will be able to derive closed-form expressions that will make evaluating perpetuities easy. Next, we survey applications and discuss how to estimate transition probabilities from data.

5.1 Migration models: spreadsheet approach

5.1.1 The buy, no-buy model

The simplest migration model assumes that during each time period customers are in one of two states—"buy" or "no-buy"—illustrated in the *state diagram* (Figure 5.1) below. This simple model is not used in practice, but it will enable us to illustrate all of the concepts in a simple setting that can be easily generalized to the more complicated models used in practice. A customer who is currently in the buy state can do one of two things during the next period: the customer will buy again with the *transition probability* p_0 or not buy with the probability $1 - p_0$. Customers who do not purchase are said to *migrate* to the no-buy state. Those who buy again return to the buy state. Likewise, a customer who currently is in the no-buy state will purchase in the next period with probability p_1 (migrating back to the buy state) and not purchase with probability $1 - p_1$ (remaining in the no-buy state).

Figure 5.1 The buy, no-buy migration model

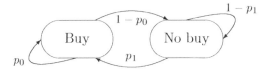

Now suppose that the firm invests c on marketing costs each period and that the net contribution for a purchase is m. Then, customers who migrate into the buy state generate cash flows $m - c$ and those migrating to the no-buy state generate $-c$. If we knew a customer's sequence of future states then we could compute CLV by summing the corresponding discounted cash flows. Unfortunately, we only know the probabilities of customers following various migration paths.

EXAMPLE 5.1:   Buy, no-buy spreadsheet example

To make this more concrete, suppose that a firm has just acquired 1,000 customers. Because all 1,000 made a purchase at the time of acquisition, they are in the buy state at time 0. Assume the probability that a customer in the buy state purchases again is $p_0 = .2$, and the probability that someone in the no-buy state purchases again is only $p_1 = .1$. The firm spends $c = \$1$ on marketing each period and buyers generate a contribution of $20 (non-buyers generate $0). We use a period discount rate of $d = 10\%$. Create a spreadsheet to forecast behavior in the next two time periods.

Solution   The future behavior and profitability can be forecasted with a spreadsheet as shown in Table 5.1 below. (See `migration.xls`.) The parameters of the model are specified in the first three rows. We would like to set up a block of cells (for example, `A5:G9`) that can be copied downward. At the beginning of time (period 0) there are 1,000 customers (cell `B7`) in the buy state and none in the no-buy state (`B8`). The next period is the previous period plus 1: `D5 = B5+1`. During period 1, 20% of the 1,000 customers buy (cell `C7 = B7*B$1`), generating a contribution of $4,000 (`D7 = C7*E$1`), and marketing costs are $1,000 (`E7 = B7*E$2`). The computations are similar for those in the no-buy state (row 8). We expect a total of `C9=SUM(C7:C8) = 200` buyers in period 1, generating a discounted profit of `F9/(1+E$3)^D5 = $2,727`. (We could also assume that marketing costs come at the beginning of the period and therefore should not be discounted, and revenues come at the end of a period).

Table 5.1 Forecasting the future value of customers

	A	B	C	D	E	F	G
1	$p_0=$	0.2		$m=$	$20		
2	$p_1=$	0.1		$c=$	$1		
3				$d=$	10%		
4							
5	Period	0	Period	1			
6	State	Count	# Buyers	Contrib.	Mkt Cost	Profit	Disc
7	Buy	1,000	200	$4,000	$1,000		
8	No-buy	0	0	$0	$0		
9	Total	1,000	200	$4,000	$1,000	$3,000	$2,727
10							
11	Period	1	Period	2			
12	State	Count	# Buyers	Contrib.	Mkt Cost	Profit	Disc
13	Buy	200	40	$800	$200		
14	No-buy	800	80	$1,600	$800		
15	Total	1,000	120	$2,400	$1,000	$1,400	$1,157
16							
17	Period	2	Period	3			
18	State	Count	# Buyers	Contrib.	Mkt Cost	Profit	Disc
19	Buy	120	24	$480	$120		
20	No-buy	880	88	$1,760	$880		
21	Total	1,000	112	$2,240	$1,000	$1,240	$932

The block `D5:G9` can be copied downward after a few modifications. The previous period must be adjusted by setting cell `B11 = D5`. The number in the buy state (`B13`) equals the total number of buyers from the previous block (`C9`), and the number in the no-buy state (`B14`) equals `B9-C9`. After these modifications, block `A11:G15` can be copied downward, for example, to `A17:G21`, `A23:G27`, and so on. CLV is the sum of the discounted cash flows $\$2,727 + \$1,157 + \$932 + \ldots$ (Depending on the application, we might wish to deduct the cost of acquisition and add the contribution from the first purchase.) Try reproducing this spreadsheet.

The spreadsheet described above implements a probabilistic model that makes certain assumptions. The forecasts from the model are accurate to the extent that the assumptions are satisfied. When the assumptions are not satisfied, a more complicated model is necessary. An important assumption is that everyone in the buy state purchases in the next period with the same probability p_0 and everyone in the no-buy state purchase with probability p_1. This assumption is not reasonable because, as we will see, the probabilities depend on factors such as the customer's recency and frequency.

5.1.2 The recency model

The buy, no-buy model is the easiest migration model to understand, but it is often inadequate for modeling future behavior. One problem, called *customer heterogeneity*, is that not all those in a state will have the same probability of purchasing in the next period. When the purchase probabilities of customers within a state are heterogeneous, the buy, no-buy model might not give accurate predictions. This subsection and the next show how to allow the purchase probabilities to depend on observable customer characteristics such as *recency* and *frequency*.

Response probabilities often depend on customer characteristics that the firm can observe. One such characteristic is *recency*, which is the *number of periods since the customer most recently purchased*. The recency model defines states based on the customer's recency. Let p_r be the probability that a customer in recency state r purchases in the current period.

For example, suppose that that are three states. Figure 5.2 shows the state diagram. Customers who have just bought in the most recent period have a recency of 0 and will buy again in the next period with probability p_0; if not, they migrate into the $r = 1$ state indicating that they have been inactive for one period. Those in the $r = 1$ state who purchase migrate back to the $r = 0$ state with probability p_1. Those who do not purchase migrate to the $r \geq 2$ state with probability $1 - p_1$.

Figure 5.2 State diagram for the recency migration model

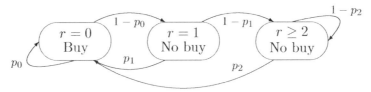

EXAMPLE 5.2: Recency spreadsheet example

Suppose that a firm has just acquired 1,000 customers who have just purchased and are therefore in the $r = 0$ state. Assume that the transition probabilities are as follows:

State	Probability of Purchase in Next Period
Recency = 0	$p_0 = .4$
Recency = 1	$p_1 = .2$
Recency $\geq$ 2	$p_2 = .1$

The firm spends $1 per customer each period on marketing and earns $20 from all buyers. The period discount rate is 10%. Create a spreadsheet to forecast buyer counts and revenues over the new periods.

Solution   The future behavior of these 1,000 customers can be forecast with a spreadsheet model as shown in Table 5.2. As of period 0 there are 1,000 customers in the $r = 0$ state. C7 shows that we expect $1,000 \times .2 = 200$ to purchase during period 1 making a contribution of $200 \times \$20 = \$4,000$ with a marketing cost of $1,000 \times \$1 = \$1,000$. We also need to program formulas to estimate the number of buyers in the $r = 1$ and $r \geq 2$ states. The number of buyers in the $r = 1$ state during period 1 equals the number starting in this state (cell B8) times the probability of a purchase (B2). Likewise, the number of buyers in the $r \geq 2$ state equals the number starting in that state (B9) times the probability of purchase (B3). Because there were no customers in these two states during period 0, the expected number of buyers equals 0 for these two states.

Table 5.2 Spreadsheet for the recency migration model

	A	B	C	D	E	F	G
1	$p_0 =$	0.4		$m =$	\$20		
2	$p_1 =$	0.2		$c =$	\$1		
3	$p_2 =$	0.1		$d =$	10%		
4							
5	Period	0	Period	1			
6	State	Count	# Buyers	Contrib.	Mkt Cost	Profit	Disc.
7	$r = 0$	1,000	400	\$8,000	\$1,000		
8	$r = 1$	0	0	\$0	\$0		
9	$r > 1$	0	0	\$0	\$0		
10	Total	1,000	400	\$8,000	\$1,000	\$7,000	\$6,364
11							
12	Period	1	Period	2			
13	State	Count	# Buyers	Contrib.	Mkt Cost	Profit	Disc.
14	$r = 0$	400	160	\$3,200	\$400		
15	$r = 1$	600	120	\$2,400	\$600		
16	$r \geq 2$	0	0	\$0	\$0		
17	Total	1,000	280	\$5,600	\$1,000	\$4,600	\$3,802

The next step is to set up a block within the spreadsheet (`A12:G17`) that describes what happens during period 1 and can be copied down for future periods. The state diagram in Figure 5.2 is helpful in setting up the formulas because it shows how customers enter and leave particular states. We begin with state $r = 0$, to which buyers from all states transition. The number of buyers at in $r = 0$ during period 1 (`B14`) is the sum of all buyers (`=C10`). Those in $r = 0$ who do not buy transition into the $r = 1$ state, and therefore the number in $r = 1$ during period 1 (`B15`) is the difference `B7 − C7 = 600`. The state diagram shows us that the $r \geq 2$ state receives customers who do not buy from the $r = 1$ and $r \geq 2$ states, so the count in `C16` equals `B8+B9-C8-C9`.

Of the 400 in the $r = 0$ state at the end of period 1 (cell `B14`), we expect $400 \times .4 = 160$ (cell `C14`) to purchase during period 2. Likewise, of the 600 in the $r = 1$ state at the end of period 1 (cell `B15`), we expect $600 \times .2 = 120$ (cell `C15`) to purchase during period 2. Thus, we expect $160 + 120 = 280$ total buyers during period 2 (cell `C17`). Profits are computed as in Table 5.1. In practice we usually want to have more than 3 recency states. The reader should now reproduce this spreadsheet from scratch.

5.1.3 The recency-frequency model

In addition to depending on recency, the probability of buying in the future period usually also depends on *frequency, the number of previous periods in which a customer has made a purchase,*[1] and our predictions will generally improve if we account for both. A state diagram for a recency-frequency model is shown in Figure 5.3 and is a little more complicated. Let p_{rf} be the probability that a customer with recency r and frequency f makes a purchase in the next period; we use the variable f for frequency despite the fact that we have also used f to denote a function in other chapters. A newly acquired customer begins in the $r = 0$, $f = 1$ state, and those who buy again in the next period transition to the $r = 0$, $f \geq 2$ state with the probability p_{01}. Otherwise they lapse into the $r = 1$, $f = 1$ state with probability $1 - p_{01}$. Recent, multi-time buyers ($r = 0$, $f \geq 2$) who buy again return to the same state with the probability p_{02}, otherwise they transition to the multi-time, one-period-lapsed state ($r = 1$, $f \geq 2$) with the probability $1 - p_{02}$.

Figure 5.3 State diagram for the recency-frequency migration model

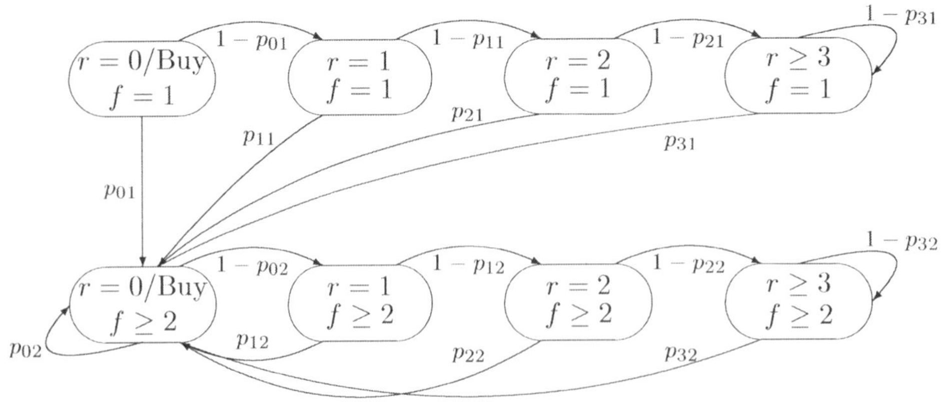

EXAMPLE 5.3: Recency-frequency spreadsheet example

A firm has just acquired 1,000 customers who are now in the $r = 0$, $f = 1$ state. The transition probabilities are given in cells `A1:E3` of the spreadsheet below. Marketing costs are \$1, the contribution is \$20 and the period discount rate is 1%. Create a spreadsheet.

Solution   The complete spreadsheet is provided in `migration.xls`. Our goal is to set up a block (`A17:G27`) representing the next period. This block is a little more complicated than the previous two examples, but the basic idea is the same. We first increment the period number: `B17 = B5+1`. The state diagram (Figure 5.3) is helpful in setting up the formulas for each of the cells. There are no arrows feeding into the $r = 0$, $f = 1$ state, so the count in the next period (`B19`) is fixed at 0; this cell count is determined by the acquisition efforts of an organization and a person determining acquisition budgets would try different numbers in this cell to understand the long-term consequences of the actions.

The next state ($r = 0, f > 1$) receives arrows from all other states, and so `B20 = C15`. The $r = 1$, $f = 1$ state receives only the non-buyers from the $r = 0$, $f = 1$ state, and so `B21 = B7 − C7`. Likewise, `B22 = B8 − C8`. This block can now be copied to forecast future periods.

5.2 Migration model: matrix approach

The spreadsheet approach requires setting up a block within a spreadsheet with formulas to describe the state diagram, which can then be copied for each additional period in the future. Although this process will produce the right answer, it can be cumbersome and error prone. For those who can remember a little bit about matrices, there is an equivalent way to forecast migration models into the future that is easier and enables us to find a closed-form expression for CLV in perpetuity. This section answers four questions:

1. What is the probability that a customer who is in the buy state, buys k periods later?

2. What is the expected profit for this customer k periods later?

3. What is the CLV for this customer?

4. What is the customer equity of a group of customers?

The answers to the first two questions are usually not of interest on their own, but we need to answer them in order to answer questions 3 and 4. This section uses an area of probability theory called *Markov chains*, which are covered in detail by many textbooks on

Table 5.3 Spreadsheet for the recency-frequency migration model

	A	B	C	D	E	F	G
1		$f = 1$	$f \geq 2$				
2	$r = 0$	0.2	0.4		$m =$	$20	
3	$r = 1$	0.1	0.2		$c =$	$1	
4	$r = 2$	0.05	0.1		$d =$	10%	
5	$r \geq 3$	0.02	0.05				
6							
7	Period	0	Period	1			
8	State	Count	Buyers	Contrib	Mkt Cost	Profit	Disc.
9	$r = 0, f = 1$	1,000	200	$4,000	$1,000		
10	$r = 0, f \geq 2$	0	0	$0	$0		
11	$r = 1, f = 1$	0	0	$0	$0		
12	$r = 1, f \geq 2$	0	0	$0	$0		
13	$r = 2, f = 1$	0	0	$0	$0		
14	$r = 2, f \geq 2$	0	0	$0	$0		
15	$r \geq 3, f = 1$	0	0	$0	$0		
16	$r \geq 3, f \geq 2$	0	0	$0	$0		
17	Total	1,000	200	$4,000	$1,000	$3,000	$2,727
18							
19	Period	0	Period	1			
20	State	Count	Buyers	Contrib	Mkt Cost	Profit	Disc.
21	$r = 0, f = 1$	0	0	$0	$0		
22	$r = 0, f \geq 2$	200	80	$1,600	$200		
23	$r = 1, f = 1$	800	80	$1,600	$800		
24	$r = 1, f \geq 2$	0	0	$0	$0		
25	$r = 2, f = 1$	0	0	$0	$0		
26	$r = 2, f \geq 2$	0	0	$0	$0		
27	$r \geq 3, f = 1$	0	0	$0	$0		
28	$r \geq 3, f \geq 2$	0	0	$0	$0		
29	Total	1,000	160	$3,200	$1,000	$2,200	$1,818

probability theory. DeGroot (1975, §2.3) gives an accessible introduction. Cox and Miller (1965, chapter 3) gives a thorough survey of the topic without using advanced mathematics. Pfeifer and Carraway (2000) introduce Markov chains for the purpose of computing CLV.

The answers to the four questions require us to define two vectors and a matrix. The first vector, $\mathbf{n}$, is called the *initial vector* and it gives the number of customers in each state at the beginning of the study. Let us return to the buy, no-buy migration model discussed in Example 5.1. There were 1,000 customers in the buy state and 0 customers in the no-buy state. Assuming the first state is the buy one and the second is the no-buy one, the initial vector for this example is

$$\mathbf{n} = \begin{pmatrix} 1000 \\ 0 \end{pmatrix} \quad \text{or} \quad \mathbf{n}' = (1000, 0).$$

The *transition matrix*, $\mathbf{P}$, consists of entries p_{ij} giving the probability that someone in state i at time t transitions to state j at time $t + 1$. Continuing the buy, no-buy example, those in the buy state buy again with probability .2, and those in the no-buy state buy again with probability .1. Therefore the transition matrix is

$$\mathbf{P} = \begin{pmatrix} .2 & .8 \\ .1 & .9 \end{pmatrix}.$$

Note that the rows of the transition matrix always sum to 1, that is, $\mathbf{P1} = \mathbf{1}$.

The *value vector*, $\mathbf{v}$, gives the value of transitioning into various states. The buy, no-buy model assumed that the period marketing costs were c, and the period contribution of buyers was m. Therefore, the value vector is

$$\mathbf{v} = \begin{pmatrix} m - c \\ -c \end{pmatrix}.$$

In the case of the example where $c = -1$ and $m = \$20$, $\mathbf{v}' = (19, -1)$.

Having defined the initial vector, transition matrix, and value vector, the questions at the beginning of the section can be easily answered. The answer to the first question, concerning the chance that someone who bought at time 0 buys at time t, comes from computing powers of the transition matrix. By definition, the transition matrix gives us the probability that someone in some state at time t buys during the next period. It turns out that row i and column j of the matrix $\mathbf{P}^k$ gives the probability that someone in state i at time t transitions to state j at time $t + k$. $\mathbf{P}^k$ is called the k-step transition matrix. The two-step transition matrix for the example is given by

$$\mathbf{P}^2 = \begin{pmatrix} .2 & .8 \\ .1 & .9 \end{pmatrix} \begin{pmatrix} .2 & .8 \\ .1 & .9 \end{pmatrix} = \begin{pmatrix} .12 & .88 \\ .11 & .89 \end{pmatrix}.$$

Someone in the buy state at time 0 has a 12% chance of buying at time 2, while someone in the no-buy state at time 0 has an 11% chance of buying two periods later.[2] Exercise 5.2 asks you to make a probability tree for this example. The three-step transition matrix is

$$\mathbf{P}^3 = \mathbf{P}^2\mathbf{P} = \begin{pmatrix} .12 & .88 \\ .11 & .89 \end{pmatrix} \begin{pmatrix} .2 & .8 \\ .1 & .9 \end{pmatrix} = \begin{pmatrix} .112 & .888 \\ .111 & .889 \end{pmatrix}$$

Someone in the buy state at time 0 has an 11.2% chance of buying at time 3. See Exercise 5.10 for a simple formula for finding $\mathbf{P}^k$ as a function of eigenvalues and eigenvectors of $\mathbf{P}$.

We can estimate future customer counts by combining $\mathbf{P}$ and $\mathbf{n}$. For example, if we start with 1,000 customers in the buy state and none in the no–buy state, then we expect the following number of customers in the next period:

$$\mathbf{n}'\mathbf{P} = \begin{pmatrix} 1,000 & 0 \end{pmatrix} \begin{pmatrix} .2 & .8 \\ .1 & .9 \end{pmatrix} = \begin{pmatrix} 200 & 800 \end{pmatrix},$$

which matches cells B13:B14 in Table 5.1. The matrix multiplication handles the fact that 20% of the 1,000 buy and 80% do not. Likewise, the customer counts for period 2 are given by $\mathbf{n}'\mathbf{P}^2 = (120, 880)$, matching cells B19:B20. It would now be instructive to copy the block in the spreadsheet to forecast counts in period 3 (hint: you already know the number of buyers is 112 from cell C21) and confirm the answer by computing $\mathbf{n}'\mathbf{P}^3$.

The second question concerned the expected value of a customer k periods in the future. The answer to this question is given by the vector $\mathbf{P}^2\mathbf{v}$. Let us return to the example where a buyer is worth \$19 and a non-buyer is worth $-\$1$. Consider a customer who has just bought. There is a 20% chance the customer will buy again in the next period generating \$19, and an 80% chance the customer will not buy again, generating $-\$1$. The expected profit in the next period is thus $0.2 \times 19 + 0.8 \times (-\$1) = \$3$. Someone who did not buy during the most recent period has an expected profit of \$1 in the next period. Multiplying these numbers by the customer counts, the profit in period 1 (cell F9) is $\mathbf{n}'\mathbf{P}^1\mathbf{v} = \$3,000$ (for you to confirm) and the discounted profit (cell G9) is $\mathbf{n}'\mathbf{P}^1\mathbf{v}/1.1^1 = \$2,727$. Likewise, the expected profit two periods from now is $\mathbf{P}^2\mathbf{v} = (\$1.40, \$1.2)'$. The expected profit in period 2 (cell F15) is $\mathbf{n}'\mathbf{P}^2\mathbf{v} = \$1,400$ (for you to confirm).

As we indicated earlier, the answers to the first two questions are not of much practical interest on their own, but they will enable us to answer the last two questions. The third question was about the CLV of a customer, which is now easy to compute by summing the discounted expected profits going forward:

$$\text{CLV} = \sum_{t=0}^{\infty} \frac{\mathbf{P}^t \mathbf{v}}{(1+d)^t},$$

assuming a discount rate d and $\mathbf{P}^0 = \mathbf{I}$. The fourth question is about the customer equity of a group of customers and is equal to

$$\text{CE} = \sum_{t=0}^{\infty} \frac{\mathbf{n}'\mathbf{P}^t \mathbf{v}}{(1+d)^t} = \mathbf{n}' \left[\sum_{t=0}^{\infty} \left(\frac{\mathbf{P}}{1+d} \right)^t \right] \mathbf{v}.$$

The expressions for CLV and CE both involve infinite sums and we will now find a closed-form expression for the sum by following an approach similar to the one we used to derive the SRM in Chapter 3. Let $\mathbf{A} = \mathbf{P}/(1+d)$ and consider the finite sum:

$$\mathbf{S}_t = \mathbf{I} + \mathbf{A} + \mathbf{A}^2 + \cdots + \mathbf{A}^{t-1}.$$

Post multiply both sides by A to obtain

$$\mathbf{S}_t \mathbf{A} = \mathbf{A} + \mathbf{A}^2 + \cdots + \mathbf{A}^t.$$

Subtract the second from the first

$$\mathbf{S}_t - \mathbf{S}_t \mathbf{A} = \mathbf{I} - \mathbf{A}^t$$

and solve for $\mathbf{S}_t$:

$$\mathbf{S}_t = (\mathbf{I} - \mathbf{A}^t)(\mathbf{I} - \mathbf{A})^{-1}.$$

If $\lim_{t\to\infty} \mathbf{A}^t = \mathbf{0}$, then $\lim_{t\to\infty} \mathbf{S}^t = (\mathbf{I} - \mathbf{A})^{-1}$. Note that $\mathbf{A}^t$ approaches 0 as t goes to infinity when $d > 0$, since all of the entries of $\mathbf{P}$ are less than 1. This expression, which does not involve infinite sums, can be substituted into the expressions for CE and CLV. We can now state closed-form expressions for CLV and CE:

$$\text{CLV} = \left(\mathbf{I} - \frac{\mathbf{P}}{1+d} \right)^{-1} \mathbf{v} \quad \text{and} \quad \text{CE} = \mathbf{n}' \left(\mathbf{I} - \frac{\mathbf{P}}{1+d} \right)^{-1} \mathbf{v}. \tag{5.1}$$

It is easy to compute these matrix products using SAS/IML (*interactive matrix language*) as shown in the program below.

EXAMPLE 5.4:   Buy, no-buy matrix example
Repeat Example 5.1. Also find CLV and CE.

Solution   The program below gives the SAS/IML code. The first three lines define the **v**, **n**, and **P** matrices. The rows of a matrix are separated by commas and the columns by white space. Thus v = {19, -1} specifies a 2×1 matrix (column vector), as shown in the output below with the `PRINT` command.

The * operator performs matrix multiplication, and therefore the line P2 = P*P multiplies the transition matrix by itself, giving the two-step transition matrix $\mathbf{P}^2$. Likewise, multiplying P2*P gives the three-step transition matrix $\mathbf{P}^3$. It is easy to evaluate equation 5.1 with SAS/IML. The `INV()` function inverts a matrix, `I(2)` specifies a 2×2 identity matrix, and n with a backquote (n') denotes **n** transpose. A customer who is currently in the buy state has a CLV of \$33 and a customer in the no-buy state has a CLV of \$11. Because we begin with 1,000 customers in the buy state, CE = $1,000 \times \$33 = \$33,000$, as computed by `ce`.

The reader should now write an SAS/IML program for Example 5.2 (see Exercise 5.3 in the supplementary exercises on the SAS web site for detailed instructions).

```
PROC IML;
v = {19, -1};
n = {1000, 0};
P = {0.2 0.8,
     0.1 0.9};
P2 = P*P;
P3 = P2*P;
clv = INV(I(2) - P/1.1) * v;
ce = n' * clv;
PRINT v n P P2, P3 clv ce;
```

v	n	P		P2	
19	1,000	0.2	0.8	0.12	0.88
−1	0	0.1	0.9	0.11	0.89

P3		clv	ce
0.112	0.88	33	330,008
0.111	0.889	11	

5.3   Estimating transition probabilities

The examples discussed above assumed that transition probabilities are known, but in practice they must be estimated from transaction histories. The goal of this section is to show how to start from a transaction history and estimate these probabilities.

EXAMPLE 5.5:   DMEF contest example

Use the data from the DMEF customer lifetime value modeling competition (Malthouse, 2009) to estimate transition probabilities for a recency-only model with a period length of a year. The transactions range from January 1, 2002 through August 31, 2006. Suppose that today is September 1, 2005 and there will be four one-year recency states. Complete Task 1 of the contest, estimating customer equity (total donation amount, not discounted) of the 21,166 customers between September 1, 2006 and August 31, 2008.

Solution   Companies and nonprofit organizations maintain transaction "tables" such as the one in `trans.sas7bdat`. The first few records are shown in Table 5.4. Every row represents a transaction. For example, ID 8128357 has made only one donation, which was for $5 on February 22, 2002. ID 9652546 has made 5 donations starting on April 2, 2002.

Table 5.4 Example rows from the transaction table and the rolled-up table for the DMEF customer lifetime value contest data

Transaction Table				Rolled-Up Table		
ID	**GiftDate**	**Amount**		**ID**	**Recency**	**Targbuy**
8128357	22FEB2002	$5		8128357	3	0
9430679	10JAN2002	$50		9430679	3	0
9455908	19APR2002	$25		9455908	3	0
9652546	02APR2002	$100		9652546	1	0
9652546	06JAN2003	$100		9791641	1	1
9652546	05JAN2004	$100				
9652546	28DEC2004	$50				
9652546	27DEC2005	$100				
9791641	17JAN2002	$50				
9791641	16DEC2002	$50				
9791641	15OCT2003	$25				
9791641	04MAR2004	$50				
9791641	13FEB2006	$100				

We would like to compute each customer's recency as of today and whether the customer donated during the next year. The rolled-up table to the right of the transaction table shows what we would like to produce. Because ID 8128357 donated on February 22, 2002, which is more than three years prior to today (September 1, 2005), this person is in recency state 3. This person did not make any donations during the target period (September 1, 2005–August 30, 2006) and consequently `targbuy = 0`.

Now consider ID 9791641. This person made a donation on February 13, 2006, which is during the target period, and therefore `targbuy=1`. The most recent donation before today was on March 4, 2004, which is between one and two years before today, so this person is assigned to recency state 1. The SAS code to accomplish the same task is as follows:

Program 5.1 CLV modeling contest rollup

```
DATA rollup;
  SET contest.trans;
  BY id;
  LENGTH targbuy targdol recency freq 4;
  RETAIN targbuy targdol recency freq;
  IF FIRST.id THEN DO;
    targbuy=0;
    targdol=0;
    freq=0;
    recency=9999;
  END;
  diff = ("31AUG2005"d - giftdate)/365.25;
  IF diff < 0 THEN DO;
    targbuy = 1;
    targdol=SUM(amt, targdol);
  END;
  ELSE DO; /* base period */
    IF diff<recency THEN recency=diff;
    freq = freq + 1;
  END;
  IF LAST.id THEN OUTPUT;
  KEEP id targbuy targdol recency freq;
RUN;
```

The output from the crosstab is below. There is a 56.9% probability that someone who is currently in recency state 0 buys in the next period. There is a 24.5% probability that someone in the one-year-lapsed state buys in the next period. These probabilities estimate the transition matrix **P**.

```
PROC FORMAT;
  VALUE recbin
    0 - <1 = "r<1 yr"
    1 - <2 = "1<=r<2"
    2 - <3 = "2<=r<3"
    3 - HIGH = "r>=3";
RUN;


PROC FREQ DATA=rollup;
  TABLE recency * targbuy / NOCOL NOPERCENT;
  FORMAT recency recbin.;
RUN;


PROC MEANS DATA=rollup MAXDEC=2;
  VAR targdol;
  WHERE targbuy=1;
RUN;
```

Table of recency by targbuy			
recency	targbuy		
Frequency	0	1	Total
r<1 yr	1993	2630	4623
	43.11	56.89	
1≤r<2	1917	624	2541
	75.44	24.56	
2≤r<3	2291	247	2538
	90.27	9.73	
r≥3	11080	384	11464
	96.65	3.35	
Total	17281	3885	21166

Analysis Variable : targdol				
N	Mean	Std Dev	Min	Max
3885	69.06	199.96	1.00	5000.00

We could have used `IF-THEN` statements to define a new variable giving the recency bin instead of using `PROC FORMAT`. There are several advantages to the `PROC FORMAT` approach.

First, defining a new variable would require taking an additional pass through the data, which would waste computational resources. Second, the resulting data set is smaller because it has one less variable. Also, if we decide to change the bins, we would have to take yet another pass through the data set to modify the bins, but with `PROC FORMAT` we avoid the extra pass.

Running `PROC MEANS` on `targdol` for all of those who are active in the future period (`WHERE targbuy=1`) estimates the value of $m = \$69.06$. Customers who make at least one donation during the target year donate an average of about $69. So the value vector is $\mathbf{v} = (69.06, 0, 0, 0)'$.

To complete Task 1 where we estimate customer equity from September 1, 2006 through August 31, 2008, we must also know the initial vector $\mathbf{n}$. We can find it by changing `31AUG2005` to `31AUG2006` in Program 5.1 and re-running it. Doing so gives us the initial vector $\mathbf{n} = (3886, 1992, 1917, 13371)'$. We can now complete Task 1 with the following estimate $\mathbf{n}'\mathbf{P}\mathbf{v} + \mathbf{n}'\mathbf{P}^2\mathbf{v}$. The first term estimates the value during the first year, and the second term estimates the value during the second year. We can compute this using `PROC IML` as in the program below. The answer is $433,703.

```
PROC IML;
n = {3886, 1992, 1917, 13371};
v = {69.0615341, 0, 0 ,0};
P = { .5689   .4311 0 0,
      .2456  0 .7544 0,
      .0973  0 0 .9027,
      .0335  0 0 .9665};
pred = (n` * P * v) + (n` * P * P * v);
PRINT pred;
```

pred
433702.82

Figure 5.4 Histogram of entries to the first task of the CLV contest, with the estimates from the recency model superimposed

```
PROC SGPLOT DATA=contest NOAUTOLEGEND;
  HISTOGRAM x / BINWIDTH=.1;
  REFLINE .5059 / AXIS=x LABEL="Correct";
  REFLINE .4337 / AXIS=x LABEL="Rec Model";
  REFLINE .5474 / AXIS=x LABEL="Data Mine";
  XAXIS LABEL="CE Estimate (Millions)";
RUN;
```

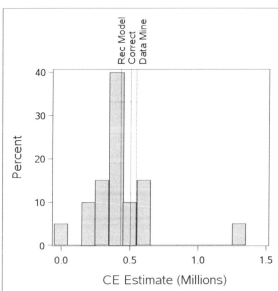

The estimate is compared with other entries from the contest in the histogram shown in Figure 5.4 (this was Figure 2 in Malthouse, 2009). The other number indicated on the plot comes from Example 6.5, where we revisit this example using a data-mining model. A total

of 24 teams ultimately submitted entries to the contest. Participants came from universities around the world, consulting firms, and research units of leading companies. They used a diverse set of methodologies. The estimate using a simple four-state recency migration model is in the same ballpark as the top entries. Could the estimate be improved by using, for example, states defined by both recency and frequency?

EXAMPLE 5.6: Recency-frequency spreadsheet example

This example shows how to compute transition probabilities for a recency-frequency model using a spreadsheet. Table 5.5 gives customer counts from a nonprofit organization. In this example, we will have a total of $3 \times 2 = 6$ states, with all combinations of 3 recency bins and 2 frequency bins. Construct a spreadsheet that can be used to forecast the customer database into the future.

Solution First consider the block A3:F11, which contains the given information and computes some other ratios. The given information includes the customer counts at the end of period 0 (B5:B10), the number who bought in period 1 (C5:C10), and the amount of all donations from each segment (E5:E10). The buy rates (D5:D10) and average donation amounts (F5:F10) are computed. The Buy Rate column is the ratio of buyers to customers, for example, D5=C5/B5. The Average Donation Amount column is the ratio of Total Donations to Buyers, for example, F5=E5/C5. The totals in row 11 are computed. For example, B11 is the sum of B5:B10 and likewise for C11 and E11. Finally, the next period is always 1 plus the current period, D3=1+B3.

Table 5.5 Spreadsheet for the recency-frequency migration model

	A	B	C	D	E	F
1	Acquisitions	0				
2						
3	Period	0	Period	1	Total	Avg Don
4	State	Count	Buyers	Buy Rate	Donations	Amount
5	$r=0, f=1$	94,542	31,520	33.3%	$1,122,896	$35.62
6	$r=0, f \geq 2$	115,994	66,145	57.0%	$2,929,523	$44.29
7	$r=1, f=1$	58,124	8,370	14.4%	$293,787	$35.10
8	$r=1, f \geq 2$	34,982	10,796	30.9%	$382,805	$35.46
9	$r \geq 2, f=1$	161,632	7,284	4.5%	$277,651	$38.12
10	$r \geq 2, f \geq 2$	24,229	3,213	13.3%	$117,971	$36.72
11	Total	489,503	127,328		$5,124,632	$40.25
12						
13	Period	1	Period	2	Total	Avg Don
14	State	Count	Buyers	Buy Rate	Donations	Amount
15	$r=0, f=1$	0	0	33.3%	$0	$35.62
16	$r=0, f \geq 2$	127,328	72,608	57.0%	$3,215,773	$44.29
17	$r=1, f=1$	63,022	9,075	14.4%	$318,544	$35.10
18	$r=1, f \geq 2$	49,849	15,384	30.9%	$545,493	$35.46
19	$r \geq 2, f=1$	204,102	9,198	4.5%	$350,605	$38.12
20	$r \geq 2, f \geq 2$	45,202	5,994	13.3%	$220,088	$36.72
21	Total	489,503	112,260		$4,650,503	$41.43

We now need to create the block B13:B21 that can be copied to make our future projections. The block B15:B20 gives customer counts as of the end of period 1, and the block C15:F20 describes their activities in period 2. We begin by setting B13=D3, that is, the next period in the previous block is the current period in this block.

The Count column comes from the state diagram. The number of $r=0, f=1$ equals the number of acquisitions, which is a parameter specified in B1, so B15=B$1. This is the number of acquisitions in every year after year 0, and we must make an additional adjustment. All new acquisitions make a donation and the number of acquisitions times the average donation amount for new donors must be added to the total in E11.

The number of $r = 0, f \geq 2$ customers is the total number of buyers in period 1, so B16=C11. Customers in the $r = 1, f = 1$ state in period 1 were in the $r = 0, f = 1$ state in period 0 and did not buy, and therefore B17 = B5-C5 (likewise for those in $r = 1, f \geq 2$). Customers in the $r \geq 2, f = 1$ state were either in $r = 1, f = 1$ or $r \geq 2, f = 1$ in period 0 and did not buy, and therefore B19 = B7-C7+B9-C9 (likewise for $r \geq 2, f \geq 2$).

We will hold the buy rates constant by setting D15:D20 = D5:D10. The buy rates can be thought of as parameters of the model. The number of buyers is then the customer count multiplied by the buy rate (for example, C15 = B15*D15).

Similarly, we hold the average donation amount constant, setting F15:F20 = F5:F10. The total donations equal the number of buyers multiplied by the average donation amount (for example, E15 = F15*C15). The sums in row 21 are the same as those in row 11. This block can now be copied. As we have done in the other spreadsheet examples in this chapter, one might want to deduct the cost of marketing, compute profits, and sum the discounted profits for several years into the future (Exercise 5.6).

Having set up the spreadsheet, we can now perform what-if analyses by modifying the parameters of this model. There are three sets of parameters, the number of acquired customers per year (B1), the buy rates (D5:D10) and the average donation amounts (F5:F10). If, for example, we decide to invest more in retaining our $r = 0, f \geq 2$ customer segment, then the buy rate should increase from 57%. We could run tests to determine that by increasing the number of solicitations to this group by two per year that their buy rate over the year increases from 57% to 60%. By entering 60% in D6, we can assess the effect on revenues in the future. We could compare this with alternative marketing actions, such as sending more contact points to recently lapsed segments ($r = 1$ and $f = 1$ or $f \geq 2$) or acquiring more customers.

The average donation amounts enable us to model the effect of cross-selling and up-selling. Such terms are more natural in the case of a company selling goods. If a firm cross-sells other product lines or up-sells to more expensive versions, then the average amounts increase. Similarly, a nonprofit could create contact points to increase the amount of a donation, as opposed to increasing the frequency of donations.

EXAMPLE 5.7: Leaky bucket problem

Use the spreadsheet from Example 5.6 to project the number of buyers and total donations for the next five years. Also, forecast buyers and donations if the organization acquires 38,000 new customers each year (periods 2 6).

Solution   We copy the block B13:B21 several times and summarize the results in Table 5.6 below. (Readers should confirm these numbers in their own spreadsheet or SAS/IML program.) Actual amounts are available for years (periods) 2 and 3. The recency-frequency model overestimates the number buyers, but underestimates the total donations.

Table 5.6 Predicted buyers and donations for Example 5.7

Year	Number Donors Predicted	Number Donors Actual	Total Donations Predicted	Total Donations Actual	38K Acquisitions/Yr Buyers	38K Acquisitions/Yr Donations
1	127,328	127,328	$5,124,632	$5,124,632		
2	112,260	108,189	$4,650,503	$4,728,080	124,929	$5,101,838
3	101,887	91,323	$4,220,194	$4,273,465	125,429	$5,119,531
4	97,190		$4,004,737		129,588	$5,275,487
5	95,287		$3,915,644		135,611	$5,515,118
6	94,994		$3,896,816		142,764	$5,803,691

What happens to these customers during the next period? Notice that the number of active customers and the total donations decrease over time. The file is said to shrink. Customers tend to migrate into states with higher recency, which also have a smaller probability of purchasing again. The longer a customer has been inactive, the harder it is to reactive the customer. Wunderman (1996, pp. 75–76) described this as the "leaky bucket problem." A customer database is like a bucket with a hole in the bottom and customers are like the water that is in the bucket. Over time, the water will leak out and eventually the bucket will be empty unless the organization adds additional water to the bucket by acquiring new customers.

The last two columns show the effect of adding water to the bucket by acquiring 38,000 new customers each year. The number buyers and total donations increase over time. This simple spreadsheet can be a powerful planning tool for determining the long-term strategies of an organization. For example, an organization that has a goal of growing will likely have to invest more resources in some combination of acquiring new customers and retaining existing ones. This spreadsheet can assist in such strategic planning efforts.

5.3.1   The law of geometric decay and frequency learning curves

The crosstab approach of estimating transition probabilities discussed in the previous section is nonparametric in that it imposes no structure on the data. The transition probability of each state is estimated independently of all other transition probabilities. A potential problem is sampling variation. When the sample sizes are small, individual estimates can be unstable. It is desirable to have a smooth curve relating recency and frequency to the probability of being active in the next time period. Malthouse and Raman (2013) propose and validate such a model across many different nonprofit organizations and retailers. They argue the following:

- *Geometric law of decay*: the probability of buying in a future period decays geometrically with recency.

- *Frequency learning curves*: the probability of a customer with recency 0 buying in the future period follows an exponential learning curve.

We begin by explaining the law of geometric decay. Let π_r be the probability that a customer with recency $r \geq 0$ years is active in some pre-specified *future* window of time such as the next period. This means that the most recent transaction occurred r years ago. The *law of geometric decay* posits that

$$\pi_r = \pi_0 \kappa^r = \pi_0 e^{\mu r}, \tag{5.2}$$

where the *initial probability* parameter $\pi_0 \in (0, 1)$ gives the probability that a customer with recency $r = 0$ buys in the future window. Some customers will be better than others and π_0 characterizes this initial level. The *decay constant* $\kappa > 0$ describes how quickly the probability of future activity decays as recency increases. It will often be convenient to re-parameterize this model with $\mu = \log \kappa$, so that $\kappa = e^\mu$. Taking logs of both sides of equation 5.2, we see that the log probability of future activity is a linear combination of recency:

$$\log(\pi_r) = \log(\pi_0) + r \log \kappa = \alpha + \mu r \tag{5.3}$$

This equation is an elegant and powerful predictor of future customer activity. Suppose, for example, that some customer who just made a purchase (and thus has recency $r = 0$) has a probability of $\pi_0 = .6$ of purchasing again within a year and that the decay constant is $\kappa = .5$, so that the probability of a future purchase is cut in half for every additional year the customer is inactive. If the customer remains inactive for one year, the probability of a purchase within the next year is reduced to .3; if the customer is inactive for two years then the probability of reactivating is only .15, and so on. Thus, it becomes substantially more difficult to reactivate customers the longer they have been inactive.

We now bring frequency (f) into the model by allowing it to affect the initial probability π_0. Figure 5.5 shows initial probability estimates for a nonprofit organization for customers

Figure 5.5 WLS estimates of initial probabilities plotted against frequency for organization 3, with an exponential learning-curve model superimposed (Malthouse and Raman, 2013, Figure 3)

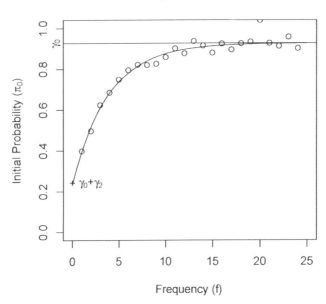

having different frequency values. For each value of frequency there were at least 100 observations. The scatter plot shows a clear pattern: the initial probability—the chance of activity in the future window for a donor with recency 0—increases steadily with frequency, but there are diminishing returns and π_0 seems to approach an asymptote. Because π_0 is a probability, it cannot exceed 1, which give an upper bound for the asymptote.

A reasonable model for a relationship of this form is the three-parameter exponential learning curve model (Neter et al., 1996, equation 13.9 and §13.5):

$$\pi_0(f) = \gamma_0 + \gamma_2 e^{-\gamma_1 f}, \quad f \geq 0, \gamma_1 > 0. \tag{5.4}$$

Parameter γ_0 specifies the asymptote because $\lim_{f \to \infty} \pi_0(f) = \gamma_0$. The y-intercept is $\pi_0(0) = \gamma_0 + \gamma_2$, and therefore γ_2 gives the distance between the y-intercept and the asymptote. The other parameter, γ_1, characterizes the steepness of the function, where large values indicate the function approaches the asymptote quickly and smaller values indicate a more gradual approach. This model has been used extensively for modeling learning curves and memory.

Nonlinear least squares was used to estimate the parameters in Figure 5.5. The asymptote is estimated as $\hat{\gamma}_0 = 0.927$, and $\hat{\gamma}_2 = -0.691$ indicates that the y-intercept is $0.927 - 0.691 = 0.236$. The steepness coefficient is $\hat{\gamma}_1 = 0.259$. The model seems to fit well, with the curve passing through the middle of the data.

Extending the model in equation 5.2 by allowing π_0 to be a function of frequency (x), we propose the following elegant four-parameter model for the probability of activity in the future window:

$$\pi_{rf} = \pi_0(f)\kappa^t = (\gamma_0 + \gamma_2 e^{-\gamma_1 f})\kappa^r. \tag{5.5}$$

The log likelihood is given by

$$l = \log L(\gamma_0, \gamma_1, \gamma_2, \kappa)$$

$$= \sum_{i=1}^{n} \{ y_i \log[\pi_0(f_i)\kappa^{r_i}] + (1 - y_i) \log[1 - \pi_0(f_i)\kappa^{r_i}] \}$$

$$= \sum_{i=1}^{n} \{ y_i \log[(\gamma_0 + \gamma_2 e^{-\gamma_1 f_i})\kappa^{r_i}] + (1 - y_i) \log[1 - (\gamma_0 + \gamma_2 e^{-\gamma_1 f_i})\kappa^{r_i}] \}$$

Figure 5.6 MLE estimates of the four parameters of the geometric-decay learning-curve model across 36 nonprofits and retailers (Malthouse and Raman, 2013, Figure 4)

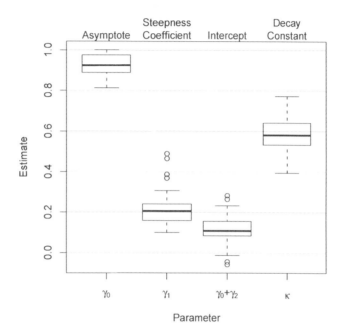

Malthouse and Raman (2013) estimate this model across six nonprofits and 30 retailers. The resulting parameter estimates are displayed in Figure 5.6. The decay constants have a median between .5 and .6. A conservative rule of thumb is that the probability of a customer being active in the future is reduced by half for every additional year that a customer is inactive. This is called the *law of annual halving*. Some organizations have decay constants in the .7s, whereas others are only in the .4s. An organization in the .4 range should investigate why its retention efforts are relatively less effective. Do they have problems with the creative execution, nature of the offer, frequency of contacts, message distribution channels, or something else (for example, corporate image)?

The steepness coefficient indicates how quickly the initial probabilities increase with purchase frequency. Larger values indicate that the initial probabilities increase more rapidly with frequency, and that the organization is doing a better job of increasing customers' behavioral loyalty (although not necessarily affective loyalty). There is substantial variation across organizations with outliers, and some are more adept at locking in a customer than others.

The asymptote and intercept give the maximum and minimum initial probabilities, respectively. Again, there is variation across organizations. Some organizations achieve a near-100% initial probability as frequency goes to infinity, whereas others only achieve an 80% initial probability.

EXAMPLE 5.8: Geometric-decay, learning-curve model estimates for CLV contest data
We now illustrate how to find the MLEs for the CLV contest data by using `PROC IML`. The program is very similar to Program 4.14, which found MLEs for the beta-geometric

distribution.

As we explained in the discussion of Program 4.14, we must do three things before calling the nonlinear optimization function `NLPNRA`: read the data, define the ML function to be optimized, and set up the optimization parameters. In contrast to the previous SAS/IML programs, where the data values were entered directly in the program, here we read data from the `rollup` data set, which was created above in Program 5.1. The `USE` command opens the data set and the `READ` command copies three columns into the matrix x. The starting values are selected based on the box plots in Figure 5.6. Each value was selected to be in the boxes.

Program 5.2 MLEs for geometric-day, learning-curve model of CLV contest data

```
PROC IML;
USE rollup VAR {recency freq targbuy};
READ ALL VAR {recency freq targbuy} INTO x;

START loglik(theta) GLOBAL(x);
  /* theta[1]=k, decay constant;  theta[2]=g0, asymptote */
  /* theta[3]=g1, steepness coef; theta[4]=g2, where g0+g2=intercept */
  pi0 = theta[2]+theta[4]*exp(-theta[3]*x[,2]);
  ll = 0;
  DO i = 1 TO NROW(x);
    ll = ll + x[i,3]*LOG(pi0[i]*theta[1]**x[i,1]) +
      (1-x[i,3])*LOG(1-pi0[i]*theta[1]**x[i,1]);
  END;
  RETURN(ll);
FINISH;


theta0 = {.5 .9 .2 -.9}; /* starting values */
con = {0 0 . .,   /* lower bounds */
       1 1 . .}; /* upper bounds */
opt = {1, 4};    /* find maximum and give lots of output */
CALL NLPNRA(rc, result, "loglik", theta0, opt, con);
```

The output is shown below. SAS gives us the message `GCONV convergence criterion satisfied` indicating that the optimization was successful. If you do not get this message, you should make sure that your objective function is defined correctly, and you might want to try some different starting values. The first parameter estimates the decay constant, $\hat{\kappa} = .54$. For every additional year a customer is inactive, the probability of being active in the future window is cut approximately in half.

Optimization Results			
Parameter Estimates			
N	Parameter	Estimate	Gradient Objective Function
1	X1	0.538803	−0.030303
2	X2	0.928941	−0.026263
3	X3	0.486594	0.020077
4	X4	−1.067428	−0.019839

Value of Objective Function = −6955.741289

The second parameter estimates the asymptote, $\hat{\gamma}_0 = .93$. The initial probability, that is, with recency zero, approaches .93 as frequency becomes large. The third parameter estimates the steepness coefficient, $\hat{\gamma}_1 = .49$. This value is large relative to others in Figure 5.6, suggesting that this organization does a better job of retaining its donors than most. The sum of the second and fourth parameters, $0.93 - 1.07 = -0.14$, gives the intercept, or the probability, of a person with frequency zero buying. We are extrapolating because we do not have any people in the sample with frequency zero, which explains the negative value.

The estimated curves can be plotted as follows. Figure 5.7 shows the probability of buying in the future period for different values of frequency as a function of recency. Figure 5.8 shows only the exponential learning curve, giving the initial probabilities (recency of zero) as a function of frequency. The points on this graph match the points for recency = 0 in the left panel. The asymptote is shown at .93.

Figure 5.7 Estimated geometric-decay model for CLV contest

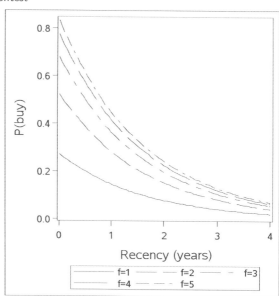

```
DATA graph;
   ARRAY y{1:5} y1-y5;
   DO r = 0 TO 4 BY .05;
     DO f= 1 to 5;
       y{f} = (0.928954 -1.067426 *
         exp(-0.486568*f))*0.538804**r;
     END;
     OUTPUT;
   END;
   LABEL y1="f=1"    y2="f=2"
     y3="f=3"    y4="f=4"    y5="f=5";
RUN;
PROC SGPLOT DATA=graph;
   SERIES X=r Y=y1;      SERIES X=r Y=y2;
   SERIES X=r Y=y3;      SERIES X=r Y=y4;
   SERIES X=r Y=y5;
   XAXIS LABEL="Recency (years)";
   YAXIS LABEL="P(buy)";
RUN;
```

Figure 5.8 Estimated exponential-learning model for CLV contest

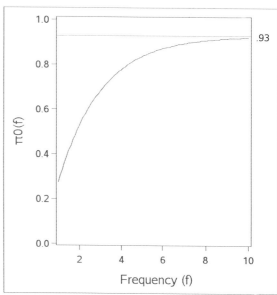

```
DATA graph2;
   DO f = 1 TO 10 BY .1;
     y = 0.928954 -1.067426*exp(-0.486568*f);
     OUTPUT;
   END;
RUN;
PROC SGPLOT DATA=graph2;
   SERIES X=f Y=y;
   REFLINE .928954 / LABEL='.93';
   XAXIS LABEL="Frequency (f)";
   YAXIS LABEL="^{unicode 03C0}0(f)"
     MIN=0 MAX=1;
RUN;
```

5.4 Chapter summary

The migration model is used to estimate CLV when customer inactivity during a period of time does not necessarily indicate that the customer will never buy again. This situation is common with retail, travel, and nonprofits, where a customer may not buy during some month, and then purchase in subsequent months. The model can also be used to account for customer *reactivation* in a retention setting, for example, a cell phone provider that has contractual relationships with its customers (retention situation) may reacquire customer who have previously canceled their contracts.

During each discrete time period, customers are in one of several segments, which are called *states* in the context of the migration model and are defined based on recency, frequency, and possibly other variables. Customers *transition* between states over time with certain *transition probabilities*. For example, a customer in the state defined by being a one-year-lapsed (recency=1), one-time buyer (frequency=1) who then purchases and transitions into a different state defined by being an active (recency ≈ 0), multi-time (frequency ≥ 2) buyer. The migration models discussed here assume that transition probabilities depend only on the state a customer is currently in.

We discuss two equivalent approaches for implementing the migration model. The *spreadsheet approach* involves setting up a block of cells in a spreadsheet program showing how customers migrate between states. This block is then copied one time for each future period. The *matrix approach* uses matrix arithmetic to implement the same model. An advantage of the matrix approach is that we can derive closed-form expressions that evaluate future cash flows in perpetuity. The model, implemented with either approach, enables decision makers to forecast important quantities such as the number of active customers and the revenues or profits the organization will have in the future as a function of the parameters, transition probabilities, number of acquired customers, and the expected spend or profit per active customer, possibly by state. These parameters can be modified to help us understand the effects of different marketing actions. For example, cross-selling and up-selling efforts typically increase the amount spent per time period while other efforts are designed to increase the chance (transition probability) that a customer will activate during some time period. The model is therefore useful to managers who must balance the allocation of resources across acquisition and retention efforts. The key results for the matrix approach are as follows. *Initial vector* $\mathbf{n}$ gives the number of customers in each state at time $t = 0$. The *transition matrix* $\mathbf{P}$ has entries p_{ij}, which specifies the probability that a customer in state i transitions to state j in the next time period. The *value vector* $\mathbf{v}$ gives the value realized by having a customer in each of the states. The *k-step transition matrix* is $\mathbf{P}^k$, where row i and column j gives the probability that a customer in state i at time 0 transitions after k periods in the future to state j. The expected number of customers at time t is $\mathbf{n}'\mathbf{P}^t$. The expected value of customers realized t periods from now is $\mathbf{P}^t\mathbf{v}$. The expected CLV and CE values are as follows:

$$\text{CLV} = \sum_{t=0}^{\infty} \frac{\mathbf{P}^t\mathbf{v}}{(1+d)^t} = \left(\mathbf{I} - \frac{\mathbf{P}}{1+d}\right)^{-1}\mathbf{v}$$

$$\text{CE} = \sum_{t=0}^{\infty} \frac{\mathbf{n}'\mathbf{P}^t\mathbf{v}}{(1+d)^t} = \mathbf{n}'\left(\mathbf{I} - \frac{\mathbf{P}}{1+d}\right)^{-1}\mathbf{v}.$$

Transition probabilities can be estimated with a crosstab of state membership in two successive time periods. A `DATA` step with the `RETAIN` statement is is a good way to prepare the data set for such a crosstab. We also discuss a parametric model relating the probability of being active in the next period as a function of recency and frequency. The *law of geometric decay* states that the probability that a customer with recency r years is active in the next period decays geometrically with r: $\pi_r = \pi_0 \kappa^r$, where π_0 is the *initial probability* that someone with recency 0 activates in the next period, and κ is the *decay constant* modeling how quickly the probability of activity decays. Across many retailing and nonprofit organizations a conservative rule of thumb is that $\kappa \approx .5$, indicating that the chance of future activity is cut in half for each additional year of inactivity. The initial probabilities follow an exponential learning curve as a function of frequency f: $\pi_0(f) = \gamma_0 + \gamma_2 e^{-\gamma_1 f}$. Combining the formulas, the probability that someone with recency r and frequency f is active in the next period is

$$\pi_{rf} = \pi_0(f) \kappa^t = (\gamma_0 + \gamma_2 e^{-\gamma_1 f}) \kappa^r.$$

Notes

[1] In other contexts, frequency is more commonly defined as the *number of previous purchases*. Migration models are simpler if we define frequency as the number of previous periods in which a customer has purchased, because then a one-time buyer can only lapse or transition to being a two-time buyer. The other definition is more complicated because one-time buyers could also transition to being three- or four-time buyers if they make more than one purchase during a period. These additional possible transitions complicate the model by adding many parameters. It is not clear whether the forecasts are more or less accurate with one model or the other.

[2] These computations can be confirmed using elementary probability theory. For example, consider someone who buys at time 0. There are two ways that this customer can return to the buy state at time 2: either the customer buys at time 1 and then buys again at time 2, or the customer does not buy at time 1 and buys at time 2. Let B_t be the event that someone buys at time t. Then $P(B_2|B_0) = P(B_2|B_1)P(B_1|B_0) + P(B_2|\bar{B}_1)P(\bar{B}_1|B_0) = .2 \times .2 + .1 \times .8 = .12$, which is exactly the computation done by the matrix multiplication.

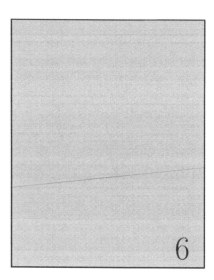

Data-Mining Approaches to Lifetime Value

6

Contents

In Chapters 3–5 we discussed *probabilistic models* for CLV. Each chapter began with a set of assumptions. For example, customers join and generate some fixed cash flow until they cancel and never return; the chance that a customer cancels is constant over time and customers; the event that a customer is retained in one period is independent of the event in other time periods. Based on such assumptions, we could derive an expected CLV. The point is that these models begin with a set of assumptions that characterize the relationship between the customer and the organization.

This chapter explores an alternative data-mining approach that begins with data rather than assumptions about the customer relationship. The value of a customer in some future period is modeled directly as a function of what is known prior to the future period. We seek a function that, above all else, fits the data well, and the quality of the fit on an independent holdout sample will be the top priority instead of the assumptions and mathematical model characterizing the relationship. The data-mining approach is also used to predict response to a single contact.

Both approaches have strengths and weaknesses and there is a long record of discussion about the topic.[1] We take a pragmatic position on this debate and recommend using the model that does the best job of answering the questions in a particular situation.

Perhaps the most important aspect of this chapter is that it provides a way to estimate both the short-term and long-term value of a marketing contact point. While this approach could be used with probabilistic as well as data-mining models, it is more closely associated with the data-mining models.

6.1 The data-mining approach to predicting future behaviors

This section is concerned with two behaviors. The first is responding to a single contact, as measured by the revenue attributed to the contact. Such models are often called *scoring models*. See Malthouse (2003c) for further discussion about scoring models and their uses. The second set of behaviors is long-term activity, as measured by the total revenue over an extended period of time in the future. We call this *long-term revenue* (LTR). Multiplying LTR by a margin and deducting relevant costs gives an estimate of a customer's long-term value. section 6.4 shows how to combine the two models to estimate the value of contacting an individual customer.

The data-mining approach to modeling these behaviors begins by identifying a proxy[2] for the behavior that has already been observed. The proxy is denoted by y. For example, if we want to estimate which customers will respond to a future contact point, a proxy is how customers responded to a similar contact point in the past. More specifically, if we want to predict how customers will respond to an e-mail offer that will be sent tomorrow, we can study a test of the e-mail offer that was mailed out last week. In the case of LTR, if we want to know how much customers will spend next year, a proxy would be how much the customer spent in the previous year.

Having identified a proxy behavior (y), we use the information available prior to the proxy period of time ($\mathbf{x}$) to predict the proxy behavior with a data-mining model, denoted by function $f(\mathbf{x})$. The y variable is called a *dependent variable* by statisticians, and an *output variable* by data miners. Statisticians call the $\mathbf{x}$ variables *independent* or *predictor variables* and data miners might call them *inputs* or *feature variables*. Data miners call the task of creating $\mathbf{x}$ variables *feature extraction*, where the variables are extracted from a relational database. The quality of the feature variables is one of the most important determinants the predictions. The set of powerful feature variables varies by industry, but versions of RFM are often in the set. We can think of the data being generated as follows:

$$y = f(\mathbf{x}) + e, \tag{6.1}$$

where e is an error, usually assumed to be homoscedastic and independent across observations. We then apply the model to the current information to predict the behavior. The following two examples should make this clear.

EXAMPLE 6.1:   CLV modeling contest, data-mining solution

Example 5.5 showed how to use a recency-only migration model to estimate the customer equity of all donors during the two-year period between September 1, 2006 and August 31, 2008. This example shows how to use a data-mining approach for the same problem.

Figure 6.1 Illustration of target and base time periods

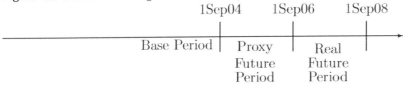

Solution   The first step is to find a proxy for the set of behaviors that we want to model. We use the two-year future period from September 1, 2004 and August 31, 2006 as a proxy for the real period. For each customer, we sum all donations during the future period so that we have a measure of long-term (two-year) revenue (the `ltr` variable in the program below), which corresponds to the dependent variable y in equation 6.1. Using the `RETAIN` statement to roll up transaction files is one of the most important programming skills covered in this book. The reader should study this program carefully.

For predictor variables, we compute RFM as of the beginning of the future period (August 31, 2004). Program 6.1 calls the RFM variables `r4`, `f4`, and `m4`, respectively, where the appended "4" signals that it is as of September 1, 2004. In terms of the equation 6.1 notation, the vector $\mathbf{x} = (\mathtt{r4}, \mathtt{f4}, \mathtt{m4})'$. We estimate a data-mining model $\hat{f}$ predicting $\hat{y} = \hat{f}(\mathbf{x})$.

Program 6.1 also computes RFM as of September 1, 2006: r6, f6, and m6. The final estimates are produced by evaluating the model $\hat{f}$, which was estimated with the 2004 data, on these new values of RFM, that is, by $\hat{f}(\texttt{r6}, \texttt{f6}, \texttt{m6})$. The predicted values can be summed to estimate the long-term value of the database.

Program 6.1 CLV modeling contest rollup

```
DATA curr.rollup;                              ELSE DO;
  SET contest.trans;                             IF diff<r4 THEN r4=diff;
  BY id;                                         f4 = f4 + 1;
  LENGTH ltr r4 f4 m4 r6 f6 m6 4;                m4 = SUM(amt, m4);
  RETAIN ltr r4 f4 m4 r6 f6 m6;                END;
  ARRAY x{*} ltr f4 m4 f6 m6;
  IF FIRST.id THEN DO;                         /* Compute RFM for 2006 */
    DO i = 1 to DIM(x);                        diff = ("31AUG2006"d - giftdate)/365.25;
      x{i} = 0;                                IF diff >= 0 THEN DO;
    END;                                         IF diff<r6 THEN r6=diff;
    r4=9999;                                     f6 = f6 + 1;
    r6=9999;                                     m6 = SUM(amt, m6);
  END;                                         END;

  /* Compute RFM for 2004 */                   IF LAST.id THEN OUTPUT;
  diff = ("31AUG2004"d - giftdate)/365.25;     KEEP id r4 f4 m4 r6 f6 m6 ltr;
  IF diff < 0 THEN ltr=SUM(amt, ltr);        RUN;
```

Figure 6.2 Histograms of log(ltr+1) for CLV contest

```
DATA contest;
  SET curr.rollup;
  logltr = LOG(targdol+1);
  LABEL logltr = "log(ltr+1)";
RUN;

PROC SGPLOT DATA=contest NOAUTOLEGEND;
  HISTOGRAM logltr;
RUN;
```

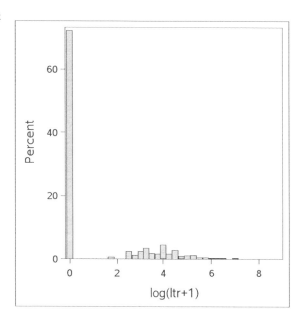

Figure 6.2 shows histograms of log(ltr+1), illustrating some of the issues that need to be addressed when building a data-mining model $\hat{f}$. The distribution of ltr is bimodal. More than 72% of its values equal 0, for those who did not make any donations during the future, two-year period. The other part of the distribution represents those who did donate, and the logarithm of this part is vaguely normal, as shown in Figure 6.3. The skewness of the log distribution *of buyers only* is 0.53 and the kurtosis is 0.85 (recall that a normal distribution has skewness and kurtosis of 0).

Figure 6.3 Histograms of `ltr` for CLV contest

```
PROC SGPLOT DATA=contest NOAUTOLEGEND;
  WHERE targdol>0;
  HISTOGRAM logltr;
  XAXIS LABEL = "log(ltr+1), where ltr>0";
RUN;
```

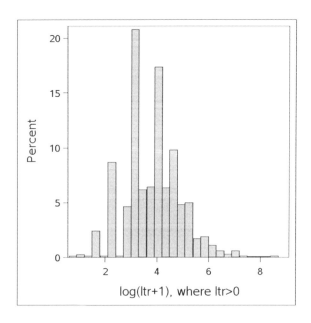

EXAMPLE 6.2:   European book retailer

We have data from a European book retailer that sells overstock books from catalogs, and this data includes transaction history from a sample of 255,189 customers between November 1997 and May 2005. This example is based on Malthouse (2010, § 4.1). We will study catalog #10, which was mailed to 104,499 customers on May 5, 2003. Our objectives are to build data-mining models that (1) predict the amount that each person receiving catalog #10 spends in response to this contact point (orders can be traced to the catalog that generated the order) and (2) estimate the long-term revenue during the period May 5, 2003–May 2005 excluding orders from catalog #10. (The total LTR could be computed by summing the two parts.) We will use RFM as of May 5, 2003 as predictor variables.

Solution   Program 6.2 gives the SAS code, again illustrating the flexibility of the `RETAIN` statement. The program is similar to Program 6.1, but is slightly more complicated. The Contact file part of the program accesses the `contact2` table, which has one record for every catalog mailed. The `id` variable identifies the recipient of the catalog, and the `book` variable is an identifier of the catalog. The identifier for catalog #10 in 2003 is `book=135`. We use macro variables for the code number so that this program could be easily reused to study other contacts.

The next part of the program rolls up the transaction file. The main difference from Program 6.1 is that two separate variables are created from the future period. The `targdol` variable records the amount attributed to catalog #10 and the `ltr` variable is the sum of all other purchases after May 5, 2003. Another difference is that, instead of having a single record for every donation, there is one record for every unique item in an order. The `qty` variable indicates the number of items purchased and the `price` variable gives the price of the item. Instead of having an `amt` variable for the amount of a donation, here we must multiply price and quantity.

Program 6.2 European book retailer

```
%LET today=05MAY2003;                         m = "monetary before &today"
%LET code = 135;                              tof = "yrs on file as of &today"
                                              targdol = "dols spent on target book"
/********* Contact file **********             ltr = "dols after &today not to target";
/* create file with list of all */           diff = (orddate-"&today"d)/365.25;
/* unique ids receiving catalog */            IF diff<0 THEN DO;  /* base period */
DATA contacts;                                   IF -diff<r THEN r=-diff;
  SET retail.contact2(WHERE=(book=&code));       IF -diff>tof THEN tof=-diff;
  BY id;                                         f = f+1;
  IF FIRST.id;                                   m = SUM(m, price*qty);
  KEEP id;                                    END;
RUN;                                          ELSE DO;    /* future period */
                                                 IF book = &code THEN
/****** Roll up transaction file *****/            targdol = SUM(targdol, price*qty);
%LET newx= r f m targdol ltr tof;                ELSE ltr = SUM(ltr, price*qty);
DATA Data1;                                   END;
  SET retail.order2;                          IF LAST.ID AND r < 9999 THEN OUTPUT;
  BY id;                                      KEEP id &newx;
  LENGTH &newx 4;                          RUN;
  RETAIN &newx;
  ARRAY x{*} &newx;                        /********* merge files *********/
  IF FIRST.ID THEN DO;                     DATA curr.all;
    DO i=1 to DIM(x);                        MERGE contacts(IN=b) data1;
      x{i} = 0;                              BY id;
    END;                                     IF b THEN gottarg=1;
    r=9999;                                  ELSE gottarg=0;
  END;                                       LABEL gottarg=
  LABEL                                        "indicator if received target cat";
    r = "recency (yrs) as of &today"      RUN;
    f = "freq before &today"
```

The third sections merges the contact and rolled-up transaction file. The `gottarg` variable equals 1 for those who received catalog #10 (indicated by having a record in `contacts`) and 0 otherwise.

Figure 6.4 shows histograms of the logged dependent variables. We see the same pattern as in Figure 6.2 and Figure 6.3. The distributions are bimodal. One mode is at the value 0 for people who have no activity in the future period. The other mode is for those active in the future period and is approximately lognormal (in this example the values of skewness and kurtosis are even closer to 0).

Many predictive models are available in SAS to estimate f, ranging from linear regression to more complicated models such as neural networks and tree-based models. It is beyond the scope of this book to survey data-mining models. The interested reader should consult Hastie et al. (2001). Instead, we will focus the discussion on issues that are particular to modeling CLV and responses to a marketing contact point. Much of our discussion applies as well to data-mining models not covered here.

The term data mining can mean many different things, and it is important to clarify our meaning. These models are all labeled as data-mining approaches in this chapter because of their motivation: they make no attempt to model the dynamics of the relationship. The models begin and end with the data. All data-mining methods provide a function that relates values during the future period to the base-period variables, and they are judged on how well they estimate the future values rather than the plausibility of their assumptions

Figure 6.4 Histograms of `ltr` and `targdol` from a European retailer

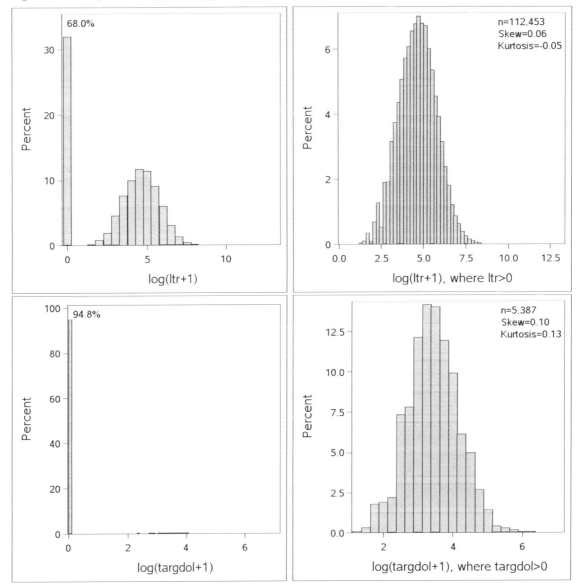

or the relationship dynamics accounted for in the model.[3]

As was mentioned in the introduction, there has been a long and lively debate about the merits and limitations of the two approaches. It is important to note some of the key points. First, extrapolation beyond the end of the future period is especially questionable. Our models will provide an estimate of long-term value over three years, and no more. Of course, probabilistic models make assumptions that may or may not be true. Many of them are difficult to confirm. When the assumptions made by a model are untrue then the conclusions drawn from it are suspect.

6.2   Regression models for highly skewed data

This book assumes that readers have had at least two courses in statistics or marketing research, including an introduction to multiple linear regression, logistic regression, and two-way ANOVA models. The purpose of this chapter is not to duplicate the introductions to these topics provided in hundreds of statistics and marketing research textbooks.

Instead, we pick up where the typical introductory statistics textbook leaves off. Most introductions stop with well-behaved data—the error distributions are usually normal, homoscedastic and without outliers. Even though some introductions discuss transformations, few cover the *multiplicative* or *two-step* models. This section provides a quick review of simple linear regression and uses it as a springboard to discuss these models, which are among the most important in database marketing, where it is common to have highly skewed, bimodal, dependent variables. Many lessons from these models also apply to more modern nonparametric methods such as feedforward neural networks.

6.2.1   Simple linear regression

The simple linear regression of y on x enables us to quantify how some dependent variable (y) depends on an independent variable (x). We observe pairs (x_i, y_i) for customer $i = 1, \ldots, n$. For example, if we know a person's age (x), what can we say about the person's purchase intent (y)? Linear regression assumes that the y values were generated as follows:

$$y_i = \alpha + \beta x_i + e_i,$$

where e_i are independent, normal random variables often called *errors*, each having a mean of 0 $[E(e_i) = 0]$ and a common *error variance* of $V(e_i) = \sigma_e^2$. Errors with a constant variance are called *homoscedastic*. It follows that

$$\mu_{Y|x} = E(Y|x) = \alpha + \beta x_i \quad \text{and} \quad V(Y|x) = V(\alpha + \beta x_i + e_i) = \sigma_e^2.$$

Therefore, if a customer has an independent variable value of x, then the mean (or expected value) of dependent variable Y is $\alpha + \beta x$ (we will use Y to denote a random variable and y_i to be a realization of the random variable). The mean of Y thus increases as a linear function of x.

The value σ_e is called the *standard deviation of the errors* and tells us the typical deviation of Y from its mean (on the regression line), α is called the *intercept* and β is called the *slope*. The slope tells us the increase in the mean of Y associated with a unit change in x and the intercept tells the expected value of Y when $x \equiv 0$.

Figure 6.5 Simple linear regression

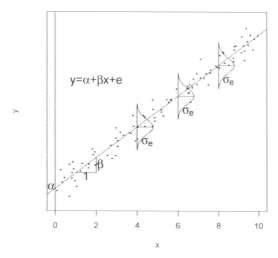

In practice, we do not know the values of parameters α, β, and σ_e, and we must estimate them from data. *Ordinary least squares* (OLS) estimates a and b are found by minimizing the *sum of squared errors* (SSE) over all possible values of α and β:

$$\min_{a,b} \underbrace{\sum_{i=1}^{n}(y_i - a - bx_i)^2}_{\text{SSE}}.$$

Predicted or *fitted values* $\hat{y}$ estimate the mean of Y for a given x_i:

$$\hat{y}_i = a + bx_i.$$

Instead of estimating parameters, data miners sometimes say "training the model," where the model "learns" to produce "model outputs" $\hat{y}$ to be as close as possible (in terms of squared distance) to the "training values" y by selecting the best values of "weights" a and b. The term *supervised learning* is often used instead of model estimation.

The value $\hat{e}_i = y_i - a - bx_i$ is called the *residual*, and it estimates the true error e_i. An unbiased estimate of the error variance is given by the *mean squared error*

$$S_e^2 = \text{MSE} = \frac{\text{SSE}}{n-2}.$$

The square root of MSE, S_e, is called the *root mean squared error* (RMSE) or the *standard error of the estimate*. Sometimes MSE and RMSE are computed with a denominator n instead of $n-2$ (or $n-p$ when there are $p-1$ independent variables and an intercept in the model). After this section we mostly use the denominator n whenever we compute the mean squared error. Because the data sets used in database marketing tend to have a large number of observations, the difference between the two is negligible in practice.

6.2.2   The multiplicative model

The multiplicative model assumes that dependent variable y^* depends on predictor variable x^* in a multiplicative, rather than additive, way:

$$y_i^* = \alpha^*(x_i^*)^{\beta} e_i^*,$$

where e_i^* has a *lognormal distribution*. That is, $\log(e_i^*) = e_i$ has mean μ_i and variance σ_e^2. Taking logs of both sides,

$$y_i = \log(y_i^*) = \log(\alpha^*) + \beta\log(x_i^*) + \log(e_i^*) = \alpha + \beta x + e_i.$$

Thus, after transforming $y = \log(y^*)$ and $x = \log(x^*)$, we have the simple linear regression model. We can estimate α^* with $\exp(a)$, and β is the same in both models.

Interpreting the parameters and obtaining fitted values is more complicated for the multiplicative model. We begin by discussing fitted values. To understand how to estimate Y^*, we must first review some properties of the *lognormal distribution*. If Y has a normal distribution with mean μ and variance σ^2, then $Y^* = e^Y$ has a lognormal distribution. In other words, $\log(Y^*) = Y$ is normal. It is easy to show with moment-generating functions that

$$E(Y^*) = \exp(\mu + \sigma^2/2).$$

This result is somewhat counterintuitive because one might expect the mean to be simply $\exp(\mu)$, but it is not. This result suggests that the mean of Y^* is a function of both the mean μ and the variance σ^2 of Y. Some intuition to explain this result is as follows. Without loss of generality, consider normal distributions with a mean of 0. Such distributions have two tails and the entire real line as a range. Exponents of real numbers, however, are strictly positive, with the negative half of the original normal distribution being mapped to the interval $(0, 1)$ and the positive half mapped to $(1, \infty)$. As the variance of the original distribution increases, there will be more area under both tails. This increases the area in the right tail of the exponentiated distribution, but has less effect on the exponentiated tail squeezed between 0 and 1. Having more area in the $(0, \infty)$ tail of the original distribution will pull the mean of the lognormal distribution to the right, which is why the mean of a lognormal distribution increases with the variance of the Y.

Figure 6.6 illustrates this. The arrows show the mean. As the variance increases, the amount of area in the tails increases, but because the distributions are bounded below at 0, the mean is pulled to the right.

Figure 6.6 Lognormal distributions with the exponentiated distribution having means of 0 and standard deviations .25, .5 and 1. Arrows show the means.

```
%LET sigma = ^{UNICODE '03C3'x};
DATA pdf;
  DO x = 0 TO 4 BY .01;
    y1 = PDF('LOGNORMAL', x, 0, 1);
    y2 = PDF('LOGNORMAL', x, 0, .5);
    y3 = PDF('LOGNORMAL', x, 0, .25);
    OUTPUT;
  END;
  LABEL y1 = "&sigma=1"
    y2 = "&sigma=0.5"
    Y3 = "&sigma=0.25";
RUN;

DATA anno; /* add arrows showing means */
  DRAWSPACE='datavalue'; FUNCTION='arrow';
  x1=EXP(.25**2/2); x2=x1; y2=0;
  y1=PDF('LOGNORMAL',x1,0,.25); OUTPUT;
  x1=EXP(.5**2/2); x2=x1; y2=0;
  y1=PDF('LOGNORMAL',x1,0,.5); OUTPUT;
  x1=EXP(1/2); x2=x1; y2=0;
  y1=PDF('LOGNORMAL',x1,0,1); OUTPUT;
RUN;
```

```
PROC SGPLOT DATA=pdf SGANNO=anno;
  SERIES X=x Y=y1 / LINEATTRS=(PATTERN=1);
  SERIES X=x Y=y2 / LINEATTRS=(PATTERN=2);
  SERIES X=x Y=y3 / LINEATTRS=(PATTERN=3);
  YAXIS LABEL="Lognormal Density";
RUN;
```

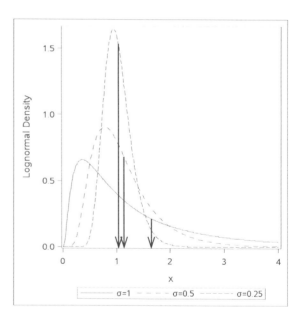

The implication of this result is that we cannot simply exponentiate $\hat{y}$ to get the fitted values in their original units. Instead, we must add half the variance before exponentiating:

$$\hat{Y}^* = \exp(\hat{y} + S_e^2/2) = \exp(a + bx + S_e^2/2).$$

We can also use moment-generating functions to find the variance of Y^*:

$$V(Y^*) = \exp(2\mu + \sigma^2)(e^{\sigma^2} - 1).$$

The variance of Y^* increases with the mean. The coefficient of variation ($CV = \sigma/\mu$) describes the variation relative to the mean. The CV of Y^* is

$$CV_{Y^*} = \frac{\sqrt{V(y^*)}}{E(Y^*)} = \frac{\sqrt{\exp(2\mu + \sigma^2)(\exp(\sigma^2) - 1)}}{\exp(\mu + \sigma^2/2)} = \sqrt{\exp(\sigma^2) - 1},$$

which does not depend on μ. The standard deviation of the untransformed dependent variable, is thus proportional to its mean. The logarithm is often called a *variance stabilizing transformation* when the standard deviation is proportional to the mean.

We now discuss the interpretation of the parameters. The slope and intercept have different interpretations. When $\beta \equiv 1$, then $y^* = \alpha^* x^*$, and y^* is proportional to x^*. The intercept is 0 and the slope is now α^*. In other words, every unit increase in x^* is associated with an increase of α^* in y^*.

As shown in Figure 6.7 below, when $\beta > 1$ there are increasing returns to scale. That is, as x^* increases, a unit change in x^* is associated with progressively larger increases in y^*. Likewise, $\beta < 1$ implies decreasing returns to scale.

Figure 6.7 Interpreting multiplicative model parameters

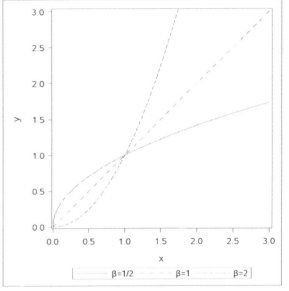

```
%LET beta = ^{UNICODE '03B2'x};
DATA functions;
  DO x = 0 TO 3 BY .01;
    y1 = sqrt(x);
    y2 = x;
    y3 = x*x;
    OUTPUT;
  END;
  LABEL y1 = "&beta=1/2"
    y2 = "&beta=1"
    Y3 = "&beta=2";
RUN;


PROC SGPLOT DATA=functions;
  SERIES X=x Y=y1 / LINEATTRS=(PATTERN=1);
  SERIES X=x Y=y2 / LINEATTRS=(PATTERN=2);
  SERIES X=x Y=y3 / LINEATTRS=(PATTERN=3);
  YAXIS LABEL="y" MAX=3;
RUN;
```

EXAMPLE 6.3:   Business failures

The `busfail.csv` data are from of the Census (1994, pp. 27), and the problem is based on one by Siegel (2011, ch. 11, problem 6). For each state and the District of Columbia, the name (`state`), number of business failures (`failures`) and population in thousands (`population`) is provided. Estimate regression models of `failures` on `population`, and log(`failures`) on log(`population`). Test whether failures are proportional to population, and estimate the number of failures in Illinois, which has a population of 11,697 (thousand). Find the coefficient of variation of the errors.

Solution   The program to the left of Figure 6.8 reads in the data, computes the logs, and runs the regressions. Note that `population` was given in thousands and that `logpop` gives the logarithm of population, not in thousands. The scatter plots of the raw (top) and logged (bottom) data, with the fitted regression line superimposed. The simple linear regression model does not fit the raw data very well for several reasons. First, California is an outlier in the upper right-hand corner that exerts a strong influence on the regression line. Without California in the data set, the estimated slope would be substantially smaller and the line would pass approximately through the middle of the remaining points. Second, estimating the model with California produces a clear pattern in the residuals: the estimated line is below all of the points for smaller states; states with populations between 7 and 20 million are all below the line; California is well above the line. Third, the variance around the line increases with mean failures (heteroscedasticity).

A fourth issue is the skewness of `population`. This issue does not violate any assumptions of the model, but does create a situation where a few observations can exert a strong influence on the regression line and increase the variance of the estimates. The

Figure 6.8 Scatterplots from the business failure problem

```
DATA busfail;
  INFILE "busfail.csv" DSD FIRSTOBS=2;
  INPUT State$ Failures Population;
  logpop = LOG(population*1000);
  logfail = LOG(Failures);
  popM = population/1000;
  failK = Failures/1000;
  _model_ = "MODEL1";
  IF state="Cal" THEN outlier = state;
  LABEL
    popM = "Population (millions)"
    failK = "Failures (thousands)"
    logpop = "log(Population)"
    logfail = "log(Failures)";
RUN;

PROC SGPLOT DATA=busfail NOAUTOLEGEND;
  REG X=popM Y=failK / DATALABEL=outlier;
RUN;

PROC SGPLOT DATA=busfail NOAUTOLEGEND;
  REG X=logpop Y=logfail / DATALABEL=outlier;
RUN;

PROC REG DATA=busfail;
  MODEL logfail = logpop;
  TEST logpop=1;
RUN;
```

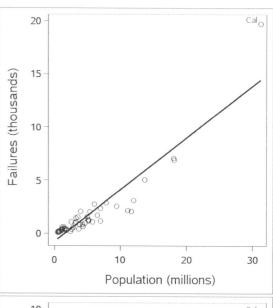

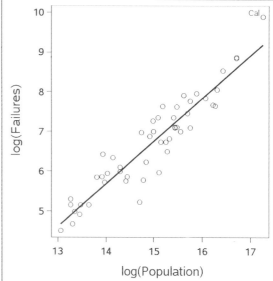

median population is 3.57 million and the maximum is 31.2 million, so half of the observations fall in a slice that is less than 10% of the entire range. The 90th percentile is 11.7 million. Thus, more than two thirds of the range is devoted to 10% of the cases. The sparseness of the observations in the right two-thirds of the scatter plot destabilizes the estimates and enables a few observations to have a strong influence on the fit.

After logging both variables, the scatter plot and estimated regression line indicate the the simple linear regression (on the logged data) fits very well. The log function has reduced the influence of California, symmetrized both distributions, and eliminated the dependence of the variance of the errors on the mean of failures (homoscedastic).

The output from the multiplicative model is shown below.

Analysis of Variance					
Source	DF	Sum of Squares	Mean Square	F Value	Pr > F
Model	1	61.31412	61.31412	349.66	< .0001
Error	49	8.59238	0.17535		
Corrected Total	50	69.90650			

Parameter Estimates					
Variable	DF	Parameter Estimate	Standard Error	t Value	Pr > |t|
Intercept	1	−9.31575	0.85834	−10.85	< .0001
logpop	1	1.07185	0.05732	18.70	< .0001

Test 1 Results for Dependent Variable logfail				
Source	DF	Mean Square	F Value	Pr > F
Numerator	1	0.27554	1.57	0.2160
Denominator	49	0.17535		

The estimated regression equation is

$$\log(\texttt{failure}) = -9.136 + 1.072 \log(\texttt{population}).$$

Recall that failures are proportional to population when the slope is 1, so we need to test $H_0 : \beta = 1$. The statement "TEST logpop=1" produces the F test shown in the output. Equivalently, we can compute the test statistic $(1.07185 - 1)/0.05732 = 1.25$, which has a t distribution with 49 degrees of freedom. Either way, the P-value is .2160 > .05, so we cannot reject the null hypothesis that failures are proportional to population. The estimated log failures in Illinois can be computed as follows:

$$\hat{y} = -9.31575 + 1.07185 \log(11,697,000) = 8.128.$$

We must add half of the mean squared error and exponentiate to estimate the raw number of failures:

$$\exp(8.128 + 0.17535/2) \approx 3700.$$

The coefficient of variation of failures is as follows:

$$\sqrt{\exp(0.17535) - 1} = 0.4378.$$

Mosteller and Tukey (1977, p. 109) gave advice on transformations that they call "first aid re-expressions." They advocate taking the logs of all count and amount variables as first aid and note, "These rules are not supposed to be a final answer—just as first aid for the injured is no substitute for a physician—but they offer a safe beginning." This advice is usually very good. In database marketing, it is generally a good idea to log all flavors of frequency and monetary value for all of the reasons illustrated in the example: logs symmetrize the distribution (avoiding data sparseness in the right tail), stabilize the variance so that it does not depend on the mean, and reduce the influence of outliers. This advice applies to many other nonparametric regression methods as well. For example, feedforward neural networks are also sensitive to outliers and implicitly assume homoscedastic errors. Trees, on the other hand, are invariant to monotonic transformations of predictor variables and therefore logging predictor variables has no effect.

Recency variables usually do not require log transformations, but there can be instances where a log (or square root) transformation is appropriate, such as when the modeler expects diminishing returns in the dependent variable as recency increases.

6.2.3   Two-step models

As illustrated in Figures 6.2 and 6.4, the distribution of the dependent variable for LTR and scoring models is usually bimodal. One mode consists of zeros, indicating that a customer does not make any purchases in the future period. The other mode consists of those who make some purchase in the future period. The right mode is usually approximately lognormal. Such a dependent variable is problematic for linear regression because, as we will see, the variables predicting whether a customer will respond are different from those predicting how much a customer will spend if the customer responds. Combining these separate behaviors—response and spend conditional on response—creates modeling difficulties. One approach to modeling such variables is to use a two-step model, which estimate separate two separate models and combine the predicted values:

1. *Response model.* Estimate the probability that the customer will respond to the contact, that is, $y = 0$ versus $y > 0$. This could be done with logistic regression or any model for dichotomous data such as the probit model or a feed-forward neural network with a sigmoidal output activation function. Recency and frequency variables tend to be the most important predictors of future response. Sometimes a *purchase rate*, frequency / time on file, is used in place of frequency, because customers with longer tenure have had more opportunities to purchase.

2. *Conditional-spend model.* For the responders only, estimate the amount spent or donated. The multiplicative model is often used for this task. Monetary value, perhaps normalized by frequency to give an *average order amount* or time on file to give an *average amount per period*, is usually the best indicator of future spend for those who are active.[4]

After both models have been estimated, the predictions from the two models are multiplied to give the final score. To understand why, let R be a random variable indicating whether a customer responds with probability $P(R = 1) = \pi$. We ultimately want to know the expected future spend, $E(Y)$, which can be decomposed as follows:

$$E(Y) = E[E(Y|R)] = (1 - \pi)\underbrace{E(Y|R = 0)}_{0} + \pi E(Y|R = 1) = \pi E(Y|R = 1), \qquad (6.2)$$

because the expected spend of someone who does not respond is 0.

Let π_i be the probability that customer i responds. Estimate the following model with logistic regression

$$\log\left(\frac{\pi_i}{1 - \pi_i}\right) = \mathbf{x}_i'\mathbf{a},$$

where $\mathbf{a}$ is a vector of slope coefficients. The estimated probability of response is

$$\hat{\pi}_i = 1/[1 + \exp(-\mathbf{x}_i'\mathbf{a})].$$

Using only observations where $y_i > 0$, estimate a linear regression predicting $\log(y_i + 1)$ from the predictor variables producing slope vector $\mathbf{b}$ and mean squared error S_e^2. Final scores for a future customer are nonlinear functions of the covariates $\mathbf{x}_0$ given by

$$\hat{y}_0 = \frac{\exp(\mathbf{x}_0'\mathbf{b} + S_e^2/2) - 1}{1 + \exp(-\mathbf{x}_0'\mathbf{a})} \qquad (6.3)$$

The exponent in the numerator converts the log-amount used as the dependent variable in the regression into raw amounts.

EXAMPLE 6.4:   Frequency, monetary value, average order amount and purchase intensity

Continuing Example 6.2, apply first-aid log transformations to frequency, monetary value, and future spend (`targdol`). Use only those who received and responded to catalog #10 to study the correlation matrix and regress future spend on frequency and monetary. Discuss the relationship with average order amount and purchase intensity.

Solution   The SAS program and output are shown below. The output is typical of scoring models. The `CORR` option produces the correlation matrix shown here, which indicates that (1) future spend has positive associations with both frequency and monetary value, and (2) frequency and monetary value are highly correlated. A multiple regression shows a sign flip for frequency. One might be tempted to attribute the flip to multicollinearity, but this example is hinting at an important fact about these variables.

```
DATA all;
  SET curr.all;
  logf = LOG(f+1);
  logm = LOG(m+1);
  logtarg = LOG(targdol+1);
RUN;


PROC REG DATA=all CORR;
  MODEL logtarg = logf logm;
  WHERE targdol > 1 AND gottarg=1;
run;
```

Correlation			
Variable	logf	logm	logtarg
logf	1.0000	0.9423	0.2426
logm	0.9423	1.0000	0.2885
logtarg	0.2426	0.2885	1.0000

Root MSE	0.69848	R-Square	0.0909
Dep. Mean	3.42067	Adj R-Sq	0.0905
Coeff Var	20.41925		

Parameter Estimates					
Variable	DF	Parameter Estimate	Standard Error	t Value	Pr > $|t|$
Intercept	1	2.12874	0.06126	34.75	< .0001
logf	1	−0.18651	0.02772	−6.73	< .0001
logm	1	0.33613	0.02441	13.77	< .0001

We can understand the relationship between the variables by letting y represent future spend (that is, `targdol`), f represent frequency, and m represent monetary value (to avoid taking the log of 0 we could let f be frequency $+1$, and likewise for m). We are estimating the model

$$\log y = \alpha + \beta_1 \log f + \beta_2 \log m + e. \tag{6.4}$$

Consider what would happen if $\beta_2 = -\beta_1 = \beta$. If this were the case the model would reduce to

$$\log y = \alpha - \beta \log f + \beta \log m + e = \alpha + \beta \log(m/f) + e.$$

We could alternatively create a new variable, m/f, and regress $\log y$ on $\log(m/f)$ instead of $\log f$ and $\log m$ separately, and save one degree of freedom. The ratio m/f has a simple interpretation as the *average order amount*, and the reduced model would have a strong intuitive appeal—predict the amount of a future order by the average amount of previous orders. After estimating equation 6.4 for dozens of organizations in different industries, I have observed that it is fairly common, although not universal, for $\beta_2 \approx -\beta_1$.

In this example, $\beta_2 \neq -\beta_1$ and regressing `logtarg` on $\log(m/f)$ produces a substantially worse fit. Average order amount is clearly not the only predictor. Consider the following reparameterization:

$$\gamma_1 = \frac{\beta_2 - \beta_1}{2} \quad \text{and} \quad \gamma_1 = \frac{\beta_2 + \beta_1}{2}.$$

Substituting this into equation 6.4,

$$\log y = \alpha + \beta_1 \log f + \beta_2 \log m + e = \alpha + \gamma_1 \log(m/f) + \gamma_2 \log(fm) + e,$$

so that γ_1 measures the effect of average order amount and $\gamma_2 = 0$ if and only if $\beta_2 = -\beta_1$. The two models, of course, have identical fits (the reader should confirm that the values of MSE and R^2 are the same). Malthouse (2010, footnote 9) interprets $\log(fm)$ as a measure of *purchase intensity* because $\gamma_2 \log(fm) = \gamma_2 \log f + \gamma_2 \log m$. Thus $\log(fm)$ is a summed scale. The strong correlation between `logm` and `logf` suggests that PCA would identify a single factor and produce scores approximately proportional to $\log(fm)$. An explanation for why the two are correlated is that they are both manifestations of the purchase intensity construct.[5]

Summarizing, when estimating models with frequency and monetary value, we can use either $\log m$ and $\log f$, or we can equivalently use $\log(m/f)$ and $\log(fm)$. Both parameterizations have natural interpretations.

Another important ratio variable is frequency divided by the length of time that someone has been a customer (sometimes called *time on file* or *tenure*). This can be interpreted as the *purchase rate* (for example, number of purchases per year if tenure is measured in years).

EXAMPLE 6.5:   CLV modeling contest, data-mining solution

Continuing Examples 5.5 and 6.1, complete Task 1 of the contest using a two-step data-mining model with RFM as predictors.

Solution   The solution uses the `curr.rollup` data set created in Program 6.1. The `r4`, `f4`, and `m4` variables give RFM as of 2004 and will be used as the predictor variables in estimating the regressions. After estimating the models, we will evaluate the function using the RFM variables as of 2006: `r6`, `f6`, and `m6`. Program 6.1 converts `curr.rollup` into a format that will facilitate this process of using RFM as of 2004 to estimate the model, and then applying it to RFM as of 2006. The idea is to create two observations for each respondent, one giving RFM values as of 2004 and the other as of 2006. The 2006 version will have the outcome variables set to missing so that they will be excluded from the estimation. We will have `PROC REG` and `PROC LOGISTIC` compute predicted values for us, and the predictions will be computed and saved for all observations—both those from 2004 and 2006.

A `DATA` step computes the final estimates from equation 6.3, and `PROC MEANS` computed the final sum, which is \$581,784.82. This answer is indicated on Figure 5.4 and is off by about the same amount, but in the other direction, as the recency-only migration model. As with the recency model, this simple two-step model compares fairly well with most of the other entries. Would a model with more predictor variables and more careful selection of transformations (not just "first aid") and interactions come even closer?

Program 6.3 CLV modeling contest rollup

```
DATA rollup;                            PROC LOGISTIC DATA=rollup DESCENDING;
  SET curr.rollup;                        MODEL targbuy = r logf logm;
  /* create variables for 2004 */         OUTPUT OUT=logitout PREDICTED=phat;
  yr = 2004;                            RUN;
  r = r4;
  logf = LOG(f4+1);
  logm = LOG(m4+1);                     PROC REG DATA=logitout CORR;
  logtarg = LOG(targdol+1);               MODEL logtarg = r logf logm;
  targbuy = (targdol>0);                  OUTPUT OUT=regout PREDICTED=yhat;
  OUTPUT;                                 WEIGHT targbuy;
                                        RUN;
  /* create variables for 2008 */
  yr = 2006;                            DATA answer;
  r = r6;                                 SET regout;
  logf = log(f6+1);                       answer = phat*(EXP(yhat+0.47246/2) - 1);
  logm = log(m6+1);                     RUN;
  targbuy = .;                          PROC MEANS DATA=answer N SUM;
  targdol = .;                            WHERE yr = 2006;
  OUTPUT;                                 VAR answer;
  DROP r4 f4 m4 r6 f6 m6;               RUN;
RUN;
```

6.3 Evaluating data-mining models

Suppose we have an estimate $\hat{f}$ of function f in equation 6.1. We need to evaluate the quality of the estimated model. This section will cover two issues: (1) devising metrics to evaluate the model and (2) estimating the metrics. Two families of metrics are commonly used in practice. One measures the typical size of the errors e in equation 6.1 and the other estimates revenues realized by using $\hat{f}$ to select a certain number of people to receive a contact point (for example, *gains tables*). We will see that both families of metrics should be estimated on a *test sample* of data rather than the *training sample* used to estimate $\hat{f}$.

6.3.1 Residual-based metrics

We have observed values of the dependent variable y_i and independent variables $\mathbf{x}_i$ for a sample of n customers. These n observations are called the *training sample* or *estimation sample* because we will use them to estimate (or train) our model, $\hat{f}$. Sometimes the word *set* or *data* is used in place of *sample* as in "training set" or "training data," but all mean the same thing.

The quality of the fit is evaluated through the residuals $\hat{e}_i = y_i - \hat{f}(\mathbf{x}_i)$. There are many metrics that are some function of the $\hat{e}_i$ values. The *sum of squared errors* is

$$\text{SSE} = \sum_{i=1}^{n} \hat{e}_i^2 = \sum_{i=1}^{n} [y_i - \hat{f}(\mathbf{x}_i)]^2.$$

Often we rescale SSE so that it measures the average squared residual, or *mean squared error* ($\text{MSE} = \text{SSE}/n$). MSE is also called the *average squared error* (ASE) by some procedures in SAS. The *root mean squared error*, $\text{RMSE} = \sqrt{\text{MSE}}$, measures the typical size of a (not squared) residual.

Another rescaled version of SSE is the *coefficient of determination*, $R^2 = 1 - \text{SSE}/\text{SST}$, which is the "fraction of variation in y explained by the model." The constant $\text{SST} = \sum_i (y_i - \bar{y})^2$ is called the *total sum of squares*, giving the sum of squared residuals from the baseline *intercept model* $\hat{f}_0(\mathbf{x}_i) = \bar{y}$ (for all i). We can think of R^2 as making a comparison between our model $\hat{f}$ and the simplest possible model consisting only an intercept, which is constant over all values of $\mathbf{x}$ and does not model any dependence of y on $\mathbf{x}$. All of these metrics are some monotonic transformation of SSE, and they characterize the magnitude of the residuals in some way.

All of the SSE-based measures discussed above have a problem: they evaluate the model using the data that was used to estimate the model $\hat{f}$. The parameters of $\hat{f}$ have been selected so that they give a good fit to the training set. For example, if we use a least-squares optimization criterion, then the parameters are selected to minimize SSE. Mosteller and Tukey (1977, p. 37) note a famous saying, "Optimization capitalizes on chance!" A learning or training analogy would be if a math teacher gave her students a set of problems to practice on, and then gave the same problems on the exam. Statisticians call this problem *optimism*, and when SSE is computed on the training data, it will give an overly optimistic assessment of the fit.

Data miners avoid the problem of optimism by computing fit measures on another data set. Such measures are called *out-of-sample estimates*. The simplest approach is to compute the fit measures on another set of data, called the *test sample*. Mosteller and Tukey (1977, p. 38) suggest that the test sample should be "kept in a locked safe where it has rested untouched and unscanned during all of the choices and optimizations." We lock the test sample in a safe while we develop model $\hat{f}$ using the training data. Then we apply the estimated model $\hat{f}$ to the test sample and compute the fit statistics.

There are different ways to produce a test sample. One way is to randomly assign the available data to training and test samples, or if the available data has few observations we use *cross validation*.[6] A stronger test is to use what Mosteller and Tukey call "fresh data," which come from, for example, another time period. Both approaches will be illustrated the examples that follow.

EXAMPLE 6.6:   European retailer—test and training MSE

Split the nonprofit data set from Program 6.2 into training and test samples. Use linear regression and the training sample to estimate the log donations to catalog #10 from recency and the logs of frequency and monetary. Compute SSE and MSE for both the training and test samples.

Solution Data mining software such as SAS Enterprise Miner make it very easy to form test sets and compute fit statistics for both the test and training set. `PROC GLMSELECT` also automates the task for linear regression models but not for logistic models. It is also fairly easy to do with a `DATA` step and `PROC REG`. We illustrate both `PROC GLMSELECT` and the `DATA` step with `PROC REG` approaches. The latter will be needed for subsequent examples that also use logistic regression.

The program below uses a `DATA` step to define a variable `train` equaling 1 if an observation is in the training set and 0 for the test set. Each observation is assigned at random to one of the two sets by comparing a uniform $[0, 1]$ variable with .5.

Program 6.4 Retailer example with a test set using linear regression and RFM as predictor variables

```
%INCLUDE "gains.sas";   /* used in a subsequent example */
PROC FORMAT;
  VALUE train
    0 = "Test"
    1 = "Train";
RUN;

DATA all;
  SET curr.all;
  IF gottarg=1;
  train = (RANUNI(12345)<.5);
  FORMAT train train.;
  logf = LOG(f+1);
  logm = LOG(m+1);
  logtarg = LOG(targdol+1);
  /* used in subsequent examples */
  logtof = LOG(tof+1);
  targbuy = (targdol>0);    /* dep var for logistic regression */
  trainbuy = train*targbuy; /* used for two-step model */
  _MODEL_ = "MODEL1";       /* used for two-step model */
  logltr = LOG(ltr+1);      /* used in last section */
  ltr01 = (ltr>0);          /* used in last section */
RUN;
```

We begin with PROC GLMSELECT, as illustrated in Program 6.5. The syntax is similar to PROC REG, with a few differences. The SELECTION=NONE statement specifies that all variables should enter the model. The PARTITION statement specifies that the train variable should be used to partition the data. The test set consists of all (formatted) values of train that equal the value 'Test', from the format specified earlier; all other observations are used as the training set. In this example we have created the train variable, which will be used in subsequent examples. If we had wanted to fit only this linear regression model, it would not have been necessary to create the train variable. PROC GLMSELECT would have split the data for us had we specified the command: PARTITION FRACTION(TEST=.5);.

Program 6.5 Computing test-set MSE with PROC GLMSELECT

```
PROC GLMSELECT DATA=all;
  MODEL logtarg = r logf logm / SELECTION=NONE;
  PARTITION ROLEVAR=train(TEST='Test');
RUN;
```

The output contains the following two pairs of lines, giving the sample sizes and average squared errors (ASE) for the training and test sets.

Number of Observations Used for Training	51930
Number of Observations Used for Testing	52563

ASE (Train)	0.58635
ASE (Test)	0.58948

An alternative approach that gives the same answer is to use PROC REG to regress logtarg on recency and the logs of frequency and monetary value. The regression is weighted by the train variable so that all observations in the training set receive a weight of 1. Those in the test set receive zero weight and are ignored in the objective function. The OUTPUT statement saves both the predicted values and residuals for all observations.

Program 6.6 Computing test-set MSE with PROC REG

```
PROC REG DATA=all;
  MODEL logtarg = r logf logm;
  WEIGHT train;
  OUTPUT OUT=regout PREDICTED=yhat RESIDUAL=ehat;
RUN;
%gains(targdol, yhat, regout(WHERE=(train=0)));
```

Analysis of Variance					
Source	**DF**	**Sum of Squares**	**Mean Square**	**F Value**	**Pr > F**
Model	3	635.76363	211.92121	361.39	< .0001
Error	51926	30449	0.58640		
Corrected Total	51929	31085			

We now show two ways of computing SSE for the test and training sets. PROC MEANS offers the USS option, which computes the uncorrected sum of squares of a variable, $\sum_i \hat{e}_i^2$. The uncorrected sum of squares of the residuals equals SSE. The "CLASS train" statement tells SAS to compute SSE separately for the test and training sets. Excerpts from the output are provided below. The USS for the training set in the PROC MEANS output, 30449.32, matches the ANOVA table from PROC REG. The Corrected Total degrees of freedom in the ANOVA table (51,929) equals the number of observations in the training set from MEANS (51,930) minus one, confirming that the WEIGHT statement caused PROC REG to use only the training data. There is no obvious way to have PROC MEANS compute MSE, and we would have to divide USS by 51,930 (or 51,926 for unbiased MSE) using a pocket calculator.

```
PROC MEANS DATA=regout USS;
  CLASS train;
  VAR ehat;
RUN;
```

Analysis Variable : ehat Residual		
train	**N Obs**	**USS**
Test	52563	30985.07
Train	51930	30449.32

PROC SQL can also be used. An advantage of using SQL over MEANS is that it will compute ASE = MSE = SSE/N for us. The typical size of a squared residual is about 0.59, matching the answer from GLMSELECT exactly. The fact that the test and training MSE values are approximately equal indicates that the regression model is not overfitting the data. When training MSE is much less than the test set MSE, the regression function overfits the data. The MSE value reported in the ANOVA table is slightly different because the denominator is 51,926 instead of 51,930.

```
PROC SQL;
  SELECT train,
    COUNT(ehat) AS n,
    SUM(ehat**2) AS SSE,
    SUM(ehat**2)/COUNT(ehat) AS MSE
  FROM regout
  GROUP BY train;
```

train	n	SSE	MSE
Test	52563	30985.07	0.589484
Train	51930	30449.32	0.586353

The %INCLUDE statement at the beginning of the program, the additional transformations in the DATA step, and the call to the gains macro will be explained in

Example 6.7.

Example 6.1 provides and example of using fresh data. The training data set comes from the period of January 2002 through August 31, 2006, and the test data set comes from September 1, 2006 through August 31, 2008. The test sample from a different period of time will detect if the model is capturing idiosyncrasies of the training period.

An even stronger test would be to evaluate the model on a different set of customers in a different time period. For example, we could build a model using the same training data from the 2002–8/31/2006 time period. All of the customers in this sample were acquired during the first half of 2002 (Malthouse, 2009). A stronger test set would consist of customers acquired during some other time period, say the second half of 2002, with a non-overlapping time period, for example, 9/1/2006–8/31/2008. Likewise, Fader and Hardie (2007) use a stronger test for the beta-geometric probabilistic model in Example 4.16 by estimating the model with the first seven years, and then predicting survival rates in the next five years.

6.3.2   Gains tables

For many applications, having small residuals is not the primary objective. For example, a model that predicts the response to some marketing contact point will probably be used to select which customers will receive the contact. The ultimate objective in this situation is to maximize revenues or profit, and it would be desirable to have a metric that directly matches this objective. Gains tables give the answer.

In practice, the predicted values from the regression function $\hat{f}(\mathbf{x}_i)$ will be sorted. The ordering will determine which customers receive the contact point, with customers having larger predicted values receiving the contact before those with smaller values. Gains table are created as follows:

1. Find the deciles of the predicted values. Quantiles other than deciles could also be used, but deciles are probably the most commonly used quantile in practice.

2. Compute actual revenue by decile.

3. Compute cumulative columns.

EXAMPLE 6.7:   Gains table for the retailer, RFM regression model
Create a gains table for the estimated regression model in Example 6.6 using the test set.

Solution   We first discuss the output below, which was generated with the call to the `gains` macro after running `PROC REG` in Program 6.6. The SAS code for the macro will be discussed after we learn to interpret a gains table.

decile	n	total	mean	cumn	cumsum	cummean
1	5,256	31,389	5.972	5,256	31,389	5.972
2	5,256	17,987	3.422	10,512	49,376	4.697
3	5,257	13,377	2.545	15,769	62,753	3.980
4	5,256	9,773	1.859	21,025	72,526	3.450
5	5,256	8,355	1.590	26,281	80,881	3.078
6	5,257	6,126	1.165	31,538	87,007	2.759
7	5,256	5,906	1.124	36,794	92,913	2.525
8	5,257	5,473	1.041	42,051	98,386	2.340
9	5,256	4,147	0.789	47,307	102,534	2.167
10	5,256	3,214	0.612	52,563	105,748	2.012
	52,563	105,748				

- **Decile** gives the decile number. Decile 1 includes the 10% of the test sample with the largest predicted values. Decile 10 comprises the 10% with the smallest predicted values.

- `N` gives the number of customers in each decile. There are approximately 5,256 in each decile. In theory, all `n` values should be the same, but the numbers might not be equal in practice because the sample size might be a multiple of the number of groups (ten for deciles) or there could be tied predicted values.

- `Total` gives the total actual revenue by decile. For example, the 10% of the test set identified by the model as having the largest predicted values generated revenue €31,389. Those in the lowest decile only generated €3,214. Clearly, the model is able to separate good customers from weaker ones. If response were independent of the predictor variables, all of the totals would be approximately equal, but that is not the case here.

- `Mean` equals `total / n` and tells the average revenue by decile. For example, we expect €5.972 from each customer in the top decile. We can interpret this as the *marginal short-term revenue*. For example, if the contact point costs €1, the margin is 50%, and we care only about short-term revenue, then we would lose money by sending the contact point to deciles 4–10. If we sent the contact to decile 3, we would expect to make €2.545/2− €1 = €0.27 per customer. Mailing to decile 4, however, would generate a loss: €1.859/2−€1 = −€0.07 per customer. Thus, the `Mean` column can help us decide where to stop making contacts with customers, although section 6.4 will introduce a long-term correction.

- `Cumn` keeps a running total of the `n` values. For example, the second row is computed as $10,512 = 5,256 + 5,256$, and we can conclude that there are 21,025 customers in the first four deciles.

- `Cumsum` is a running total of the `total` column. We can conclude, for example, that the top three deciles generate €62,753 in revenue.

- `Cummean` equals `cumsum / cumn`. This column tells us the average amount we will make on a customer for a given mailing depth. For example, if we used this model to select the best 30% of customers (top three deciles), we would expect to make €3.980 per customer. If we chose names at random from the database (or contacted everyone), we would expect to make €2.012. This column is used to compare models. If we had another model (see next example) that did a better job of identifying high-value customer, then it would enable us to make more than €3.980 at the third decile.

The output was created by Program 6.4. The first line of code includes the file `gains.sas`, which is shown below in Program 6.7. Because this macro is used often it makes sense to have it in a separate file that can be included whenever a gains table is desired. The last line of Program 6.4 call the `gains` macro with three arguments: `y=targdol` is the name of the variable recording the actual purchase amounts for each customer, `score=yhat` is the name of the variable giving the predictions, and the third `data` argument gives the name of the data set. In this case, we pass only observations from the test set by attaching a `WHERE` statement to the file specification.

Program 6.7 The gains macro for creating gains tables, stored in `gains.sas`

```
%MACRO gains(y, score, data);
PROC RANK DATA=&data OUT=&data GROUPS=10 DESCENDING;
  VAR &score;
  RANKS decile;
RUN;

PROC SUMMARY DATA=&data NWAY;
  CLASS decile;
  VAR &y;
  OUTPUT OUT=gainout(DROP=_TYPE_ _FREQ_) N=n MEAN=mean SUM=total;
RUN;

DATA gainout;
  SET gainout;
  RETAIN cumn cumsum 0;
  decile = decile + 1;   /* SAS numbers deciles 0, 1, ..., 9 */
  cumsum = cumsum + total;
  cumn = cumn + n;
  cummean = cumsum / cumn;
  OUTPUT;
RUN;

PROC PRINT DATA=gainout NOOBS;
  VAR decile n total mean cumn cumsum cummean;
  SUM n total;
  FORMAT n cumn total cumsum COMMA8. mean cummean 7.3;
RUN;
%MEND;
```

At the beginning of this section, we gave three steps for creating a gains table, and these steps are implemented in the macro. `PROC RANK` finds the deciles of the predicted values and stores them in the variable `decile`. To specify a different number of groups, for example, demideciles with 20 groups, change the `GROUPS=10` option (or make the number of groups an argument to the macro). The second step was to compute actual revenue by decile, which is accomplished with `PROC SUMMARY`, creating the variables displayed in the `n`, `total`, and `mean` columns of the output. The third step was to compute the cumulative columns, which is done in a `DATA` statement using the `RETAIN` statement. `PROC PRINT` displays the output.

EXAMPLE 6.8:   Two-step models for retailer example

Compare the regression model in Example 6.7 with two other models: (1) a two-step model using RFM as predictors and (2) a two-step model with predictors RFM and the log of time on file. Use a gains table on the test set and a 30% mailing depth for comparison. This example illustrates a problem that is commonly encountered in practice. The modeler has built several models and must select one for rollout.

Solution   The code is shown below in Program 6.8. It uses the data set `all` created in Program 6.4. The program defines the `twostep` macro with parameters `data` specifying the analysis data set, `y` specifying the dependent variable of the conditional spend model, `y01` specifying the dependent variable of the respond model, and `x` listing the predictor variables. It assumes that the following variables have been defined: `targbuy` indicates whether the customer responded at all, `logtarg` gives revenue, `train` indicates training or test set, and `trainbuy` takes the value 1 if an observation is in the training set and the customer responded (buys). These variables could be made parameters of the macro.

Program 6.8 Additional two-step models for the retailer example

```
%MACRO twostep(data, y, y01, x);
TITLE "two-step: &y = &x";
PROC LOGISTIC DATA=&data DESCENDING;
  MODEL &y01 = &x;
  WEIGHT train;
  OUTPUT OUT=logitout PREDICTED=phat;
RUN;

PROC REG DATA=logitout OUTEST=betas;
  MODEL &y = &x;
  WEIGHT trainbuy;
  OUTPUT OUT=regout PREDICTED=yhat;
RUN;

DATA answer;
  MERGE regout betas;
  BY _MODEL_;
  EY = phat*(EXP(yhat+_RMSE_**2/2)-1);
RUN;
%MEND;

%twostep(all, targdol, targbuy, r logf logm);
%gains(targdol, EY, answer(WHERE=(train=0)));
%twostep(all, targdol, targbuy, r logf logm logtof);
%gains(targdol, EY, answer(WHERE=(train=0)));
```

The macro first uses PROC LOGISTIC to predict response (y01=targbuy) from the predictor variables &x using only cases from the training set (the WEIGHT statement). The estimated response probabilities for all cases are saved in the variable phat in the logitout data set. Next, the macro uses PROC REG to estimate the log spend (&y) from &x using only responders in the training set (weighting by trainbuy). The predicted values for all cases are saved in regout, and the parameter estimates, including the root mean squared error, are saved in betas. The DATA step multiplies the response probabilities from the logistic regression with the expected revenues from the conditional spend model. Note that the _RMSE_ variable comes from the betas data set. The macro concludes by calling the gains macro.

The output below shows an improvement. If we use the linear regression model from Program 6.4 to select 30% of the names to receive that catalog, we would expect to make €3.980 per customer. If we used the RFM model to select 30%, we would expect to make €4.074 per customer (the first gains table below). Adding the log of time on file to the RFM model suggests that we could make €4.155 for each customer. Adding the log of time on file enables us to model important ratio variable such as the purchase rate, frequency / time on file.

These are important differences. Using the third model instead of the first, we would expect to make €4.155 − €3.980 = €0.17 more per name. If the total mailing consists of 100,000, then revenues would €17,500 higher by using the third model. Building a careful regression model pays well!

two-step: logtarg = r logf logm						
decile	n	total	mean	cumn	cumsum	cummean
1	5,256	32,288	6.143	5,256	32,288	6.143
2	5,256	18,214	3.465	10,512	50,502	4.804
3	5,257	13,741	2.614	15,769	64,243	4.074
4	5,256	9,305	1.770	21,025	73,548	3.498
5	5,256	8,110	1.543	26,281	81,658	3.107
6	5,257	6,747	1.283	31,538	88,405	2.803
7	5,256	5,550	1.056	36,794	93,955	2.554
8	5,257	4,986	0.948	42,051	98,940	2.353
9	5,256	3,540	0.673	47,307	102,480	2.166
10	5,256	3,268	0.622	52,563	105,748	2.012

two-step: logtarg = r logf logm logtof						
decile	n	total	mean	cumn	cumsum	cummean
1	5,256	36,017	6.853	5,256	36,017	6.853
2	5,256	17,240	3.280	10,512	53,257	5.066
3	5,257	12,255	2.331	15,769	65,513	4.155
4	5,256	10,566	2.010	21,025	76,079	3.618
5	5,256	7,503	1.428	26,281	83,582	3.180
6	5,257	5,350	1.018	31,538	88,932	2.820
7	5,256	5,632	1.072	36,794	94,564	2.570
8	5,257	4,763	0.906	42,051	99,327	2.362
9	5,256	3,528	0.671	47,307	102,856	2.174
10	5,256	2,892	0.550	52,563	105,748	2.012

In practice, one would want to investigate other predictor variables. For example, perhaps previous purchases of certain types of books are better indicators than overall frequency and monetary.

EXAMPLE 6.9:   DMEF4: upscale retail catalog

This example uses a data set made available by the Direct Marketing Educational Foundation and is known as the DMEF4 data set.[7] It gives an unusual example of overfitting by showing that having a test set with the same problems as the training set will not detect overfitting, emphasizing the importance of having fresh test data.

The data are from an upscale gift business that mails general and specialized catalogs to its customer base several times each year. The problem is to model how likely a customer is to make a purchase during the Fall 1992 season based on purchase history. There are 101,532 customers in the sample. According to the data,[8] the response rate was 9.4%.

The first step in developing a scoring model is to create a modeling data set from a relational database. This step has already been done for us. The target period is the fall season of 1992 and every customer in this data set received a catalog in October 1992. The `targdol` variable records the amount spent during the target period.

The base period is through July 1992, and the data set provides dozens of feature variables. These variables illustrate the types of variables that are often predictive for retailers, but we restrict our attention to only one variable: `datelp6` gives the date of the most recent purchase before the fall of 1992 and will be used to compute recency. This example will thus consider only recency as a predictor variable.

Recency is usually a good predictor of response, but sometimes there will be seasonal patterns. For example, the catalog in this example was mailed during the fourth quarter, and it could be that some buyers are seasonal, buying only at, for example, Christmas. Such seasonality would complicate our models.

We can investigate such nonlinearities by plotting the response rates for different values of the predictor variable (x). The problem is that there is often insufficient sample size for any given day to make a reliable (small margin of error) estimate of the response rate. One way to solve this is to plot the response rates for groups of dates. This approach is called a *bin smoother* or *regressogram*. Many more complicated smoothers have been proposed such as splines and kernels, but these newer methods assume that the underlying function is continuous. There are many situations in practice (for example, a temporary price cut or promotion) that produce discontinuous functions. Regressograms can be useful in detecting such discontinuities, and also have the virtue of being simple to implement on any system.

Figure 6.9 plots response rates after grouping recency by quarter. It first extracts the relevant variables from the DMEF4 data set and computes the number of quarters since the most recent purchase using the QTR date function, which returns 1=January–March, 2=April–June, and so on. The VLINE command in PROC SGPLOT computes the mean (STAT=MEAN) of the targbuy variable for each unique value of recq. Recall that the mean of a 0-1 variable such as targbuy is the fraction of 1 values, which in this case is the fraction responding within the target period (response rate). The LIMITS option causes SAS to superimpose 95% confidence intervals around each point. The WHERE statement restricts the cases to those who have purchased within the past five years.

Figure 6.9 Response rates with 95% confidence intervals for different values of recency measured in quarters

```
DATA four;
  SET dmef.four(KEEP=datelp6 targdol);
  recq = 4-QTR(datelp6)
    + 4*(1992-YEAR(datelp6));
  LABEL
    recq="Quarters since most recent purch";
  targbuy = (targdol>1);
RUN;

PROC SGPLOT DATA=four;
  VLINE recq / STAT=MEAN LIMITS=BOTH
    RESPONSE=targbuy;
  WHERE recqtr<=20;
RUN;
```

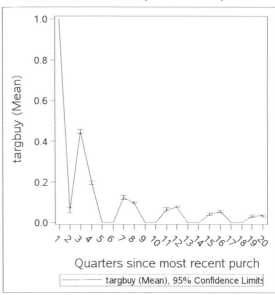

The plot has a very strange pattern. With the exception of the most recent second quarter, those who have recency during quarters 2 or 3 have 0% response rates. This seems highly implausible. At this point, one should question the source of the data to understand why this has happened. I did this, and learned that the company had a strange way of updating their database, where purchases were updated in batches. I also learned that it was impossible to get cleaner data.

We should investigate the relationship between recency and response further by computing response rates by day rather than by quarter. Table 6.1 gives the response rates for the days with the largest counts of records in the training data. We implement this with PROC SQL, although the same output could be produced using a combination of PROC MEANS, PROC SORT and PROC PRINT (it would be a good exercise for the reader to try this). As with PROC SGPLOT above, we compute the mean of targbuy for each unique value of datelp6 (the GROUP BY statement). The rows are sorted in descending order of the second column (ORDER BY 2 DESC), which is the count of customers who purchased most recently on each date. It would be a good exercise for the reader to compute the 95% confidence interval for each response rate as well.

Table 6.1 Counts of records and response rates for different values of recency using training data, sorted in descending order of count

```
PROC SQL;
  SELECT
    datelp6 FORMAT=date9.
    COUNT(targbuy) AS n LABEL="Count",
    MEAN(targbuy) AS rate LABEL="Response Rate"
      FORMAT=PERCENT7.1
  FROM four
  GROUP BY datelp6
  ORDER BY 2 DESC;
```

Date of Last Purchase	Count	Response Rate
01MAR1992	3264	96.2%
15NOV1991	2380	90.0%
15NOV1990	1113	87.2%
15NOV1989	775	83.6%
01MAR1991	719	82.8%
15NOV1988	485	72.8%
23NOV1990	431	0.0%
23OCT1990	403	0.0%
08OCT1991	320	0.0%
17OCT1989	301	0.0%
01MAR1990	297	81.1%
21NOV1990	288	0.0%
29NOV1989	284	0.0%
⋮	⋮	⋮

The numbers are bizarre. There are some extremely large counts for 3/1/92 and 11/15/91 and the dates 3/1 and 11/15 show up multiple times, showing further effects of the batching procedure. Moreover, the response rates for 3/1 and 11/15 of any year are unusually high, whereas the response rates for other dates tend to be 0. I also computed a crosstab of response and whether recency was 3/1 or 11/15 of any year. About 95% of all responders in the training data had recency on one of these two days and 88% of those with recency on these two days responded.

This illustrates some important points. First, a scoring model that mails everyone with recency on 3/1 or 11/15 will fit and perform very well on both the training *and test* sets, but will such a model perform well in real life? The batching procedure seems to give responders a recency date of 3/1 or 11/15, but obviously response is not known before the mailing. Second, this illustrates the importance of having a fresh test set from a different time period.

We must now discuss a sensible way of modeling recency in a response model. We should use a model for dichotomous dependent variables such as logistic regression. Given the problems around 3/1 and 11/15 we should constrain the response probability to be a smooth function of recency. Although it is desirable to have a discontinuous bin smoother for exploratory analyses, having a smooth function is necessary for a good model in this case. Two reasonable models would be to make the logit of response a linear function of recency or the log of recency. The log model assumes diminishing returns as recency increases, which seems reasonable. Without a strong theory, we should fit both models and use model fit to decide between the models.

This example makes an important point about understanding how each predictor variable is related to the dependent variable. Linear and logistic regression are particularly interpretable models while many data mining models such as neural networks are not so interpretable. The interoperation of the model is always important, but the modeler has less control over whether the model captures idiosyncrasies of the training data. In this example, a tree-based model such as CART or CHAID, which are high-dimension versions of a bin smoother, would pick up on the fact that, in this training set, people who have recency on 3/1 or 11/15 of any year have a very high response rate and therefore assign them high scores. A test set from the same data *would not reveal the problem*.

6.4 Accounting for the long-term effects of a marketing contact

The scoring models developed in Examples 6.2, 6.6, 6.7 and 6.8 estimated the short-term revenue from a marketing contact. The dependent variable is the revenue directly attributed to orders generated from the contact. It may seem like these revenues from the order are the only thing to consider when estimating the value of contacting a customer and deciding whether to contact some customer. But it turns out that the firm receives something else of value beyond the order—responders will have migrated to a better RFM state and will thus be more responsive to future marketing efforts. This is defined more precisely below and is called the incremental CLV effect of the contact.

We illustrate this with a concrete example. Consider a person in the retailer's database who received catalog #10 and places an order for €30. Suppose further that this customer had placed' one previous order (frequency = 1) three years ago (recency = 3 years). The retailer receives €30, the short-term revenue. In addition to the €30 order, the retailer now has a two-time buyer who has recency zero years. We know from section 5.3.1 that the more often a customer has purchased in the past the more likely the customer will purchase again. We also know that the more recently a customer has purchased, the more likely the customer will purchase again. This customer is now more loyal and is a better customer as shown by the fact that she has a larger value of frequency and a smaller value of recency. If the contact would not have been made, she would still be a one-time buyer with an even larger value of recency. In quantifying the value of the contact point, the value of this improved RF state should be considered.

Let CLV be the expected lifetime value of some customer *after* a contact. The *incremental CLV correction* is given by

$$\Delta\text{CLV} = E(\text{CLV}|\text{contact}) - E(\text{CLV}|\text{no contact}).$$

In other words, the difference between the expected CLV of a customer if he receives the contact and expected CLV if no contact is made. In principle, one could use this definition to estimate incremental CLV, but we will introduce an assumption that will make this expression more tractable.

At the time of the contact, let x_1 be a customer's recency, x_2 be the customer's frequency, and x_3 be the customer's monetary value. One could also have additional predictor variables $x_4, x_5, \dots$. Let $f^*(\mathbf{x}, \mathbf{c})$ be a function that predicts CLV from RFM ($\mathbf{x}$) and contact vector $\mathbf{c} = (c_1, c_2, \dots)'$ that consists on indicators whether the customer receives various future contacts. Modeling f^* is difficult because organizations do not know the values of $\mathbf{c}$, as they usually depend on responses to future mailings. A customer who buys in the future will receive more contacts, whereas one who stops buying will receive fewer contacts. The contact vector therefore depends on responses to future contacts. We can avoid these problems by simplifying function f^* with the *additivity assumption*: the effects of future contacts do not interact with previous purchase history (RFM) in predicting CLV. That is,

$$f^*(\mathbf{x}, \mathbf{c}) = f(\mathbf{x}) + g(\mathbf{c})$$

for functions f and g.

Under this assumption, we now derive an expression for ΔCLV that can be more easily implemented. Let π be the estimated probability of response to the current contact. Let μ be the estimated revenue from the contact given that the customer responds. Multiplying μ by the margin and deducting the cost of the contact gives the short-term profit (given response). Both π and μ come from predictive scoring models. Let δ be the length of time between the contact points or some appropriate period of inactivity. Then

$$\Delta\text{CLV} = E(\text{CLV}^*|\text{contact}) - E(\text{CLV}^*|\text{no contact})$$

$$= E(\text{CLV}|\text{contact}) + g(\mathbf{c}) - E(\text{CLV}|\text{no contact}) - g(\mathbf{c})$$
$$= \pi E(\text{CLV}|\text{resp}) + (1 - \pi)E(\text{CLV}|\text{no resp}) - E(\text{CLV}|\text{no contact})$$
$$= \pi f(0, x_2 + 1, x_3 + \mu) + (1 - \pi)f(x_1 + \delta, x_2, x_3) - f(x_1 + \delta, x_2, x_3)$$
$$= \pi[f(0, x_2 + 1, x_3 + \mu) - f(x_1 + \delta, x_2, x_3)].$$

The second and fourth lines of this derivation are especially important. In the second line the effects of future contacts, $g(\mathbf{c})$, cancel out due to the additivity assumption. In the fourth line, a customer who receives the contact will respond with probability π and, after responding, will have $\text{CLV} = f(0, x_2 + 1, x_3 + \mu)$. In other words, given that the customer responded, recency is 0, frequency is one greater, and monetary is μ larger. CLV for someone who responds to the contact must be averaged with the CLV if the customer does not respond. With probability $1 - \pi$ the customer will not respond and have $\text{CLV} = f(x_1 + \delta, x_2, x_3)$. That is, frequency and monetary will remain the same, but recency increases by δ. If no contact is made, CLV will also be $f(x_1 + \delta, x_2, x_3)$.

We can think of making the contact as taking a chance at improving the customer's RFM state. With probability π the customer will migrate to the improved state of RFM = $(0, x_2 + 1, x_3 + \mu)$. If the organization does not make the contact, or the customer does not respond, then the customer migrates to a longer-lapsed state of RFM = $(x_1 + \delta, x_2, x_3)$.

One can use any CLV model for f in the above expression, as long as RFM are part of its domain. This expression for the correction is easy to implement by any organization that has a CLV model. For each customer the organization needs to evaluate their CLV functions only two times, compute the difference, and multiply by the response probability.

Program 6.9 SAS program to compute incremental CLV for retailer example

```
%twostep(all, logltr, ltr01, r logf logm logtof);
%twostep(all, logtarg, targbuy, r logf logm logtof);


%MACRO clv(r, f, m, tof);
(EXP(1.78563 -0.25347*(&r) +0.45974*LOG(&f+1) +0.54046*LOG(&m+1)
  -1.03268*LOG(&tof+1) + 1.86937/2) -1) /
(1 + EXP(-( 0.5626 -0.6168*(&r) +0.4863*LOG(&f+1) +0.0395*LOG(&m+1)
  -0.4193*LOG(&tof+1) )))
%MEND;


DATA score;
  SET answer;
  clv1 = %clv(0, f+1, m+mu, tof+1/12); /* CLV if they buy */
  clv2 = %clv(r+1/12, f, m, tof+1/12); /* CLV, no buy */
  incclv = phat * (clv1-clv2);
  total = EY + incCLV;
  KEEP targdol mu phat incclv EY id clv1 clv2 total;
  label phat = " ";
RUN;


PROC MEANS DATA=score;
  var phat mu EY incclv total;
RUN;
```

EXAMPLE 6.10:   Incremental CLV model for retailer example
We illustrate the model by continuing Example 6.8. The SAS program below implements the model. It first calls the `twostep` macro from Program 6.8 twice, once for predicting LTR and then for predicting response to catalog #10 (`logtarg`). It next defines a macro that estimates CLV based on a customer's RFM and time on file using equation 6.3. The

numbers are the estimated regression coefficients from the response model and conditional-spend model.

The `DATA` step computes CLV conditional on buying from catalog #10 (`clv1`) and separately for not buying (`clv2`). EY is the expected short-term revenue computed using equation 6.2. The `incclv` variable computes the incremental CLV value according to equation 6.5. `Total` is the sum of short-term revenue (`EY`) and incremental CLV (`incCLV`). The output shows that LTR increases by €3.91 on the average, and ignoring long-term effects underestimates the value of a contact point.

Variable	N	Mean	Std Dev	Minimum	Maximum
phat	165287	0.0455927	0.0332070	0.0010016	0.4076337
mu	165287	37.2760445	12.8203793	4.5080898	573.4827523
EY	165287	1.7668701	1.8055916	0.0188155	57.2708266
incCLV	165287	3.9098722	6.2754719	0.0107379	600.2163074
total	165287	5.6767423	7.8162084	0.0295534	628.3309470

6.5   Chapter summary

The data-mining approach can be used to estimate how much, if anything, a customer will spend in response to receiving a marketing contact. Such a model is called a *scoring model*. It can also be used to estimate the amount a customer will spend in some extended future period of time, which we call *long-term revenue* (LTR).

While the retention and migration models discussed in previous chapters begin with a set of assumptions describing the dynamics of a customer relationship, the data-mining approach begins and ends with data. The analyst turns back the clock so that there are two disjoint periods, the *base period* from which predictor feature variables ($\mathbf{x}$) are extracted and the *future period* from which the dependent variable (y) comes. Some sort of regression, supervised learning or predictive analytics model $\hat{y} = \hat{f}(\mathbf{x})$ is used to predict the future-period behaviors from the base-period variables. The ultimate objective is to produce accurate predictions on a holdout sample.

The dependent variables tend to have two characteristics that complicate models. The distributions are usually bimodal, with the left mode consisting of the value 0 indicating that no purchases are made in the future period, and the right mode consisting of active customers. It is customary for the left mode to be comprised of a substantial percentage of customers, and it is not uncommon for it to be 95% or even 98% of the distribution. The other model is typically very right skewed with outliers, and a logarithm transformation will often make the distribution approximately normal.

The *two-step model* is often used to predict such dependent variables and involves estimating two separate models. First, the *response model* predicts whether a customer is active (right mode) or not (left mode) in the future using a model for dichotomous dependent variables such as logistic regression. The *conditional-spend* model predicts future spend for those who are active in the future period. When the dependent variable has a lognormal distribution, unlogged predicted values can be computed with $\exp(\hat{y} + S_e^2/2)$, where $\hat{y}$ is the predicted log of the dependent variable and S_e is the standard error of the estimate.

As a rule of thumb, log all count and amount variables, such as future spend amounts in the conditional-spend model and all versions of frequency and monetary value. Logging the dependent variable that is an amount acts as a variance stabilizing transformation. Logging right-skewed independent or dependent variables symmetrizes the distributions and reduces the influence of outliers in the tails. The best predictor variables in the response model will be recency, frequency, and a purchase rate (frequency / time on file). The best predictor variables in the conditional-spend model will be monetary value, frequency, and ratios such as average order amount (monetary / frequency) and amount per period (monetary / time on file).

Data-mining models are evaluated by some *metric* on a *hold out sample*. There are two general types of metrics, residual-based metrics and *gains tables*. Residual-based metrics measure the typical size of a residual. For example, the *mean squared error* is

$$\text{MSE} = \sum_{i=1}^{n}(y_i - \hat{y})^2.$$

Gains tables estimate the revenues that would be generated by using model $\hat{f}(\mathbf{x})$ to select a specified percentage of names to receive a contact from some list. Residual-based metrics and gains tables should be computed using a *test sample* (also known as a *validation* or *holdout* sample) that was not used to estimate the model. The simplest way to have a test sample is to randomly divide the available data into test and training samples before estimation. *Fresh data* from another time period or cohort of customers provide stronger test sets.

The value of a marketing contact point to an organization can be divided into short-term and long-term components. The short-term component consists of the revenues generated from the sales immediately attributed to the contact point and are estimated with a scoring model. For example, an e-mail prompts people to place orders generating short-term revenues. The long-term value comes from the customer migrating to a better RFM state, implying the customer will be more responsive to marketing efforts in the future. The change in CLV due to the customer migrating to a better state is the incremental CLV and should be considered when evaluating the financial value of a contact point.

Notes

[1] See (Breiman, 2001) for an excellent description of the data-mining approach, and discussion from David Cox, Brad Efron and others pointing up the limitations of this approach. See also (Malthouse, 2009) for discussion of a CLV-modeling competition that included a wide variety of models. The conclusion was what the modeler, rather than the model, determines the quality of the forecasts. There were probabilistic and data-mining models that produced answers close to the best one, as well as models from both families that were way off.

[2] The proxy could also be multiple behaviors. See Malthouse and Derenthal (2008) for discussion of how multiple models can be aggregated to produce better models.

[3] With this characterization of data mining, a model like linear regression could be a probabilistic model or a data-mining model depending on the rationale. A linear regression model, perhaps with appropriate transformations, that used to "fit a curve" is a data-mining model. If our understanding of the process that generated the data (that is, theory) implies a linear functional form and independent, homoscedastic, Gaussian errors, then it is a probabilistic model.

[4] See Elkan (2001) for a further refinement using the Heckman correction. The basic idea is to include the predicted probabilities from the response model as an additional predictor in the conditional-spend model.

[5] Explaining the correlation between $\log m$ and $\log f$ through a latent variable seems more plausible than assuming M is dependent on f or vice versa. The variable $\log(fm)$ is an example of a *behavioral score* (Calder and Malthouse, 2003).

[6] Cross validation divides the available data into K parts of approximately equal size labeled $k = 1, 2, \ldots, K$, and then estimates the model K times. In estimating the model time k, all data except part k are used, and the estimated model is then applied to the left-out part k. Fit statistics are then summed over the left-out parts.

[7] See http://www.directworks.org/academics for details.

[8] This response rate seems high and it is possible that responders were oversampled when the data set was prepared, although this was not mentioned in the documentation.

References

Agresti, A. (1990). *Categorical Data Analysis*. Wiley, New York.

Allison, P. (2010). *Survival Analysis Using SAS: A Practical Guide*. SAS Institute INC., Cary, NC, second edition.

Bartholomew, D. and Knott, M. (1999). *Latent Variable Models and Factor Analysis*. Arnold, London, second edition.

Berger, P. and Nasr, N. (1998). Customer lifetime value: Marketing models and applications. *J. of Interactive Marketing*, 12(1):17–30.

Blattberg, R. and Deighton, J. (1996). Manage marketing by the customer equity test. *Harvard Business Review*, July-August:136–144.

Blattberg, R., Malthouse, E. C., and Neslin, S. (2009). Customer lifetime value: Empirical generalizations and some conceptual questions. *J. of Interactive Marketing*, 23:157–168.

Blattberg, R. C., Getz, G., and Thomas, J. (2001). *Customer Equity: Building and managing relationships as valuable assets*. HBS Press, Boston.

Blattberg, R. C., Kim, B.-D., and Neslin, S. A. (2008). *Database Marketing*. Springer, New York.

Breiman, L. (2001). Statistical modeling: The two cultures (with discussion). *Statistical Science*, 16(9):199–231.

Calder, B. and Malthouse, E. C. (2003). The behavioral score approach to dependent variables. *Journal of Consumer Psychology*, 13:387–394.

Calder, B. and Malthouse, E. C. (2004). Managing media and advertising change with interactive marketing. *Journal of Advertising Research*, 43:356–361.

Cox, D. R. and Miller, H. D. (1965). *The Theory of Stochastic Processes*. Chapman and Hall, London.

DeGroot, M. (1975). *Probability and Statistics*. Addison Wesley, Reading, Massachusetts.

Delwiche, L. and Slaughter, S. (2008). *The Little SAS Book*. SAS Institute, Inc., Cary, NC.

Elkan, C. (2001). Magical thinking in data mining: Lessons from coil challenge 2000. In *Proceedings of* KDD-2001, pages 426–431.

Elsner, R., Krafft, M., and Huchzermeier, A. (2004). Optimizing rhenania's direct marketing business through dynamic multilevel modeling (dmlm) in a multicatalog-brand environment. *Marketing Sci.*, 23(2):192–206.

Fader, P. and Hardie, B. G. (2007). How to project customer retention. *J. of Interactive Marketing*, 21:76–90.

Fader, P. and Hardie, B. G. (2010). Customer-base valuation in a contractual setting: the perils of ignoring heterogeneity. *Marketing Science*, 29:85–93.

Fraley, C. and Raftery, A. (2002). Model-based clustering, discriminant analysis, and density estimation. *Journal of the American Statistical Association*, 24(2):123–140.

Gupta, S. and Lehmann, D. (2003). Customers as assets. *J. of Interactive Marketing*, 17(1):9–24.

Hastie, T., Tibshirani, R., and Friedman, J. (2001). *The Elements of Statistical Learning*. Springer, New York.

Hatcher, L. (1994). *A Step-by-step approach to using the sas system for factor analysis and structural equation modeling*. SAS Institute Inc., Cary, NC.

Hyndman, R. and Fan, Y. (1996). Sample quantiles in statistical packages. *American Statistician*, 50:361–4.

Johnson, R. A. and Wichern, D. W. (2002). *Applied Multivariate Statistical Analysis*. Prentice Hall, Upper Saddle River, NJ.

Kotler, P. and Keller, K. (2012). *Marketing Management*. Pearson Education, Inc., Upper Saddle River, NJ, 14th edition.

Kumar, V., Aksoy, L., Donkers, B., Venkatesan, R., Wiesel, T., and Tillmanns, S. (2010). Undervalued or overvalued customers: Capturing total customer engagement value. *Journal of Service Research*, 13:297–310.

MacQueen, J. (1967). Some methods for classification and analysis of multivariate observations. In *Proceedings of 5th Berkeley Symposium on Mathematical Statistics and Probability*, pages 281–297. University of California Press.

Macready, G. B. and Dayton, C. M. (1977). The use of probabilistic models in the assessment of mastery. *Journal of Educational Statistics*, 2:99–120.

Malthouse, E. and Raman, K. (2013). The geometric law of annual halving. *J. of Interactive Marketing*, 27(1).

Malthouse, E. C. (2001). Checking assumptions of normality before conducting factor analyses. *Journal Consumer Psychology*, 10(1-2):81.

Malthouse, E. C. (2003a). Database subsegmentation. In Iacobucci, D. and Calder, B., editors, *Kellogg on Integrated Marketing*, pages 162–188. Wiley, New York.

Malthouse, E. C. (2003b). Latent class software. Technical report, Medill/IMC, Northwestern University.

Malthouse, E. C. (2003c). Scoring models. In Iacobucci, D. and Calder, B., editors, *Kellogg on Integrated Marketing*, pages 227–249. Wiley, New York.

Malthouse, E. C. (2007). Mining for trigger events with survival analysis. *Data Mining and Knowledge Discovery*, 15:383–402.

Malthouse, E. C. (2009). The results from the lifetime value and customer equity modeling competition. *J. of Interactive Marketing*, 23:157–168.

Malthouse, E. C. (2010). Accounting for the long-term effects of a marketing contact. *Expert Systems with Applications*, 37:4935–4940.

Malthouse, E. C. and Calder, B. (2002). Measuring newspaper readership: A qualitative variable approach. *International Journal on Media Management*, 4:248–260.

Malthouse, E. C. and Calder, B. J. (2005). Crm and relationship branding. In Tybout, A. and Calkins, T., editors, *Kellogg on Branding*, pages 150–168. Wiley, New York.

Malthouse, E. C. and Derenthal, K. M. (2008). Improving predictive scoring models through model aggregation. *J. of Interactive Marketing*, 22(3):51–68.

Malthouse, E. C. and Elsner, R. (2006). Customization with crossed-basis subsegmentation. *Journal of Database Marketing and Customer Strategy*, 14:40–50.

Malthouse, E. C. and Mulhern, F. (2007). Understanding and using customer loyalty and customer value. *Journal of Relationship Marketing*, 6(3/4):59–86.

Mardia, K., Kent, J., and Bibby, J. (1979). *Multivariate Analysis*. Academic Press, London.

Mosteller, F. and Tukey, J. (1977). *Data Analysis and Regression: a second course in statistics*. Addison Wesley, Reading, MA.

Neter, J., Kutner, M. H., Nachtsheim, C. J., and Wasserman, W. (1996). *Applied Linear Statistical Models.* Irwin, fourth edition.

of the Census, U. B. (1994). *Statistical Abstract of the United States.* U.S. Bureau of the Census, Washington D.C., 114 edition.

Pfeifer, P. and Carraway, R. (2000). Modeling customer relationships as markov chains. *Journal of Interactive Marketing,* 14:43–55.

Pfeifer, P., Haskins, M., and Conroy, R. (2005). Customer lifetime value, customer profitability, and the treatment of acquisition spending. *Journal of Managerial Issues,* XVII:11–25.

Roberts, M. L. and Berger, P. (1999). *Direct Marketing Management.* Prentice Hall, Upper Saddle River, New Jersey, second edition.

Rossiter, J. and Percy, L. (1997). *Advertising Communications & Promotion Management.* Irwin McGraw-Hill, Boston, second edition.

SAS Institute (2011). *SAS© Certification Prep Guide: Advanced Programming for SAS© 9.* SAS Institute INC., Cary, NC, third edition.

Shepard, D. (1999). Back to basics: The economics of classical direct marketing. In Shepard, D., editor, *The New Direct Marketing,* chapter 33, pages 420–476. McGraw Hill, New York, third edition.

Siegel, A. (2011). *Practical Business Statistics.* Academic Press, Burlington, MA, 6 edition.

Stone, B. and Jacobs, R. (2001). *Successful Direct Marketing Methods.* McGraw-Hill, Chicago, seventh edition.

Therneau, T. and Grambsch, P. (2010). *Modeling Survival Data.* Springer, New York, second edition.

Tufte, E. (2001). *The Visual Display of Quantitative Information.* Graphics Press, Cheshire, Connecticut.

Venables, W. and Ripley, R. (1999). *Modern Applied Statistics with S-PLUS.* Springer, New York, 3rd edition.

Wunderman, L. (1996). *Being Direct.* Random House.

Index